LET'S DANCE

Let's Dance

❧

Popular Music in the 1930s

❧

ARNOLD SHAW

EDITED BY

BILL WILLARD

New York   Oxford

Oxford University Press

1998

Oxford University Press

Oxford   New York
Athens   Auckland   Bangkok   Bogotá   Bombay
Buenos Aires   Calcutta   Cape Town   Dar es Salaam
Delhi   Florence   Hong Kong   Istanbul   Karachi
Kuala Lumpur   Madras   Madrid   Melbourne
Mexico City   Nairobi   Paris   Singapore
Taipei   Tokyo   Toronto   Warsaw

and associated companies in
Berlin   Ibadan

Published by Oxford University Press
198 Madison Avenue, New York, New York 10016

Oxford is a registered trademark of Oxford University Press

Library of Congress Cataloging-in-Publication Data
Shaw, Arnold.
Let's dance : popular music in the 1930s /
Arnold Shaw; edited by Bill Willard.
p.   cm.   Includes index.
ISBN 0-19-505307-9
1. Popular music—United States—1931–1940—History
and criticism.   2. Big band music—History and criticism.
3. Jazz—1931–1940—History and criticism.
I. Willard, Bill.   II. Title.
ML3477.S4753   1998   781.64'0973—dc21   97-45584

1 3 5 7 9 8 6 4 2

Printed in the United States of America
on acid-free paper

To my wife, Ghita,
who makes my life a song

Contents

Foreword

Arnold Shaw's last book caught me by surprise when I discovered that it covered popular music of the thirties. At one time he had mentioned a possible novel, and I assumed it would have a Las Vegas theme and plot, with tentacles in popular music amid show business. During a period of several months he was confined to a wheelchair with little physical mobility but with an obviously active mind. It seemed that his principal object and pursuit was the Popular Music Research Center that he converted into reality in 1985. His base was the University of Nevada, Las Vegas (UNLV), as adjunct faculty member teaching popular music history courses—rock, black music, songwriting techniques, as well as Broadway's eminent composers.

Our friendship expanded into a team to develop varied projects of the Research Center. To achieve heightened community interest I produced a show starring blues/ballad-singing star Joe Williams, warmed by a notable collection of entertainers from the Las Vegas Strip and downtown "Glitter Gulch" showrooms, supported by the internationally famed UNLV Jazz Ensemble. The producer role emanated from my post as Las Vegas news reporter/show reviewer/columnist for *Variety*, the "bible" of show business, an occupation from 1950 with occasional veering into "showbiz" on the Strip as actor/straightman/writer/composer/columnist/radio and television reporter/ commentator, with additional Screen Actors Guild and Actors Equity roles, plus several one-man gallery art shows in Las Vegas and New York City.

It was a shock to the academic and many other communities when on

September 26, 1989, Arnold Shaw died of cancer. During the memorial service, UNLV Provost John Unrue stated that his name would be added to the Popular Music Research Center's title. Shaw's widow, Ghita, requested that I be appointed director. In 1990, I was contracted by UNLV to be associated with the Music Department of the College of the Fine and Performing Arts to continue Arnold Shaw's valuable Research Center legacy. The new name for the Center, Arnold Shaw Research Center for Popular Music, honors the work he began with its immense growing store of LPs, CDs, audio and videotapes, music and show business memorabilia, artifacts, serials, standing files, and gift collections from honored music and entertainment stars. The Center lives on in total perception of Arnold Shaw's exploration of "The Culture and Sociology of the Las Vegas Popular Performer."

There were several examples of the Shaw-Willard collaboration in the eighties. One included themes or subject matter for *Variety*'s enlarged special January edition, tended with tender loving care by doughty editor Abel Green. Shaw's journalistic journeys into the offbeat happenings associated with what he dubbed "casinotels" should not conflict with my "roundups," normally laden with entertainment specifics including show reviews, we agreed.

The other opportunity occurred with his twelfth book-in-progress, *The Jazz Age*, about the Roaring Twenties. My role in the post-genesis of that Oxford University Press book was to comb the manuscript for any errors and make suggestions that might add additional credence to the author's already staunchly experienced and further researched accounting of that era.

The responsibility of editing and additional writing on this volume, *Let's Dance*, followed a request to the publisher by Shaw's brilliant widow and amanuensis, Ghita Shaw. The task proved to be distinctly different from working on *The Jazz Age*. It was a joy to visit the thirties again with Arnold Shaw, as I recalled my hegira in the Big Apple from 1933 to 1938 as a jazz disciple of such mentors as Don Redman and Fats Waller.

The new manuscript, I found, had often repeated numerous situation accounts and names, necessitating proper juxtaposition to keep the Shaw continuity and meticulously glowing writing style a fascinating adventure into a marvelously productive musical timespan. The process was to index every page with name and subject matter for positive placement or omission, while being careful not to interfere with or despoil Shaw's masterful depictions of the turbulent thirties.

A cherished gift from Arnold Shaw was his autograph, signed September 3, 1987, in the front of *The Jazz Age*: "To Bill Willard—a friend and an anachronism—a Renaissance Man of the Arts in the 20th century."

Las Vegas, Nevada   —Bill Willard
December 1997

Preface

The early thirties were a traumatic time for Americans. The Great Depression was not only an economic catastrophe but a psychological and emotional shock. Confusion, frustration, despair, even suicidal tendencies were rampant. With the advent of Franklin D. Roosevelt as president, the New Deal, and the many back-to-work programs, a feeling of hope began to emerge. "There is nothing to fear but fear itself," FDR said. And America began to dance the Depression away to the jubilant bounce and blare of the Big Bands. At the beginning of the era, they were singing "Brother, Can You Spare a Dime?," which with the rise of Roosevelt optimism turned to "Who's Afraid of the Big Bad Wolf?," and finally at the end of that period became "God Bless America."

Although the thirties are remembered as the big band era, they were years that brought vital changes in the entertainment scene. After "talkies" had weathered the Depression, musical films filled the screen with mammoth chorus spectacles and made stars of dancers like Fred Astaire, Ginger Rogers, and others. The center of New York entertainment moved from Harlem to midtown's 52nd Street, soon known as Swing Street. Musical theatre moved delicately away from cliché boy-girl romance and began to tackle sociological and political subjects, with a satire by the Gershwins winning the first Pulitzer Prize awarded to a musical. Radio, especially in the form of coast-to-coast shows featuring name bands, superseded vaudeville as the major medium for creating song hits. Popular music had its first significant barometer of popularity as well as a powerful hit-maker in radio's *Your Hit Parade*, heard weekly in prime time on Saturday evenings. In all these respects, the thirties represented an innovative turn away from the past. In short, the deprivations of the early years made the era one of change, experimentation, and esthetic adventuring.

In the thirties, the popular song acquired new stature, as few films were produced without a specifically written theme song that gave identity to the film. The popular song also became notable as the signature of each of the big bands. Perhaps the most significant change was in the addition of substance, occasioned by the desperation—economic and psychological—produced by the Depression, which promoted a certain number of writers to write social commentaries or uplift songs.

By the end of 1931, almost ten million men were out of work. Major cities were marked by lengthening breadlines, a growing number of soup kitchens, desperate citizens selling apples at street corners, and shantytowns springing up to "house" those who could no longer pay rent. In 1931, over 28,000 businesses and almost 2,300 banks went bankrupt. Major corporations like U.S. Steel, General Motors, U.S. Republic, and Ford cut wages by 10 percent and more. Film attendance was off 40 percent, so that movies were offering double bills, free dishes, and bank nights in an effort to bring audiences back and away from their radio sets and *Amos 'n' Andy*. Many Broadway theatres shuttered their doors; others turned into movie houses. By 1932, the Dow Jones average had dropped from 381.17 in 1925 to 41.22. General Motors, listed on the New York Stock Exchange at 79 in 1929, was down to 8; U.S. Steel down from 262 to 22; and A.T.& T. from 304 to 70.

It was only in a musical that one could warble, "Who cares if banks fail in Yonkers . . . it's love that conquers." More people were then wailing, "Brother, Can You Spare a Dime?"

The headlines of the decade tell a devastating tale, starting with echoes of *Variety's* gag line, "Wall St. Lays an Egg" in 1929. For example, "Troops Drive Veterans from Capitol, Fire on Camps There and at Anacostia" (7/ 32). A slight lift came with "Roosevelt Sweeps the Nation in Landslide; Congress Democratic and Wet" (11/32) and "Roosevelt Opens Recovery Drive, Five Million Jobs His Goal" (6/33). But soon: "Big Italian Force Invades Ethiopia; Mussolini Rallies 20,000,000 Fascisti" (10/35); "4 Killed, 84 Hurt as Strikers Fight Police in Chicago" (at a Republic Steel plant) (5/37); "Hitler Invades Austria" (3/38); "Hitler starts Hostilities, Poland Is Invaded, Danzig Annexed; Cities Bombed from Air; Britain, France, U.S. Prepare to Meet Crisis" (9/39). It was a decade that began in scarcity and ended in violent conflict.

In this troubled and turbulent atmosphere, the thirties nevertheless succeeded in becoming an extremely creative era. No field of entertainment remained untouched, and many enjoyed innovative developments. With the silver screen now possessed of a voice, the musical film became a major new form, featuring dancing as an art and, later, introducing audiences to child actors.

LET'S DANCE

Prologue

From 1950 into 1966, I served as Vice-President and General Professional Manager of three major music publishing firms: Duchess Music, Hill & Range Songs, and, for eleven years, the venerable Edward B. Marks Music Corporation. They were critical years, encompassing the changeover of popular music from its set 32-bar form with the pivotal position of the piano and the use of large orchestras to accompany singers to the guitar-dominated years of Elvis, Little Richard, and Chuck Berry, and finally into the rock era of Bob Dylan, the Beatles, and the Rolling Stones.

As general professional manager, my function was to audition and evaluate songs submitted for publication and exploitation; to make "demo" records for audition purposes and arrange for commercial recordings by leading record companies and artists; and also to supervise the activities of the song-plugging and record-promotion staff. In short, my tenure depended on my ability to find and develop hits. It was a grueling enterprise, and the fate of any given song was as unpredictable as a throw of the dice.

I will state without embarrassment that I was quite successful at it. At Duchess, I was able to develop such hits as "Petite Waltz," an instrumental by a Belgian café pianist; "It Is No Secret What God Can Do," a pop religioso, extensively recorded by a wide variety of artists, including country, sacred, and pop; and "Have I Told You Lately That I Love You?," the revival of a country ballad popularized by Bing Crosby. The most valuable copyright I developed, and one not then a hit, was "The End of a Love Affair." To the sister firms of Duchess, Pickwick, and the potent Leeds Company, I contributed "Meet Mr. Callaghan," which I found during a visit to London and which was recorded by Les Paul and Mary Ford; and "Now Is the Hour," a Maori song resting quietly in the files of G. Schirmer, with whom I negotiated a deal involving joint ownership by Leeds and Schirmer, which led to its becoming a pop hit via a recording by Crosby.

An attractive offer from the Aberbach brothers led me to Hill & Range Songs, where I was involved with such hits as "Let Me Go Lover" (whose title, originally "Let Me Go Devil," I changed to make it viable for a television show); "The Things I Didn't Do," a million-seller whose bid for stardom was frustrated by its "B" side, "Papa Loves Mambo"; and "Sh-Boom," owned by Atlantic Records, with whom I made a joint-ownership arrangement—I paid $6,000 for a half share based on the record by the unknown Chords—with the "cover" by the Crew Cuts yielding a No. 1 hit and the first national rock 'n' roll hit.

I joined Edward B. Marks Music in the spring of 1955 when the company, the oldest firm still owned by the family of its founders, was in the doldrums. A trip to Nashville and a sojourn at the home of Col. Tom Parker brought me into contact with the recordings of the then-unknown Elvis Presley. It was when I brought these disks to the attention of Bill Randle of Station WERE in Cleveland, then one of the nation's most powerful disc jockeys, that bidding for Elvis's contract began among the major labels, and RCA Victor emerged the winner, paying Sam Phillips of Sun Records $40,000.

Starting with "Dungaree Doll," a song I conceived and on which I collaborated, I developed a long list of hits at Marks that included "More"; "Wonderful, Wonderful" (Johnny Mathis's first recorded song); "Lollipop," on which I made the original record released by RCA Victor, but was swamped by a Chordettes million-copy seller; "Banana Boat Song," which catapulted Harry Belafonte, who grew up in Jamaica, into the realm of calypso hits; "Born Too Late"; "Tell Laura I Love Her"; and a Top Ten revival of "What a Diff'rence a Day Made" by Dinah Washington.

My work at Marks included nursing *Bye Bye Birdie* through several rewrites, only to lose its publication when the firm refused to advance $19,000 requested by the producer. I published six Bacharach-David songs, including "I Cry Alone" (Dionne Warwick's first recording)—but that was before the duo produced an incredible succession of song hits.

I bought the American rights to ten Jacques Brel songs from his Belgian publisher at the nominal sum of $50—but that was two years before he became nationally known through the off-Broadway hit show *Jacques Brel Is Alive and Well and Living in Paris*. The American lyrics to "Ne Me Quitte Pas" ("If You Go Away") and to "Seasons in the Sun" were written by a man who later established a worldwide reputation as a poet—Rod McKuen.

Shortly before I left the music business, I published a number of Paul Simon songs, and he worked as my assistant for a period of months.

I offer this thumbnail sketch to give the reader a conception of the depth and scope of my involvement in popular music, which includes writing songs and instrumental music for piano.

Out of these experiences have come a dozen books. But this tome on the thirties covers an era before I became involved in publishing—an era in which I played the piano on the radio, led a small band for weekend gigs, and when I knocked—not too successfully—on the doors of music publishers and producers.

✤ 1 ✤

The Thirties: Turbulent and Creative

On the evening of January 14, 1930, a jubilant George Gershwin (1898–1937) raised his baton in the pit of the Times Square Theatre for the premiere performance of his new musical, *Strike Up the Band.* Sporting a large gardenia in his lapel and wearing an oversized white tie with his tails, he hummed, sang, and whistled his songs with such verve and volume that he appeared to be on stage rather than in the pit, conducting songs like "Soon," "I've Got a Crush on You," and the breezy title tune.

Strike Up the Band was the first musical of the year as well as the decade. Although the title referred to a marching or military band, it was most apropos as the kickoff show of the decade that soon became known as the Swing Era or the Era of the Big Bands. By some happy coincidence, the pit band was that of jazz trumpeter Red Nichols and included in its clarinet section the man who later launched the Swing Era, Benny Goodman.

If the show fortuitously foreshadowed the turn that popular music took in the middle of the decade, it pioneered a new trend in the musical theatre. Instead of the traditional boy-girl romantic story—boy meets girl/boy loses girl/boy wins girl, as musicals of the twenties were humorously capsuled—*Strike Up the Band* was a satirical caricature of war and international diplomacy. It was the forerunner of musicals that were concerned with the growth of the labor movement (*Pins and Needles*), life in a company town (*The Cradle Will Rock*), urban corruption (*Face the Music*), the foibles of Wash-

7

ington politics (*Of Thee I Sing, I'd Rather Be Right*), and other sociological and political themes.

Despite its sociological substance, *Strike Up the Band* was a lively show, its satire light enough to leave them laughing and its turns memorable enough to set them whistling. Forgotten during its presentation was the havoc wrought by the Great Depression.

In 1927, Warner Bros. produced *The Jazz Singer* with Al Jolson—the first "talking picture." The success of *The Jazz Singer* and the introduction of the talkies prompted what became known as the California Gold Rush of Tin Pan Alley songwriters. But by the early thirties, the devastation wrought by the Depression and a glut of second-rate talkies motivated studios to cut their talkie schedules, reversing the flow of songwriters. But Harry Warren and Al Dubin, responsible for *42nd Street*—the film that revived the talkie market—remained; they were later joined as permanent residents by Jerome Kern, Jimmy McHugh, Sammy Fain, and others. By 1935, when the studios were singing "Happy Days Are Here Again," Warren and Dubin had competition from Robin (Leo) and Rainger (Ralph), Gordon (Mack) and Revel (Harry), and other teams who became part of the Hollywood coterie.

By 1934, the Academy of Motion Picture Arts and Sciences decided that songs were as important to a film's success as actors, directors, and so on, and added a Best Song category to the Oscar awards. The first went to "The Continental" by Con Conrad and Herb Magidson, a song written especially for *The Gay Divorcée*, the film version of Cole Porter's *Gay Divorce*. The year before was the first in which a movie musical—in fact two, *42nd Street* and Mae West's *She Done Him Wrong*—made the Top Ten box-office leaders.

Tin Pan Alley remained as aloof as Hollywood when it came to probing topical issues. Its approach to the world crisis was unequivocally optimistic, whether songwriters and publishers believed it or not. Their role was to elevate the spirits of the citizenry. Look "Beyond the Blue Horizon" to a brighter day; "Get Happy"; "Smile, Darn Ya, Smile!"; "Wrap Your Troubles in Dreams (And Dream Your Troubles Away)"; "Life Is Just a Bowl of Cherries," don't take it too seriously; and, of course, the anti-Depression theme, "Who's Afraid of the Big Bad Wolf?" Rather than reflecting or anatomizing the woes of the time, they sought to avoid reminding listeners of their problems and instead instill hope and positivism.

In 1932, an announcer on station KFWB in Los Angeles launched a program called "The World's Largest Ballroom." Al Jarvis's playing of records by bands and singers became so popular that he was on the air for three hours a day. It is said that his plugging of Benny Goodman records contributed to the enthusiastic reception of the band at the Palomar Ballroom.

In New York on February 3, 1935, Martin Block, a $20-a-week staff announcer on WNEW, began playing records while he awaited bulletins on the trial of Bruno Hauptmann, who was convicted of kidnapping and killing the Lindbergh baby. Because WNEW had no record library, Block went over to the Liberty Music Shop on Madison Avenue and 50th Street and purchased five Clyde McCoy disks. As he played them, he pretended they were coming live from a dance hall while he held an imaginary conversation with McCoy. It was estimated that within four months, Block had four million listeners, and, before the year was out, his "Make-Believe Ballroom" was on the air two-and-a-half hours daily. The era of the disc jockey did not really arrive until the forties, but surely it had its beginnings with Jarvis and Block in the thirties.

Apart from FDR, who was hated as well as loved, a number of men arose in the thirties to capture the imagination of the people—and did so, because people badly need heroes for distraction and support. One such super figure was J. Edgar Hoover, the head of the newly formed FBI, an organization that then possessed a magical kind of aura, and its leader a power to be admired and feared. The hunt for John Dillinger, "Public Enemy No. 1," and his eventual entrapment by the Lady in Red, made headlines for days and inflamed the imagination of the tabloid-reading public. The day the mobster was slaughtered in the hail of G-men bullets (July 23, 1934), the *Daily News* gave over its entire front page to two lines in giant type:

DILLINGER
SHOT DEAD

Another celebrity of the era, Walter Winchell, helped mythologize Hoover, and his gossip column boosted the circulation of the tabloid *Mirror* enormously. "Winchell caught the tempo of New York of the Twenties and Thirties," the city editor of the *New York Herald-Tribune* observed. "He was brittle, cheap, garish, loud and full of dissonance." Winchell was not only the first but the most powerful of a growing group of "peep-holers" who included Jack Lait, Lee Mortimer, Danton Walker, Earl Wilson, Dorothy Kilgallen, and Leonard Lyons; and, on the West Coast, Hedda Hopper, Sheilah Graham, and Louella Parsons. Before long, Winchell's daily column was supplemented by one of the most-listened-to Sunday night radio shows.

With the uproarious rise of the big bands after 1935, an aura developed and surrounded the leaders and even some of the musicians, which may have accounted for the way dancers crowded around bandstands and just stood there, gazing in awe and admiration at the players. Big band leaders had the status of stars of the screen and stage. How deeply involved the public was in the music (and the musicians) was apparent from the enormous popularity of *Your Hit Parade*, the prime-time, Saturday night, coast-to-coast show that tabulated and performed the week's top hits.

Despite the turbulence—economic, political, and psychological—of this era, what a glorious assortment of songs—gorgeous melodies and perceptive lyrics—poured from the pens and pianos of the decade's songwriters: "Just One of Those Things," "The Way You Look Tonight," "My Romance," "Night and Day," "Lovely to Look At," "September Song," "I Can't Get Started," "I've Got My Love to Keep Me Warm," "I've Got You Under My Skin," "Through the Years," "Sophisticated Lady," "Time on My Hands," "Dancing in the Dark," "April in Paris," "Autumn in New York," "Embraceable You," "You're the Top," and so many more. And from inspirational folk songwriters who eventually became seminal figures, although they were not too well known during the era, came "This Land Is Your Land" (Woody Guthrie) and "Goodnight Irene" (Leadbelly).

Born the son of ex-slaves in Morringsport, Louisiana, c. 1888, raised in Texas, Huddie Ledbetter (Leadbelly) called himself King of the Twelve-String Guitar. It took strength to play the guitar with the doubled strings, and Leadbelly was a powerful man and a strange combination of compassion and murderous temper. He was twice sent to prison for murder, but managed to win his freedom by singing the blues. His singing and his songs so impressed John W. and Alan Lomax of the Library of Congress that they arranged for the first of his many college tours. The year was 1934, and he began making recordings at the same time. He continued to be an itinerant bluesman who collected a large number of traditional blues and also wrote a number of blues that are now classics.

Doubtless the best known is the ballad "Goodnight Irene," which became a pop hit by the Weavers in 1949, the year Leadbelly died of amyotrophic lateral sclerosis, or "Lou Gehrig's Disease," a disease that, fortunately for Leadbelly, does not affect the mind.

Six years later, "The Rock Island Line," a traditional blues he popularized, became a hit for British singer Lonnie Donegan. One of Leadbelly's best recordings was "The Midnight Special," based on the susperstition that if the headlight of a train shines into a prisoner's cell, he will be freed. Perhaps the most evocative of his songs and recordings is "Good Morning Blues," overpowering in the simplicity of the imagery he uses to describe the blues.

In 1976, Paramount released a biofilm, *Leadbelly*, starring Robert F. Moseley in the title role and directed by Gordon Parks.

Woody Guthrie (1912–1967), songwriter and singer, was born in Okemah, Okfuskee County, Oklahoma, the son of Charley Guthrie, a Texan of rancher–cattle people who developed a cattle and real estate business, and Nora Bell Sherman, a rural schoolteacher. Their third child was named Woodrow Wilson Guthrie after the Democrat who was elected president. Although the family endured tragedies in Okemah—a sister was burned to death and the mother began displaying mental symptoms of Huntington's chorea—Woody remained in the town with an older brother, Roy, when the rest of the family moved to Pampa, Texas. He completed his junior year at Okemah High School, serving as the humor editor of the school annual. To raise money for the class treasury, he danced jigs and played harmonica on the streets of the town, which he left in his sixteenth summer to rejoin the family in Pampa. Here he developed his ability as a guitarist, performing at dances with a trio that included his uncle on fiddle and aunt on accordion and playing with a country-and-western band.

In 1937, after marrying Mary Jennings and fathering two daughters, he suddenly left for California. He was soon performing daily on a sing-and-talk program on Station KFVD in Los Angeles that became extremely popular because of his Will Rogers type of humor. It led to a friendship with newscaster Ed Robbins, through whom he made contact with California's progressive left-wing movement. In 1939, at the urging of actor Will Geer, he traveled to New York City, again leaving behind his family, which now included a son. In New York, he acquired admirers in folk singer Pete Seeger and historian Alan Lomax, whom he met through Will Geer at a benefit concert for Spanish Loyalist refugees. Lomax presented Woody on his CBS network show, *Folk School of the Air*; taped songs and conversation with him for the Library of Congress Archives of American Folk Song; and arranged for him to record on RCA Victor. Released early in July 1940 in two volumes, the twelve sides constituting the legendary "Dust Bowl Ballads" were Woody's first commercial disks, brought him renown, and remain a landmark in American folk balladry.

In 1941, again through Alan Lomax, he was hired by the Department of the Interior to write songs and act in a film produced about the Bonneville Power Administration in the Northwest. Twenty-five years later, in 1966, his contribution was given recognition when a power substation was named after him, and the Secretary of the Department of Interior, Stewart Udall, posthumously granted him the department's Conservation Service Award.

During World War II, Woody and folk singer Cisco Houston joined the merchant marine and sailed on three ships that were torpedoed. Woody wrote anti-Hitler songs and inscribed his guitar with the legend, "This Machine KILLS FASCISTS!" He was drafted as the war was ending and served almost a year before receiving an honorable discharge. In this period Dutton published *Bound for Glory* (1943). Although it was regarded as an autobiography because it portrayed his childhood, family tragedies, and life in Okemah, Woody always referred to it as his "novel." A novel, *Seeds of Man*, which contained edited stories he had written about his search for a silver mine in Texas, was published posthumously in 1976. Other publications included *American Folksongs* in 1946 and *Born to Win*, published by Macmillan in 1965.*

On his return to New York after a cross-country trek in 1952, the symptoms of Huntington's disease, inherited from his mother, were beginning to manifest themselves so that Woody voluntarily entered a hospital at his wife's urging. Finding it difficult to perform and even to write, he remained hospitalized until his death in 1967 at Creedmore State Hospital in Queens, New York.

Although Woody's father actively fought socialism—the Socialist Party was a strong third party in some rural areas in Woody's youth—Woody's own political development was steadily leftward. In the early forties, he joined the Almanac Singers, formed by Seeger, Lee Hays, and Millard Lampell to promote the singing and writing of leftist songs, and performed at factories, union meetings, and anti-fascist conclaves. "Woody briefly embraced communism," *The Rolling Stone Encyclopedia of Rock & Roll* reports, "although he was denied membership in the U.S. Communist Party because he refused to renounce his religion, but he did write a column for a daily communist paper."

Woody is said to have written more than a thousand songs between 1932 and 1952. A number of them were popularized by the Weavers, the most successful folk group of the fifties, whose personnel overlapped that of the Almanac Singers. Among the Guthrie best-sellers in their repertoire were "Hard, Ain't It Hard" and "So Long, It's Been Good to Know You," one of the celebrated Dust Bowl ballads. "This Land Is Your Land," also introduced by the Weavers, enjoyed renewed commercial acceptance in 1961 when it was recorded by the New Christy Minstrels. In 1986, the reigning giant of rock music, Bruce Springsteen, included the song in a five-volume best-selling compendium, prefacing his rendition by observing that it was written by Woody as an angry response to Irving Berlin's "God Bless America."

*In addition to these autobiographical works, the reader will find valuable material in *Woody Sez* by Woody Guthrie, preface by Studs Terkel; compiled and edited by Marjorie Guthrie, with a bibliography by Guy Lodsdon (1975); and in Alan Lomax's *Hard-Hitting Songs for Hard-Hitting People: American Folk Songs of the Depression and the Labor Movement in the 1930s.* Notes on the songs by Woody Guthrie; music transcribed and edited by Pete Seeger (1967).

Other popular numbers in the Guthrie oeuvre included "Pastures of Plenty" and "Oklahoma Hills," both extolling the scenic beauty of America; "You've Got to Go Down" and "Union Maid," fervent labor songs; "Blowing Down the Old Dust Road" and "Do Re Mi," detailing the hardships of migratory workers; "Tom Joad," written after he had seen the film *The Grapes of Wrath*, based on the John Steinbeck novel; "Pretty Boy Floyd," a ballad in the Robin Hood tradition; and "Hard Traveling," one of many songs based on his experiences as a hobo. Of the latter songs Guthrie wrote: "It's the kind of song you sing after you had been booted off your little place and had lost out, lost everything. . . . It tells about a man who had ridden the flat wheels, kicked up cinders, dumped the red-hot slag, hit the hard-rock traveling."

Woody was the poet of the Oklahoma Dust Bowl, of unionization and anti-fascism, and, above all, of the American hobo and the West. "He sang the beauty of his homeland," the *New York Times* observed in his obituary, "—a beauty seen from the open door of a red-balling freight train or from the degradation of the migrant camps and the Hoovervilles of the Depression years. His vision of America was bursting with image upon image of verdant soil, towering mountains and the essential goodness and character of its people."

In *The New Yorker* in the early forties, book editor Clifton Fadiman wrote: "Someday people are going to wake up to the fact that Woody Guthrie and the two thousand songs that leap and tumble off the strings of his music box are a national possession like Yellowstone and Yosemite, and part of the best stuff this country has to show the world."

Through his impact on Bob Dylan, who was drawn to his hospital bed from his Minnesota origins, Woody became a major influence on the popular music of the early sixties. In his debut album (1962), young Dylan not only sang his "Song to Woody" but imitated his singing style as well as his mode of writing in songs like "Talkin' New York." Dylan introduced poetry and protest into rock 'n' roll, heading a phalanx of singer-songwriters who included Paul Simon, Janis Ian, Neil Young, and Joni Mitchell.

In the late sixties, Pete Seeger organized several memorial concerts for Woody. The concerts at Carnegie Hall in 1968 and the Hollywood Bowl in 1970, featuring Bob Dylan, Joan Baez, Judy Collins, Richie Evans, Tom Paxton, and Country Joe McDonald, among others, were recorded and released as albums. Seeger has also appeared periodically in concerts with Arlo Guthrie, Woody's son of his second marriage, who carried his father's folk tradition into the music scene of the 1970s and 1980s.

In 1976, Woody's book *Bound for Glory* became the title of a well-received motion picture in which David Carradine gave an in-depth portrayal of Woody.

⚡ 2 ⚡

"All Talking! All Singing! All Dancing!"

In 1933, Warner Bros. rented a railroad train, named it *The 42nd St. Special*, filled it with stars and starlets Bette Davis, Preston Foster, Laura La Plante, and others, and sent it steaming across the country. It was their way of celebrating the fantastic success of the musical film *42nd Street*, with a score by Harry Warren and Al Dubin, the film that launched a movie musical renaissance—"musicals were back with a bang."

As we know, the birth of the movie musical, the historic occasion on which the magic of sound was added to sight on the screen, occurred in October 1927 when Warner Bros. presented the first showing of Al Jolson in *The Jazz Singer*. Advertised as a talking picture, it introduced singing into film, although it was basically a drama with several songs added. It was not until 1929, when MGM made *The Broadway Melody*, that the world had a film that could be described as "100% All Talking! All Singing! All Dancing!"

The thirties were the golden decade of the musical film. But this was also the era in which the form floundered, fumbled, and flourished before it developed a self-sufficient creative group of singers, dancers, actors, directors, songwriters, and, especially, choreographers. Shortly after *The Jazz Singer* made Tin Pan Alley aware that Hollywood was a market for music, the so-called California Gold Rush of songwriters to the coast occurred. This was followed in 1930 by a large-scale migration of stage stars, as legitimate theatres were darkened by the Depression. That year, studios turned to the Broadway musical and to radio for material. There was a cascade of movie musicals, employing among others, scores by Jerome Kern, Sigmund Romberg, Harry Tierney, and Irving Berlin. The characters of the very popular radio show, *Amos 'n' Andy*, played their radio roles in *Check and Double Check*, with Bert Kalmar and Harry Ruby writing their first movie score.

Paul Whiteman and his Rhythm Boys were brought to the coast to film *The King of Jazz*, with songs by Tin Pan Alley kingpins Jack Yellen, Milton Ager, Billy Rose, and others. The "horse opera" was born at the same time, with cowboy stars like Ken Maynard and Bob Steele singing in their cowboy films. By 1939, the studios had turned out thirty-one musical westerns.

By 1931, as the Depression deepened and queues in front of movie houses telescoped, costly musicals were cut from production schedules, and the number made dropped from sixty-six in 1930 to seventeen in 1931, then to a low of twelve in 1932.

42nd Street, which arrived with the ascendance of FDR and the New Deal, marked the turnaround. Not only did it establish the songwriting team of Warren and Dubin, but it introduced the showman of the screen, Busby Berkeley, whose lavish musical numbers matched if not surpassed all others. No bird's eye view of the thirties could possibly avoid consideration of this man who left an indelible imprint on the movie musical. Born William Berkeley Enos in Los Angeles in 1895, he was to the movie musical what Ziegfeld was to the Broadway stage, creator of mammoth song-and-dance spectacles. His trademarks, as seen on many of his films, were "endless vistas of interminable numbers of chorines, usually dressed in as little as possible; formations photographed from above, with the girls becoming Catherine wheels, kaleidoscopes, and opening flowers, or holding up cards and joining them together to become giant American flags, N.R.A. symbols or portraits of FDR. . . . Choruses sung endlessly, with variations over and over again."

In *42nd Street*'s title song, Berkeley initiated the use of large numbers of girls—as many as forty-four—arranged in parallel, diagonal lines doing a thundering tap dance. It was a show-stopper on its first production and has remained one even in the eighties Broadway revival. In a series of musical films that he directed and choreographed, he continued the use of massive groups, forming geometric patterns and performing routines in unison. In "Pettin' in the Park," a number in *Gold Diggers of 1933*, forty couples were involved in the maneuvers. Among the songs introduced by Dick Powell and Ruby Keeler was "Shadow Waltz," a number in which sixty chorus girls played illuminated violins, arranged in patterns until they coalesced at the climax to form one giant violin.

In *Gold Diggers of 1935*, Berkeley began a sequence in "Lullaby of Broadway" with Wini Shaw's face appearing as a speck on a black screen. The face grew in size as the song progressed. When it was in close-up at the song's end, her profile turned into the Manhattan skyline. The more than one hundred dancers crowded the screen in a show-stopping routine. The number ended with Shaw's face receding from its full-size close-up to the initial speck on a black screen. In *Gold Diggers of 1937*, Berkeley filled the stage with nearly one hundred girls, arranged in geometric sections as parts of a military band led by Joan Blondell, with ninety-five drummers, forty-four trumpeters, and twenty-four flag girls.

Berkeley's massive choreography undoubtedly contributed to the emphasis on dancing that marked the musicals of the thirties. Starting in 1933 in *Flying Down to Rio*, Fred Astaire joined forces with Ginger Rogers. Together they danced in nine scintillating musicals, the last in 1939, so that their work was entirely encompassed by the thirties (excluding, of course, their nostalgic 1949 reunion in *The Barkleys of Broadway*). Vincent Youmans's *Rio* was followed by Cole Porter's *The Gay Divorcée* (1934), Jerome Kern's *Roberta* (1935), Irving Berlin's *Top Hat* (1935) and *Follow the Fleet* (1936), Kern's *Swing Time* (1936), the Gershwins' *Shall We Dance* (1937), Berlin's *Carefree* (1938), and *The Story of Vernon and Irene Castle* (1939). Irene Castle herself chose Astaire to play her late husband.

Astaire had class, which dance critic Marshall Stearns defines as "poise, charm, nonchalance, grace, sophistication, elegance." He adds: "In spite of his real uneasiness about it, the almost stereotype image of the debonair aristocrat in top-hat-and-tails has remained indelibly."

As for style, Astaire has himself described it as "a sort of outlaw style," a blend of ballet, tap, and ballroom dancing. Brilliant tap dancer Honi Coles observes: "Astaire sells body motion, not tap." Stearns concurs, contending that one of Astaire's greatest contributions to American vernacular dance is "the use of his arms and body, and indeed his entire body."

Astaire was a descriptive dancer, working to find motions that conformed to melodies and rhythms; he used spatial movements to express sound. But he also worked painstakingly with the words of songs. (He was an accomplished songwriter himself.) Possessing a limited voice at best, he was most concerned that the lyric should be heard and was deeply involved in finding a way to project it in dance. He was not just a hoofer, but a man who told a story through the motions of his body.

Of Eleanor Powell's tap dancing, Fred Astaire, who worked with her in *Broadway Melody of 1940*, wrote in his autobiography: "She put 'em down like a man, no ricky-ticky-sissy stuff with Ellie. She really knocked out a tap dance in a class by herself." Neatly described as "a long-stemmed American Beauty from Mt. Vernon, N.Y.," Powell tapped her way to stardom in George White's *Scandals of 1935* and *Broadway Melody of 1936*.

For another Powell, Dick Powell, Busby Berkeley used his penchant for numbers in staging the song "I Only Have Eyes for You" in *Dames*. He placed Powell in a subway dream sequence in which everywhere he looked, including the subway advertisements, he saw the face of his loved one, played by Ruby Keeler. Powell and Keeler were another "hot" dance team of the era. Dancing also played a major role in popularizing Olympic skating champion Sonja Henie, who tripped the light fantastic on ice; her novel style was introduced in *One in a Million* in 1937. That same year was a big one for Dick Powell, who had the singing-dancing lead in four musicals. A new dance team made its appearance when George Murphy, an amateur boxing champion in his college days, joined forces with Alice Faye.

The Hollywood film of the thirties was also a bonanza for child stars. Discovered by songwriter Jay Gorney in the lobby of a Los Angeles movie theatre, Shirley Temple was put under contract at the age of five and made her feature film debut in *Stand Up and Cheer* (1934). That year she made five smash films, and after the first two was stealing the show from such stars as Gary Cooper and Carole Lombard. It was not long before other youngsters became big box office: Jane Withers, a singing moppet presented by 20th Century-Fox; nine-year-old Bobby Breen, an RKO star discovered by Eddie Cantor; Deanna Durbin, out of Canada, who made her debut at fourteen in *Three Smart Girls*; and Mickey Rooney, who was a veteran at sixteen—he appeared in his first film at five—when he made the first of the popular *Andy Hardy* films and later appeared with the great Judy Garland, then fifteen. The climax of the moppet parade came, of course, with Garland's spellbinding performance in *The Wizard of Oz* (1939), for which she received a special Oscar.

"The movie musical," Gene Kelly said in 1953, "is one of the few American art forms. . . . outside of a few pleasant Jessie Matthews British films of the thirties, what movie musicals even worth noting have been produced under any auspices except Hollywood?"

The thirties did witness an influx of a large number of talented actors and actresses. *The Big Broadcast* of 1933 introduced Bing Crosby as a featured player. The decade's female newcomers included Betty Grable in *Collegiate*, big-mouthed Martha Raye in *Rhythm on the Range*, Marlene Dietrich in *The Blue Angel* (her American screen debut), Jean Harlow in *Hell's Angels*, Mary Martin in *The Great Victor Herbert*, and others. Gene Autry galloped to horse opera stardom in five films, introducing the sagebrush classic "Tumbling Tumbleweeds," and Roy Rogers, whose real name was Leonard Slye, came riding out of Cincinnati to become a Republic Pictures star in four cowboy musical westerns. Don Ameche scored in two 1938 Top Ten box-office hits: *Alexander's Ragtime Band* and *In Old Chicago*.

The year 1987 marked the fiftieth anniversary of *Snow White and the Seven Dwarfs*, featuring "a group of whimsical characters, created with pen and brush by the artists of the Walt Disney studios—the seven little dwarfs who 'whistled while they worked,' broke the spell cast by the wicked old witch on Snow White, and made her wish ["Some Day My Prince Will Come"] come true."

Their fame was international. The band of the Royal British Grenadiers switched from "Pomp and Circumstance" to "Heigh Ho, Heigh Ho, It's Off to Work We Go" for the changing of the guard at Buckingham Palace, and even Adolf Hitler, we are told, was powerless to purge Germany of them. The seven little dwarfs attracted the then astronomical sum of $6 million at Canadian and American box offices, and over three million rubber replicas of the seven—factories worked twenty-four hours a day to keep up with the demand—were snatched up by toy buyers and an eager public. Westbrook Pegler, a columnist not noted for his amiability, claimed that the Disney cartoon was "the happiest thing that has happened in the world of music since the armistice."

By 1933, Hollywood was no longer entirely dependent on Tin Pan Alley and Broadway for song material. A group of songwriting teams had developed, including some émigrés from the East: Leo Robin and Ralph Rainger, Arthur Freed and Nacio Herb Brown, Sam Coslow and Arthur Johnston, Mack Gordon and Harry Revel, Bert Kalmar and Harry Ruby, Jimmy McHugh and Dorothy Fields, and Al Dubin and Harry Warren, the latter duo the most consistent hit producers of all in the thirties.

Impressed by the impact of their score for what was little more than a corny Cinderella story (*42nd Street*), Warner Bros. retained Warren and Dubin to write songs for what became a series of successful films, *The Gold Diggers* (1933–37). It was hardly what one of the least publicly known and most prolific hit writers, Harry Warren of Brooklyn, anticipated when he stepped uneasily off the Atchison, Topeka and Santa Fe's Super Chief in 1932. He had been a drummer in a band at fourteen, sold fruit in a Brownsville theatre presenting a Yiddish stock company, was a stagehand at a Loew's theatre, picked up enough piano playing so that he was Corrine Griffith's unofficial pianist at Vitagraph Studios in Brooklyn, played piano in a silent movie house, led a small band at the Montauk Point Naval Air station during the war, and got his first job in the music business with Stark and Cowan, a small publishing firm, at $20 a week. In the 1920s, he produced modest hits in "Rose of the Rio Grande" and "I Love My Baby (My Baby Loves Me)."

By 1930, he was collaborating with Ira Gershwin and Billy Rose, composing "Cheerful Little Earful" for the musical *Sweet and Low*. In 1931, Warren produced hits in "I Found a Million Dollar Baby" in *Crazy Quilt*, words by Mort Dixon and Billy Rose, and "You're My Everything," words by Mort Dixon and Joe Young and presented in Ed Wynn's *Laugh Parade*.

The year 1934 brought two standards from the pens of Warren and Dubin: "I'll String Along with You" in *Twenty Million Sweethearts* and the perennial

"I Only Have Eyes for You" in *Dames*, a song that continues to be revived. By 1935, *The Gold Diggers* series brought Warren and Dubin an Academy Award. The lilting "Lullaby of Broadway" was chosen Best Film Song over Irving Berlin's "Cheek to Cheek" and Jerome Kern's "Lovely to Look At." It also appeared on the first program of the newly launched *Your Hit Parade* in the No. 2 slot. To Al Jolson, who had then passed his prime, they contributed "About a Quarter to Nine" in *Go into Your Dance*, a song that became a permanent part of his repertoire. In the same year, they wrote the songs for six other musical films.

In 1937 came the moody "September in the Rain," written for the film *Stars Over Broadway* but used only as an instrumental. James Melton introduced the song with a lyric late in *Melody for Two*.

Although Warren and Dubin continued to collaborate, Warner Bros., having hired Johnny Mercer and Richard Whiting, began urging Dubin to collaborate with Mercer when Whiting died. "Dubin was outright furious at being forced to collaborate with the young Johnny Mercer on lyrics for *Garden of the Moon*," Mercer's daughter wrote in her biography of him. "He demanded that Warner's buy out his contract, even though his friend, Harry Warren, was exhorting him to stay. But Al wanted out, wanted to go back to New York to try to forget his humiliating experience of working with another lyricist. So Al, whose primary sense of pleasure at the time was drugs, climbed aboard the Super Chief once again and settled down at the Taft Hotel in New York City." He quickly landed a job with Olsen and Johnson's show, *Street of Paris*, collaborating on the songs with composer Jimmy McHugh.

In the meantime, Harry Warren was paired with Johnny Mercer, and the two created top-hat material for two 1938 films. For Louis Armstrong in *Going Places* they wrote "Jeepers Creepers," a song that went to No. 1 on *Your Hit Parade* and was an Academy Award nominee, competing with Irving Berlin's "Change Partners" and "Now It Can Be Told," Jimmy McHugh–Harold Adamson's "My Own," Ben Oakland–Oscar Hammerstein II's "Mist Over the Moon," and losing out to "Thanks for the Memory" by Ralph Rainger and Leo Robin, the song that became Bob Hope's theme. In 1938, Warren and Mercer also wrote "You Must Have Been a Beautiful Baby," introduced by Dick Powell in *Hard to Get*, another song that went to the top of *Your Hit Parade*. The prolific Warren's songs totaled 178, according to Robert Lissaur's *Encyclopedia of Popular Music in America*.

✲ 3 ✲

"Life Begins at 8:40"

Two musicals, Marc Blitzstein's *The Cradle Will Rock* and Harold Rome's *Pins and Needles*, are representative of a major turn that musicals took during the thirties—reaching beyond the well-marked boundaries of the typical romance into social and political areas. Even when the main story line was "boy-meets-girl, loses girl, wins girl," songs were interpolated with a sociological perspective. In this period, a new depth of thought marked major works and the musical began to move, as it tackled more challenging subjects, toward integration of plot, songs, and characters.

That bookwriters were insecure about audience reaction to their newfound interest in topical subjects and current problems is suggested by their frequent resort to a dream framework. This technique was used in *Strike Up the Band*, *The New Yorkers*, and *I'd Rather Be Right*, among other topical musicals. For the theatregoer, the dream device permitted an escape from realities they might prefer to discount.

The concern with topical matters could have been a result of the general economic decline. But the theatre world itself did not escape the havoc wrought by the Great Depression. Of the sixty-eight playhouses on Broadway in 1930, more than a third went out of operation. Between 1930 and 1934, twelve theatres—including the Eltinge, Selwyn, Sam H. Harris, George M. Cohan, and New Amsterdam—were transformed into "grind houses" offering a continuous showing of second-and-third-run movies around the clock. Twelve more legitimate theatres were converted into movie houses between

1935 and the outbreak of World War II, and the colossal Hippodrome, famous for aquatic and circus specialties, was torn down and replaced by a parking lot in 1940. Unquestionably, both radio and musical films contributed to make the thirties a lean decade for the theatre.

"Backers who had cavalierly given thousands of dollars to mount new shows," theatre historian Gerald Bordman reports, "were declaring themselves bankrupt. So were many of the greatest producers—Arthur Hammerstein, Charles Dillingham, even the Shuberts." And Florenz Ziegfeld, E. Ray Goetz, Edgar Selwyn, among others, were in serious straits.

From a high of thirty-two musicals produced in 1930, the figures sank to a low of ten in 1935 and finished with thirteen in 1939. As for performances, only two shows ran over the 500-performance mark—and they were both flukes: *Pins and Needles* (1,108 performances) and Olsen and Johnson's madcap vaudeville-type revue, *Hellzapoppin*. In a period when there was a movement toward the integrated musical, this jigsaw revue ran for an amazing 1,404 performances.

The other "long-run" leaders of the thirties were: *Of Thee I Sing* (441), *Anything Goes* (420), *Du Barry Was a Lady* (408), *The Cat and the Fiddle* (395), *Flying High* (357), *Music in the Air* (342), *I Married an Angel* (338), and *On Your Toes* (315).

With the theatregoing audience vastly reduced, it is, perhaps, not surprising that every one of the major show composers suffered a flop during the decade. For George Gershwin, it was *Pardon My English* (48 performances, 1933); Jerome Kern, *Very Warm for May* (59 performances, 1935); Vincent Youmans, *Through the Years* (20 performances, 1932); Cole Porter, *You Never Know* (78 performances, 1938), and Arthur Schwartz, *Virginia* (60 performances, 1937). The flops were not saved by the magnificent melodies that went on to become classics, such as "All the Things You Are" from Kern's *Very Warm for May* or "Through the Years" from Vincent Youmans's show of the same name.

The most productive composer of the period was Richard Rodgers, who wrote the largest number of musical shows of any composer and whose shows displayed a persistent search for fresh story material and subjects. The weakest were *Simple Simon* (1930), starring Ed Wynn, and *America's Sweetheart* (1931). Yet from the former came the touching lament by a taxi dancer, "Ten Cents a Dance," while the latter yielded the Depression-inflected "I've Got Five Dollars." In *Jumbo* (1935), the last show to play the mammoth Hippodrome, Rodgers and Hart worked with Billy Rose, who attempted to interweave the most attractive aspects of carnival, circus, and comedy. It added two evergreens to popular music: the lilting "My Romance" and the unforgettable torch ballad "Little Girl Blue."

For *On Your Toes* (1936), Rodgers and his brilliant lyric writer Lorenz Hart collaborated on the book, pioneering the use of legitimate ballet in a Broadway musical. For the two most ambitious numbers, one a satire on the classic ballet and the other a takeoff in jazz style on gangster mores, they enlisted the help of George Balanchine, one-time master of Diaghilev's Ballets Russes of Monte Carlo. "Slaughter on Tenth Avenue," an extended orchestral composition with a doleful blues for strings and an accelerating jazz theme, was used in a climactic flight of a hoofer and his girl from gangsters and became a show-stopper. When the show was revived in 1954, critic Richard Watts, Jr., commented: "A sizable number of jazz ballets have passed this way since *Slaughter on Tenth Avenue* first appeared, but it is still something of a classic in the field." Ray Bolger, who succeeded Fred Astaire as Broadway's favorite dancer, played the hoofer, and George Abbott, with whom Rodgers and Hart had collaborated on *Jumbo*, was co-author of the book. "There's a Small Hotel" was the show's ballad hit, and "Quiet Night," a moody song, offered a melody that remained with you.

Babes in Arms (1937), an idea created by R & H, dealt with the rebellion of youngsters against the older generation; but from its opening marching song, it was clear that the work was an analogue to the world situation. The score was one of Rodgers's best, and included such standards as "Where or When," the witty, sarcastic "Lady Is a Tramp," the miniature tour de force "Johnny One Note," the humorous "I Wish I Were in Love Again," and the classic torch ballad "My Funny Valentine," not to mention the militant marching title song.

By contrast, *I'd Rather Be Right* (1937), a satire on Washington politics, was largely devoid of hit melodies, partly because the songs were interwoven with the text of the book. George M. Cohan, playing FDR (whom he hated), did not hesitate, as an accomplished songwriter, to make changes in the lyrics until he was reprimanded by the producer.

I Married an Angel (1938) was an adaptation by R & H from a European play. With George Balanchine again as choreographer, ballet dancer Vera Zorina, a graduate of the Ballets Russes of Monte Carlo, achieved her first success on the Broadway musical stage. Rodgers expanded his role as a song composer, writing ballet music, interludes, and rhythmic dialogue. But the score did include the hit title song and the lively and tuneful "Spring Is Here." "Musical comedy has met its master," Brooks Atkinson wrote in the *New York Times*, characterizing the show as "one of the best musical comedies of many seasons, and imaginative improvisation with a fully orchestrated score."

Still searching for fresh material, R & H turned to George Abbott, who developed a book based on Shakespeare's *Comedy of Errors*. At least two hits brightened the score of *The Boys from Syracuse* (1938): the sparkling waltz "Falling in Love with Love" and the arhythmic "This Can't Be Love." *Life* called it a "fantastically funny and bawdy show in the best musical tradition."

R & H's final show of the decade, *Too Many Girls* (1939), added "I Didn't Know What Time It Was" to their catalogue of scintillating songs. The show that followed in 1940 was the iconoclastic *Pal Joey*, with an anti-hero, but it died at the box office. When it was revived in 1952 it became the longest running of any revival at that point in the history of the American theatre (542 performances).

Next to Richard Rodgers, Cole Porter was the most productive show song writer in the thirties. Creating his own lyrics as well as music, he did not quite equal the number of hits achieved by Rodgers, whose songs, in the estimation of Alec Wilder, "show the highest degree of consistent excellence, inventiveness and sophistication."

Porter's biggest show of the thirties was a musical written in the flippant buoyancy of the twenties—*Anything Goes* (1934). Historian Stanley Green calls it the "quintessential of the lavish, bawdy, swift-paced, uninvolved musical comedy." This was hardly surprising. Born of a millionaire family, Porter married a multimillionairess. While most citizens suffered the travail and trauma of the Depression, Porter continued to occupy the presidential suite in the Waldorf Towers, maintained homes in New England and Brentwood, California, and employed a staff of butler, maid, and secretary. A fresh carnation daily adorned his lapel and a fresh pair of white socks his feet, regardless of the suit he wore—this in memory of his wealthy grandfather. A member of the social elite of New York's upper crust and sought after for the most elegant and exclusive parties, "Cole was the most self-indulgent and pleasure-loving man I have ever known," playwright Moss Hart has said. "But pleasure and indulgence stop dead the moment songwriting begins."

That dedication continued even after the 1937 accident in which a horse he was riding slipped and fell on him, injuring his legs so badly he was in constant pain. In an effort to avoid the amputation of his right leg that finally occurred in 1958, he endured numerous operations. Even during years of pain and bandages, it was not unusual on opening nights to see him carried into the theatre. Porter remained a man of the twenties, and his shows reflected the glamour, glitter, and nonsensical gaiety of the era.

Starring Ethel Merman as an evangelist turned nightclub singer, comic Victor Moore as a chicken-hearted hoodlum posing as a priest, and debonair William Gaxton as a playboy, *Anything Goes* gave the world of popular music "I Get a Kick Out of You," "Blow, Gabriel, Blow," the haunting "All Through the Night," and the pileup of literate, social, and topical metaphors in "You're the Top." It was the longest running of Porter's shows in the period—420 performances.

The songs for *Anything Goes* were composed while Porter was cruising down the Rhine. During a world tour, he wrote the score for *Jubilee* (1935), producing a number of exotic melodies as a result of the places he had visited. "Begin the Beguine" came to him as he was listening to native music on the island of Kalabali in the Dutch East Indies. Another, less impressive, song, "The Kling-Kling Bird on the Divi-Divi Tree," came out of Jamaica in the British West Indies. The exotic material did not eliminate Porter's love for the good ballad—and he wrote one of his minor-keyed tunes of romantic disillusionment in "Just One of Those Things."

With a book by Russel Crouse and Howard Lindsay and a cast that included Ethel Merman, Jimmy Durante, and Bob Hope, *Red, Hot and Blue* ran for only 183 performances, but it is remembered for "Down in the Depths (On the Ninetieth Floor")," a favorite of cabaret queen Mabel Mercer, and for the tongue-twisting "It's De-Lovely."

Despite his style of living and his sophisticated outlook, Porter's work did not remain entirely out of the arena of current events. *The New Yorkers* (1930), with songs mostly by Porter, advertised itself as a "Sociological Musical Satire." Only one song emerged from its short run and it was heard, if at all, only melodically. Radio judged its lyrics too risqué, and Charles Danton of *The Evening World* thought that "Love for Sale" was "in the worst possible taste." It was neither risqué nor in bad taste, but it was realistic at the time when banks were closing their doors, as the Bank of the United States did three days after *The New Yorkers* opened on December 8, 1930.

Before the thirties were over, Porter tackled another topical show. *Leave It to Me* (1938) was a spoof of the Soviet Union, with a book by Bella and Samuel Spewack. It was not one of Porter's stronger scores, but it did bring unexpected stardom to a newcomer named Mary Martin, who stole the show from Sophie Tucker, William Gaxton, Tamara, and Victor Moore with her delivery of an offbeat number titled "My Heart Belongs to Daddy."

Next to *Anything Goes*, successfully revived on Broadway with a slightly altered book in 1988, *Du Barry Was a Lady* (1939) was Porter's most successful show of the 1930s. With Ethel Merman as Du Barry and Bert Lahr as a washroom attendant fantasizing that he is Louis XIV, the show was stopped cold nightly by their tongue-in-cheek delivery of "Friendship." The show also contained one of Porter's elegantly ribald ditties in "But in the Morning, No."

Noël Coward, "the one foreign songwriter to capture the imagination of the American theatergoers," in the words of *The New Yorker*'s Douglas Watt, had several things in common with Cole Porter. He wrote both words and music and he was a master of wit, sophistication, and the ribald. In the words of Alastair Cooke, "he was the idol of an upper crust that he kidded but embraced." Porter was upper crust, no kidding!

Musically, Coward owed a debt to two non-American traditions: the European operetta and the British music-hall style. The former is represented in songs like "I'll Follow My Secret Heart," "Zigeuner," "I'll See You Again," and others that caught on and became American standards. We hear the British music hall in such songs as "Mad Dogs and Englishmen," "The Stately Homes of England," and "Mad About the Boy."

During the thirties, when he was quite productive as a playwright, actor, and songwriter, Coward created such well-remembered songs as "Someday I'll Find You" (*Private Lives*, 1930), "The Party's Over Now" (*Set to Music*, 1938), and "If Love Were All" (*Bitter-Sweet*, 1929). The last-mentioned was his most successful operetta, and it saw its first revival in 1940.

The reference to Coward as "the one foreign" songwriter is not quite accurate, since it disregards Kurt Weill, a German émigré, and Vernon Duke, a Russian émigré. What is true is that Weill and Duke mastered the Broadway idiom in a way that Coward did not.

For Vernon Duke, born Vladimir Dukelsky, 1930 brought the publication of his first American song. A symphonic composer who wrote ballets for Diaghilev, he migrated from his native land to settle in London, where he composed half a dozen shows. "I'm Only Human After All," with a lyric by E. Y. Harburg, was submitted originally to *The 9:15 Revue* but was dropped even before rehearsals. It gained a welcome spot in *The Garrick Gaieties of 1930*.

It was only the first of a very elegant, freshly harmonized, and unique set of songs that Duke contributed to the Broadway stage, including, "April in Paris" (1932), "I Like the Likes of You" and "What Is There to Say?" (1934), "Autumn in New York" (1935), and "I Can't Get Started" (1936). Like a number of his great songs, "April in Paris" initially stirred little interest. A recording on a minor label, Liberty, by a little-known society chanteuse, Marian Chase, opened the door to the worldwide recognition the song eventually received. But H. T. Parker, the Boston critic, early applauded the song's marvelous, evocative power: *"April in Paris is worthy of that city in Spring. There is a catch in the throat if one has too many memories."* And historian Isaac Goldberg wrote Duke: "If I had my way, I'd make the study of *April in Paris* compulsory in all harmony classes. It is one of the finest musical compositions that ever graced an American production." "Autumn in New York," with words as well as music by Duke, also had to wait a period of years before it found the large appreciative audience it merited, having been introduced in the musical *Thumbs Up!* (1935).

For Hyman Arluck, better known as Harold Arlen, 1930 brought the publication of his first song. He was then serving as rehearsal pianist and "gofer" for Vincent Youmans's ill-fated show, *Great Day*. Arlen, who had a good singing voice, was scheduled to do a number that unfortunately was dropped from the show. During rehearsals, Arlen frequently improvised introductions for the various songs. A phrase that caught the ears of many also impressed Will Marion Cook, conductor of the black male chorus. When it was brought to the attention of songwriter/publisher Ted Koehler, he agreed to write a lyric, and Arlen had his first published song. Described as a "hallelujah" number, "Get Happy" was introduced by Ruth Etting in the *9:15 Revue* (1930). During an out-of-town tryout of the short-lived *Revue*, George Gershwin made a point of complimenting young Arlen on the number.

It was the beginning of a remarkable career, little publicized, in which Arlen accounted for some of the finest, best-selling songs of our time, many of them blues inflected. A partial list of his perennials would include: "Between the Devil and the Deep Blue Sea" (1931), "I've Got the World on a String" (1932), "I Gotta Right to Sing the Blues" (1933), "Stormy Weather" (1933), "It's Only a Paper Moon" (1933), and "Let's Fall in Love" (1934). In 1939, he produced the award-winning score of *The Wizard of Oz* with its imperishable melody "Over the Rainbow." And this list of gems covers only the thirties in a career rich with hits into the sixties.

On Arlen's death in 1986 at the age of eighty-one, Irving Berlin paid the following tribute: "Arlen wasn't as well known as some of us. But he was more talented than most of us and he will be missed by all of us."

Although he was a newcomer, Arthur Schwartz, a barrister turned Broadway composer, was responsible for most of the songs, with Howard Dietz, in *The Little Shows* of 1929 and 1930, and *Three's a Crowd* (1932). The hits were by others: Ralph Rainger, with "Moanin' Low" in *The Little Show* (1929); Herman Hupfeld, with "Sing Something Simple" in the second *Little Show*; and Johnny Green, with "Body and Soul" in *Three's a Crowd*.

But when it came to *The Band Wagon* (1931), Schwartz and Dietz are said to have created what has been called "the greatest of all revue scores." One scintillating number followed the next: "I Love Louisa," with its beer-barrel rhythm; the melodically descriptive "High and Low"; the frisky "Hoops"; the jaunty "New Sun in the Sky," with its promise in the dark days of 1931 of good things to come; and the climactic, brooding "Dancing in the Dark."

That the thirties were a lean period, despite aesthetic advances, is made clear when we realize that the great Irving Berlin wrote only two shows. But he did write six film musicals, several showcasing the elegant and nimble dancing of Fred Astaire and Ginger Rogers. Both *Face the Music* (1932) and *As Thousands Cheer* (1933) were in the new vein of bringing the contemporary world onto the stage, particularly the latter, which used the format of a newspaper as part of its structure. *As Thousands Cheer* (400 performances) was one of the first Broadway shows to star a black singer—and Ethel Waters walked off with honors, performing "Heat Wave" and one of the earliest anti-lynching songs, "Supper Time." The show's hit song was the well-known "Easter Parade," based on a melody Berlin had used in 1917 for a song he called "Smile and Show Your Dimple."

For George Gershwin, who died in 1937, the thirties marked the pinnacle of a distinguished career. Not so much because of the musicals, though there were substantial shows like *Strike Up the Band* (1930), *Girl Crazy* (1930), and *Of Thee I Sing* (1931) (the first musical to win a Pulitzer Prize); but because of *Porgy and Bess* (1935), "the season's masterpiece" in Gerald Bordman's evaluation. The folk opera was hardly a winner in its initial presentation. Theatregoers apparently did not want to spend an evening reliving the woes that were so prevalent in the world around them. *Porgy and Bess* had more than its share of memorable melodies: "I Got Plenty o' Nuttin'," "Summertime," "It Ain't Necessarily So," "A Woman Is a Sometime Thing," "Bess, You Is My Woman Now," and "I Loves You, Porgy." But the basic story, set in a black community in Charleston, was tragic and sordid, involving violence and a crippled man in love with a lusty woman. It was not an entertainment for 1935. Since then, it has been revived countless times, playing in countries all over the world, including the Soviet Union, and has gone on to recognition as America's most important if not its greatest operatic work. In the thirties, many songwriters journeyed to the bank; others journeyed to Hollywood or the Hit Parade; George Gershwin journeyed to greatness.

Harold Rome (1908–1993)

Born May 27, 1908, in Hartford, Connecticut, Rome attended public high school and Trinity College in Hartford. Torn between an interest in law and architecture, he studied both at Yale, earning a bachelor of arts and bachelor of fine arts degree. He also took courses in music, played in the band that toured Europe, and played piano with the Yale Collegiates at proms. Settled in New York City by 1934 and unable to find work as an architect, he worked with the WPA for $23.50 a week, studied piano, improvisation, and orchestration, and supplemented his income by playing jazz. Turning from architecture to songwriting for a livelihood, Rome worked for three summers at the Green Mansions adult camp in the Adirondacks. While the ninety songs and sketches he wrote failed to attract publishers or producers, they caught the ear of the Entertainment Director of the ILGWU. When Charles Friedman, producer of the Green Mansion Show, was hired to direct an intimate, modest topical revue, Rome was retained to write the songs.

The huge success of *Pins and Needles* (1937) was not duplicated in a number of shows Rome later wrote. But *Call Me Mister*, written after he was mustered out of service in World War II, was a winner, and it yielded a million-selling hit in "South America, Take It Away," introduced by Betty Garrett and recorded by Bing Crosby and the Andrews Sisters (1946).

Rome's first book musical on Broadway was *Wish You Were Here* (1952), whose title song saved the show and became a best-selling record for young Eddie Fisher. *Fanny* (1954) was Rome's greatest Broadway success (888 performances).

Rome and his wife Florence celebrated their fiftieth wedding anniversary on February 3, 1989. Painting was his hobby, as it was Irving Berlin's. In 1965, he exhibited forty of his works at the Marble Arts Gallery in New York, with special music written by Rome played through loudspeakers.

Rome's last work for the musical theatre was *Scarlett*, an adaptation by Herbert White of the famous movie *Gone With the Wind*. It was introduced in Tokyo, where it was a huge success. It played in London, Los Angeles, and San Francisco in 1972 and toured the United States without making it to Broadway.

Interview with Harold Rome

I have a theory about the success of *Pins and Needles*. Originally, when the Ladies' Garment Workers Union decided to do a show, they got a professional company so that the first *Pins and Needles*, presented in 1936, was a professional production, staged by Philip Loeb. Earl Robinson, who later wrote *A Ballad for Americans*, and I played the two pianos. It had two performances. Brooks Atkinson came to one and gave it a very good review. Chester Erskine, who at that time owned the Biltmore Theatre, said he would put it on.

But Louis Schaffer, head of the ILGWU Entertainment Department, said: "No! If it's that good with these outsiders, it'll be much better with our own." So we spent a whole year, rehearsing ILGWU workers from 7:00 P.M. to

10:00 P.M. every single night after work. We taught them to sing. We taught them to walk and dance.

The show was supposed to open just for weekends for union members. But when the critics saw it, they gave it great reviews. So it opened as a steady show, and all the workers had to join Equity.

My theory is that when these people came on the stage and said, "We're from the shops," they were from the shops. And so there was an immediacy, a recognition by the audience and an immediate participation by them. They were with them because the people on stage were who they were singing and talking about.

Now, I used the same formula again in 1946 in *Call Me Mister* when I dealt with ex-servicemen. They came on stage and they said: "Sound-Off, 1–2 . . ." And then whatever they did, they were doing as ex-servicemen, as guys who had come from defending their country. And there was an immediate, personal rapport between them and the audience.

A current example of that is *A Chorus Line*, where the kids who come on stage are chorus people. Even though their lines are written for them, they are the people they are talking about, doing what they do as chorus people—and the immediacy of recognition and appreciation by the audience is very strong. I think that's one reason it's lasted so long—it's not that great a show. It's that personal feeling that you get only in the theatre. You can't get it on television or in the movies. *Pins and Needles* had what *A Chorus Line* has now. I didn't know it then. But that was one of its strongest points. Besides that, it was a very good show, with some very strong songs, and a step forward in its time.

Don't forget. We were getting out of the doldrums in 1937 and looking forward to more prosperous times. The WPA was working. The whole country was on the UP from way DOWN. And that was part of the spirit of the show.

Sing Out the News, which came in 1938, was not a success. It ran for only nine months. It was the uptown version of *Pins and Needles*. And it, too, was part of its time. It made fun of Wall Street. There were many newsworthy numbers. But, by that time, *Pins and Needles*, which ran until 1941, had stolen the glory as being the first.

But just as *Pins and Needles* had a hit song in "Sunday in the Park," which made the Hit Parade, *Sing Out the News* had "Franklin D. Roosevelt Jones"—a black family that wanted to honor their son as best they could and named him FDR Jones.

To *Streets of Paris*, the Olsen-Johnson revue of 1939, I contributed one song, "History Is Made at Night." The girls did a number wearing pillows on their heads. I know that Gerald Bordman, in his book, *American Musical Theatre*, mentions a number titled "The French Have a Word for It." But it does not ring a bell.

Incidentally, although it's chronologically somewhat outside your time span, I also did one number for the Gypsy Rose Lee "Burlesque Revue," *Star and Garter*, which has an interesting history. The show was produced by Mike Todd to capitalize on Mayor La Guardia's closing of New York's burlesque houses. The number was called "Bunny, Bunny, Bunny," and the girls came out holding small bunnies against their midriffs. The song had nothing to do with Playboy clubs. The girls just sang that you couldn't get their bunny, bunny, bunny for no amount of money, money, money. After a year, we received a complaint from the city. I can't remember and I don't believe I knew whether it was from the Mayor's office or the Police Department. But they claimed the song was risqué and ordered Todd to have it changed. So "Bunny, Bunny, Bunny" became "Money, Money, Money." Regardless of the city's attitude, I got a letter from Cole Porter asking for a copy of the song, which was not published. He was very much interested in its construction—it was written like a South American song.

Turning back to *Pins and Needles*, there was optimism in that part of the thirties. We had just been through a terrible time. The Roosevelt economy was getting us out of it. That was one reason the union did the show. They wanted good publicity, they wanted to promote an image, and they had a whole entertainment department working on it. The funny thing is that our work was never censored or edited. And because of that, we had a very good show.

Louis Schaffer made all the wrong decisions—and they all turned out to be right. Like to have his own people do the show instead of pros. Then, after six months, he had us put in new numbers to take the place of those that had gotten outdated. After we had put in four or five, he said: "I'm gonna call the critics in to see the NEW *Pins and Needles*. We said: "You're crazy. You got great reviews before we made the changes. Why take chances?"

But he did; he called in the critics to see the *new* edition. And we got even better reviews than the first time. When it came to a road company, he had us train a second company. But instead of sending the second, he sent the first company on the road. He said: "I wanna make the best impression!" All the judgments he made, which were against sound theatrical policy, worked out fine for him and for us.

Burton Lane (1912–1997)

Burton Lane was born February 2, 1912, in New York City. Through the thirties and into the sixties, he composed catchy melodies for Broadway shows and Hollywood films. That he had a feeling for fantasy is suggested by his two most successful shows: *Finian's Rainbow* (1947) and *On a Clear Day You Can See Forever* (1965). In addition to the title song of the latter, his catalogue of hits includes "Everything I Have Is Yours" (1933), "Says My Heart" (1938), "The Lady's in Love with You" (1939), and, of course, "How Are Things in Glocca Morra?" from *Finian's Rainbow*, along with "That Old Devil Moon."

Interview with Burton Lane

My mother died when I was two years old. From what I heard from my father, she played the piano and they loved musical shows. After they returned from a performance, she would play the scores, remembering many of the tunes. Papa loved popular songs. He loved music, and when I played the piano, he would dance around the room. We had a player piano—they existed in those days—and I would pump the pedals, and my father would bounce around in rhythm. Music brought a lot of joy into our modest surroundings.

I did take piano lessons when I was about seven or eight. I took to them very quickly. But my uncles and aunts thought I was too young, and they convinced my father to cut them out. I didn't start studying again until I was ten or eleven years old. One day my father brought home a piece of music—I was studying to read music by then. In trying to read it, I struck a wrong chord that led me into something else. I didn't know what I was doing, but I guess that was the beginning of writing. It became a kind of adventure for me to fool around with chords that were not on the sheet music. And so I began to write melodies.

It was Harold Stern who opened the door of professional writing for me. Stern not only led the band at the Brighton Beach Hotel but was the musical director for the Shuberts. At that point, I was about fifteen years old and my father was a builder. He was putting up an apartment house in Brooklyn, and the steel girders were just going up when one night, at two o'clock in the morning, the phone rang. It was the most unusual thing that could have happened. And I heard my father's voice on the telephone in the next room; he was trembling, thinking that something terrible had occurred: that the girders had fallen; that somebody had got hurt. But it was Harold Stern calling from the Shubert office. They did hold their auditions after midnight. Stern had told J. J. Shubert about me and had arranged for me to come down the following night at 12 or 1:00 in the morning to audition.

I had written quite a few songs with my first lyric writer. He was a friend of my brother's and was studying law. We were both brought down the next night and auditioned for J. J. Shubert, who was very, very impressed and signed us to a contract to write the score for the *Greenwich Village Follies*. Blossom Seely and Lew Fields, later her husband, were starring in a current *Follies*. The next one was going to star James Barton, the actor who later played in *Tobacco Road* for something like ten years. But James Barton became ill and the show was called off. I had turned in a lot of songs to the Shuberts. In fact, I didn't know how to make piano parts. They had a man by the name of Maurie Rubens, who was their arranger and man of all trades. He would sit alongside me as I played these melodies and would take down the tunes and make piano parts. They got all this music.

Three or four years later when I was in Philadelphia—I was the rehearsal pianist for *Three's a Crowd,* starring Fred Allen, Clifton Webb, and Libby Holman—I wrote two songs for that show. Suddenly I had a call from my father, who said that on a hunch he had gone to the opening of a new Shubert show in Newark. The music, my father said, was by Maurie Rubens, and nine-tenths of the score was made up of the tunes that I had turned in. Then it happened in Brooklyn; another one opened in Boston. There were four shows altogether in which my tunes were used, tunes that I had written when I was fifteen years old for the unproduced *Greenwich Village Follies*. We didn't sue them, but my father and J. J. Shubert agreed on a contract; that is, the terms of a contract. My father was a businessman, but not in show business, and he didn't know that when you had tunes in a show, the producers would give you a contract. My father was told to get a lawyer to draw up a contract with the terms agreed upon. When he brought back the contract a couple of weeks later—it was on a Friday—Shubert asked for the weekend to look it over. When we came back on Monday, all the terms had been changed. We started suit. Then the songs came out of the shows and all four shows closed in one week. And that was the end of it. Rather than pay me something like $25 or $30 a week for each show, they closed them. It was weird.

The Shuberts had Sigmund Romberg under contract. They bought shows from European producers, and Romberg got a pittance. There was *The Student Prince* and other great operettas of the period—and he got practically nothing from them for his scores. But writers didn't have any protection. There was no Dramatists Guild and no organizations that protected writers. That came much later.

Through some friends, I met Joe Young socially—he teamed with Sam Lewis, with whom he wrote "Rock-a-Bye Your Baby with a Dixie Melody" and other big hits of the twenties—and, to test me, he and Lewis gave me a lyric to set to music. I think I set it in ten minutes. They were pleased with it, and Young took me up to Remick Music. Joe Keith was then head of Remick's and he gave me a contract for a year. I received $17.50 a week as an advance against royalties.

I used to come down there every day after school. It was in my first year at the High School of Commerce in Manhattan. This was in the days when publishers had little cubbyholes with small upright pianos. Vaudeville performers would come in. Although I played the piano for them, that was not my job. I did it because I enjoyed it. I met Fats Waller. Harry Warren was the only other composer under contract at the time; he was writing with Joe Young and Sammy Lewis. It was a great experience for me. Harry and I were friends throughout his life. I met Harold Arlen when he brought his first song in: "Get Happy." After I met Irving Berlin, I placed a number of songs with his publishing company. Saul Bornstein, later Saul Bourne, was then a partner of Berlin. It was the Berlin publishing company that sent Harold Adamson and me to California in 1933. They gave us a six-week contract to see if we could place songs in films. Our first song was "Everything I Have Is Yours" in *Dancing Lady*. I lived in California for twenty-two years and Harold lived there until he passed away several years ago.

I wrote two songs with Howard Dietz for *Three's a Crowd*. Jack Robbins had called Dietz, having heard that Arthur Schwartz was in the hospital for an operation. He said: "I've got a guy over here whom you should hear." And he sent me over to Dietz. I played a few melodies for him and Howard wrote up two: "Forget All Your Books" and "Out in the Open Air." Later, when Arthur came out of the hospital and heard me play, he asked me to become the rehearsal pianist. I loved the idea because it gave me a chance to see how a show is put together. Because I was so young, Max Gordon, who was the producer, had me at all the meetings—kind of adopted me. I was able to sit in on all the production meetings, a great learning experience for me.

I had one song in *The Third Little Show* ["Say the Word"]. I did an *Earl Carroll's Vanities* (1931) with Harold Adamson, which opened up a new theatre on 50th Street and Seventh Avenue—it no longer exists. I had two songs in *Singin' the Blues*, which was a straight play. It had two songs by Dorothy Fields and Jimmy McHugh. When Alex Aarons of Aarons and Freedley heard me play, he bought two of our songs. In *Americana* (1932), I had one song that I wrote with Yip Harburg: "You're Not Pretty but You're Mine."

One of my earliest songs was called "Tony's Wife." I wrote it with Harold Adamson. It was a rhumba, probably the first American-written rhumba. When we played it for Saul Bornstein, he said: "Why do you call it *Tony's Wife*? Why not *gal* or Tony's *sweetheart*. Let's go in and play it for Irving." He took us into Berlin's office—that's when I met him—and we played the song for him. He said: "Fellers, don't change a thing, not a note or a word. Just leave the song as it is." The song never became a big hit, but it became a much-played song for that period. I think there was a singer by the name of Ramona with Paul Whiteman's band who recorded it, and the song made a lot of noise.

I met Vincent Youmans in New York, but we became quite friendly in California. We got quite close to him in the period when he was working on

Flying Down to Rio. Harold Adamson was under contract to Youmans for a brief time when Youmans established his own publishing company. Youmans would play new tunes for me and it became quite a close relationship. We were friendly until the end of his life. He was a wonderful composer.

I'll tell you one little incident. I played a melody for him that I had just written. Two or three days later, we were at a party—one of those parties where you meet a lot of directors, conductors, musicians. Alfred Newman, who won many Oscars for his movie scores, was there. In one room, there was a piano. Youmans was a great demonstrator of melodies. He had a gorgeous whistle. He would accompany himself as he whistled his melodies. I was in one room and the piano was in another. Suddenly, I head him whistling the new tune that I had played a few days earlier. The people I was sitting with said: "Just listen to that. That Youmans writes marvelous melodies." Harold Adamson said: "That happens to be Burton's melody."

Bottoms Up came after *Dancing Lady.* I don't know how or when I met Richard Whiting. He and Gus Kahn were doing *Bottoms Up.* They had a falling-out with Buddy De Sylva, who was the producer. Dick Whiting had raved about Harold Adamson and me to Buddy, and we got a call. We were signed to do the picture. There was one song we did not write. It was called "Waiting at the Gate for Katie," and that was by Dick and Gus Kahn. It became the hit song, the one that stepped out of the picture; a very cute song. That was my first meeting with Buddy De Sylva, and we became great friends as time went on.

In 1934, Harold Adamson and I were put under contract to Metro. The Paramount Theatre in Los Angeles was downtown. It had a stage show and used to show films. I went down to see a film one night. On the bill were two teenagers, the Gumm Sisters. They were about eighteen or nineteen. They sang and were okay. For a finale, they brought out their kid sister, who was just eleven. I was so impressed by her that I went out into the lobby to telephone and called the head of the music department, who happened to be Jack Robbins.

I said: "Jack, I've just heard a kid who I think has tremendous talent. She's just wonderful and I believe that Metro ought to hear her." He asked me to go backstage and see if I could arrange an audition. I went backstage, and I met the father, and arranged to have him bring the young kid out when they finished their stint at the Paramount. She came out with her father, and I played her audition. It lasted from nine o'clock in the morning until about seven-thirty at night. It started with Jack Robbins, who was bowled over by this kid. And then it would go to the head of the studio, L. B. Mayer, and the top executives, then it went to the producers, directors, and it went on all day long. At the end, no one said "Thank you" to me. Not a word. I'm sure that Robbins took credit for himself. I was twenty-two at the time. I was very naïve. So I didn't take advantage. Anyway, the kid was Judy Garland, of course, who changed her name. I was the one who got her into Metro. In 1941, I did a film for her and Mickey Rooney, *Babes on Broadway*.

The strange thing is that once they signed her, I didn't run into her until 1941, when I was signed again at Metro. I was at Metro for only one year in 1934 and was let out. I freelanced and went to Paramount and other studios. By 1941, Judy was a big star, and it was then that I came back to Metro. It was Arthur Freed who signed me to do *Babes on Broadway*. One day when we were in the commissary, Freed told us that "the kids," meaning Judy and Mickey, were going to be on a certain stage, and urged us to go over after lunch and start breaking them into songs. So I went over with Harold Adamson. As I opened the door, I suddenly became aware that somebody was running toward me. It was Judy. She threw her arms around me and said: "Burt, I never had a chance to thank you for what you did for me."

She did this again many years later. This was during a very bad period in her life. I was having dinner at Chasen's one night, and Judy came in with a group of people. I said to my wife—we had just been married—"Would you like to meet Judy?" Of course, the idea delighted her. So we went over to the table, and Judy again gave me this warm, wonderful greeting. She turned to my wife and said: "I owe everything to Burt. He was the turning point in my life." I looked at my wife when we left the restaurant, and said: "You know, she's in such bad shape, I hope that she doesn't blame me for all the bad things." She looked very bad at the time, overweight—and she looked ill.

During the Paramount period, around 1938, I wrote a number of songs with Frank Loesser. For *Cocoanut Grove*, we wrote "Says My Heart" and for *College Swing*, "Moments Like This" and "How'dja Like to Love Me." That last song reminds me of an interesting incident. When we were assigned to the picture, I suggested to Frank that we take advantage of the way Lyda Roberti, who was Hungarian or Polish, pronounced certain words. She had been in a show called *Sweet and Hot* on Broadway for which Harold Arlen wrote the music, and when she sang the title song, she pronounced it "Sweet and Chot" [a guttural "ch"]. That's how we came to write "How'dja Like to Love Me," in which she could also pronounce the "h" with the guttural "cha" sound.

This is the sad part of the tale. I was sent over to Lyda Roberti's apartment to teach her the songs. She lived in a small house in a very modest area of Hollywood. I got there, rang the doorbell, kept ringing the doorbell, but nobody came. I checked the address to make sure it was the right place. Finally, I went back to the studio and told the producer I could get no response. It turned out that she had had a heart attack and had died. It must have happened just before I got there. Martha Raye ended up assuming her role.

Most of the pictures we did in this period were hardly the kind you'd want to remember—or, for that matter, the tunes. We did the best we could with the material we were given. *Spawn of the North* was not a musical picture, but Frank and I had four or five songs in it. John Barrymore sang one of them. This picture has been shown on television more times than any picture I've written. And yet it was really a second-rate movie. We had a song called "I Like Humpback Salmon." What the hell is "humpback salmon"?

Going back to my earliest days before I went to California, I met Edgar Leslie, who was a very great and well-established lyric writer. We wrote two songs together; both were published. One of the songs was called "Under Vesuvius Skies." I didn't know what "Vesuvius" was. I was about seventeen years old and had never heard the word. The day the song was published by Walter Donaldson's firm, Mt. Vesuvius erupted. There were big headlines, of course, in all the newspapers, and that was when I found out what Vesuvius was. That was also the end of the song.

One of the songs I wrote with Frank Loesser became a hit. It was in the 1939 film *Some Like It Hot* and was called "The Lady's in Love with You." Gene Krupa and his orchestra were in it, and the stars were Bob Hope and Shirley Ross. They introduced the song, which was on *Your Hit Parade* for eight weeks during June and July of 1939. Although it was in low positions on the *Parade*, it did finally climb to No. 2 one week.

The thirties were a busy decade for me. It was fun and not so much fun. I had an unhappy marriage. An awful lot of the work I did, I did not have respect for. The quality of my work would rise or fall with what I thought of the assignment. Most of the time, in those days, I was not too happy with the projects I was assigned to. Everything goes in cycles in Hollywood. You have a series of gangster pictures and finally the grosses would drop, and they would turn to musicals. There'd be a heyday for musicals, and then that would start to fall apart. Most of the pictures were not very good. All pictures made money at one time, and then, suddenly, everything starts to fail. And there was period when I couldn't get a job.

I wanted to put an orchestra together to earn a living. I was in Chicago and about to take over somebody's band—they weren't doing too well but I thought I could do something with it—when I got a call from Alex Aarons of Aarons and Freedley. They produced all of Gershwin's musicals and Fred Astaire's shows. Aarons was a great fan of mine. We had become close friends in California. He called me from New York, having found out that I was in Chicago, and he asked: "Do you want to do a show?"

Without asking what it was, I said, "Yes." He told me to come to New York immediately and I borrowed some money and went. It was 1939 or the end of 1938. It was a show for which Yip Harburg was doing the lyrics. I had met Yip through Ira Gershwin when I was a teenager. The show turned out to be *Hold on to Your Hats*, starring Al Jolson. It was the last Broadway show in which Jolson appeared.

We wrote a hell of a score. The show got wonderful reviews. Jolson had gone into the show and put money into it because he was trying to win back his wife [Ruby Keeler]. He said: "She's agreed to do the show with me. She's never worked with me. When she sees how wonderful I am, she'll fall in love with me again, and we'll get back together."

We opened in Detroit. We played one week and then went to Chicago. During a matinee, Jolson is on stage with Ruby, doing a reprise of a song, which was very touching. In the middle of the dialogue scene, he says: "You know, Ruby"—he's now calling her by her real name instead of the stage name—"if your mother hadn't walked into the kitchen that day and gotten involved in this discussion we were having, you and I would still be together." Her mouth dropped open, her eyes opened wide, she turned around and walked off the stage, and never came back. Her understudy finished the performance. Eunice Healy was hired to take her place.

The show opened in New York and was doing standing-room business when Jolson closed the show. It was about four months later, and he had gotten his money back. He claimed he was sick and went down to Florida. Dance director Georgie Hale, who was a co-producer, managed to get photographs of Jolson at the racetrack in Florida. He sued him, and Jolson was forced to reopen the show. But by that time, the juice had run out of it—like letting air out of a balloon. But it started out to be a big show.

Another bad break happened. This was in 1939. In 1940, one minute after midnight, all ASCAP music went off the air. That was during the fight with the broadcasters and BMI. There were three songs in *Hold on to Your Hat* that had begun to develop hit potential: "There's a Great Day Coming Mañana," "The World in My Arms," and "(Love Is a Lovely Thing) Don't Let It Get You Down." One minute after midnight, 1940, those songs were off the air.

How would I compare the thirties with the present? I think that with the advent of BMI and the control that changed hands at record companies and the pushing of rock 'n' roll, the public has been fed a lot of junk. A lot of good songs have been written during this period. From personal experiences, I know that unless you have a hit show running, you can't get recordings. I've written songs that I'm very proud of. They're contemporary. I can't get recorded. It's very, very tough. At one point, Arthur Schwartz was heading a class-action lawsuit against the broadcasters. I remember one inter-office communication that went out to the disc jockeys. It had to do with a record that had an ASCAP song on one side and a BMI song on the other—and the word to the disc jockeys was to play the BMI side. "Don't play the other side. The public will never miss what they don't hear."

This is a hell of a handicap when the outlet of songs is controlled, and you can't get a recording unless there is an outlet. When there's this kind of control over what the public is allowed to hear, the public doesn't make any choice. They can only choose from what they're allowed to listen to. They don't know what's written for them because they never had a chance to hear it. I think this is the tragedy of our times.

There were always a lot of songs, bad and good, that publishers thought might make it. They got recordings and the public would make a choice. But when you're limited to what people in control want to feed the public, and nothing else, and you can't get through with a legitimate song.

When I wrote "On a Clear Day You Can See Forever," people at Chappell said: "Beautiful song! It's not going to mean anything. It's not in the groove. We're going to have a rough time getting recordings." It took a while for the song to catch on; it did have a show behind it. Robert Goulet made a recording of it. But if I brought in a song like that now without a show, you can't get a record and nobody hears it. Yet it turned out to be the biggest hit I've ever had. The problem today is that it's not a free market. The groups write their songs, record them, publish them, and plug them.

4

The Cradle of Swing

Although the spots where swing detonated as a musical phenomenon were Los Angeles (Palomar Ballroom) and Chicago (Congress Hotel), there is a street and a club that may lay claim to being the Cradle of Swing. The street was 52nd Street West, between Fifth and Seventh Avenues, and the club was the Onyx, originally one of the earliest speakeasies on that street. The concept of a cradle and a period of gestation seems relevant, for, as we have seen, the format, style, instrumentation, tempo, and the very personnel all developed over a period of years in the twenties and early thirties, even though the energy of Benny Goodman in the summer of 1935 had the quality of the musical "Big Band" appearances of Sinatra, Elvis, or the Beatles.

The ink had hardly dried on Utah's ratification of the Repeal Amendment abolishing Prohibition in December 1933 when the Onyx, a popular speakeasy, sealed its Judas hole and moved from its parlor-floor flat in the rear of a 52nd Street building to a street-level club. "Street level" is not quite right, for most of 52nd Street's clubs were located in what were once English basements, the servants' quarters of the turn-of-the-century rich, and were two or three stone steps down from the street pavement.

The Onyx's move was well timed. Repeal dealt Harlem, Prohibition's roistering entertainment center, a mortal blow. With liquor now legally available, New York City was ripe for a new entertainment center—and before long the Harlem entertainers and even their chicken joints moved downtown and settled on 52nd Street—*The Street*, as it was known during the thirties and later.

When the formal opening of the Onyx occurred on February 4, 1934, with a bill that included the Spirits of Rhythm and vocalist Red McKenzie, it became the pioneer jazz club, a major launching site for what was to be known as Swing. In fact, after a time it became known as Swing Street, a cognomen given official recognition in 1978 when the title was affixed to lampposts at the corners of Fifth and Sixth Avenues.

As a speakeasy, the Onyx was mainly frequented by musicians who played at nearby CBS, NBC, and the pit bands of the Broadway theatres. It was a place to park their instruments between shows, receive messages, and get letters they wanted kept away from home. Quite appropriately, its password was "802," the number of the local Musicians Union. Keyboard giants like Art Tatum, Joe Sullivan, Frank Signorelli, and others were constantly noodling at the corner upright—no pay except free booze. In 1933, owner Joe Helbock apparently put Joe Sullivan on a small stipend for the cocktail hour, a fact disputed by Willie "The Lion" Smith, who claims that he was being given some pay as early as 1930.

After it became a legal club at 72 West, on the north side, with paintings of Paul Whiteman and the Rockin' Chair Lady, Mildred Bailey, adorning the walls of the lounge on the second floor, the Onyx continued as a musicians' hangout until the fall of 1935. Then, a swinging brass duo, Mike Riley and Ed Farley, introduced a novelty song titled "The Music Goes 'Round and 'Round" (music Ed Farley and Mike Riley; words Red Hodgson). They performed it with a clowning routine, describing with wide gestures the passage of sound through the curves and bends of a trombone of French horn. Decca records, a fledgling company tottering under the impact of the Depression, rushed to record the duo and produced a company-saving best-seller. In the early weeks of 1936, the song rose to No. 1 on *Your Hit Parade*, and the Onyx and The Street were off to a riotous start.

As a coincidence, the Onyx furor occurred in the same period that Benny Goodman, playing a tumultuous engagement (November 1935 to May 1936) at Chicago's Congress Hotel, was being crowned King of Swing and launching jazz as a nationwide popular music fad.

Throughout the thirties, other clubs and other songs contributed to the popularization of The Street. There was hoarse-voiced Louis Prima at the Famous Door, one-armed Wingy Manone at the Hickory House, effervescent Fats Waller at the Yacht Club, Coleman Hawkins at Kelly's Stable, Frances Faye at the Yacht, Mabel Mercer at Tony's, and fiddler Stuff Smith, Maxine Sullivan, and the John Kirby Sextet, all at the Onyx. Billie Holiday and her hurting balladry were a draw at every club she played, and virtuoso Art Tatum brought the greats of classical music, notably Sergei Rachmaninoff, to marvel at his artistry. One of The Street's great moments was, of course, the appearance of the Count Basie Band at the Famous Door in 1938.

Joe Helbock, who founded the Onyx, was an active bootlegger on 52nd Street before Leon & Eddie's opened and the celebrated 21 Restaurant moved onto The Street in 1930. He told me that he could "age" a bottle of liquor between the time that someone phoned and he sent a boy out to deliver it. He had a wide acquaintance among jazz musicians, having shared an apartment with saxophonist Jimmy Dorsey, who was best man at his wedding. He hung out with the musicians at Plunkett's, a dark, narrow speakeasy on 53rd Street, just west of Broadway, that was a gathering place for the players who worked with Paul Whiteman. When he opened the Onyx as a speakeasy in 1927, he was able to get the Plunkett crowd to go with him. Like other club owners, Helbock was either lucky or he really had an ear for talent, considering the number of stars who helped jam his club.

John Popkin, who ran the Hickory House near Seventh Avenue and 52nd, always claimed that his was the first club on The Street, not the Onyx, since he opened his doors in what had been a used-car salesroom in 1933. By 1934, when he bought out his partners, he had Wingy Manone with the Marsala brothers and Eddie Condon playing jazz. To the elevated, elongated bandstand that occupied the center of an egg-shaped bar, he brought a remarkable succession of pianists through the forties and fifties. Popkin was what is known as a degenerate gambler, a man who would bet a patron leaving the restaurant $100 as to whether the number on the license plate of the next passing car would be odd or even. Eventually he lost the restaurant to a group of bookies, who occupied a conspicuous booth in the fifties.

A few club owners had musical backgrounds. Ralph Watkins, who was involved in the ownership of a number of clubs, played saxophone with Irving Alexander, another club owner, at Ben Marden's Riviera, and led his own band at the Yacht Club and the Frolics Club, situated in 1938 over the Winter Garden Theatre. Alexander married Ralph Watkins's sister, who arranged for the first wife of another club owner, Arthur Jarwood, to lend Alexander the money for Kelly's Stable, which he ran as a partner of Jarwood and George Lynch, owner of a cafeteria on Seventh Avenue.

Woody Herman remembered the owners of the Famous Door—it went through several transformations—as a Mutt and Jeff pair. "Brooks was small and short and looked like a jockey," he told me. "Felshin was over 300 pounds—he was a giant. But Brooks could be as hard as his partner. When I bucked for a bit of bread, they'd put me through such a grilling that I never wanted to approach them." Like Popkin, Brooks was a compulsive gambler. Once when he pawned his partner's overcoat, Felshin lifted him and hung him on a coat hook.

The club that Jimmy Ryan opened in September 1940 remained a bastion of Dixieland jazz long after Bop divided The Street into warring factions after World War II. Originally a chorus boy, Ryan remained a frustrated singer who boasted about the number of songs he knew, including verses, and occasionally performed in a crooning style in his club. He was a compulsive drinker who started on the bottle early in the day and who, not unexpectedly, died of cirrhosis of the liver. The club outlived him for many years. His partner, Matty Walch, a distant relative, moved it to 54th Street after the demise of The Street and continued to pursue the Dixieland policy.

Tony Soma boasted the most elegant of The Street's music clubs, attracting the elite of society and the intellectual world. His drawing card was, of course, the venerable Mabel Mercer, whose unique style of phrasing brought Sinatra, Billie Holiday, Peggy Lee, and other top vocalists to sit at her feet. It was Mercer, too, who drew the members of the celebrated Algonquin Round Table—Dorothy Parker, Alexander Woollcott, FPA (Franklin P. Adams), and a host of columnists, writers, and critics. Among those who came to listen and to hope that they could interest Mabel in their songs were such songwriters as Alec Wilder, Bart Howard, and others whose work was closer to the Broadway theatre than Tin Pan Alley. Soma himself occasionally sang, usually standing on his head, for he was a yoga enthusiast.

"On 52nd Street," jazz pianist Marian McPartland has said, "in several hours, nursing a few drinks, you could travel musically from New Orleans up to Harlem and Bop."

The street became the hangout of Tin Pan Alley publishers such as Lou Levy, record executives Leonard Joy of RCA Victor and John Hammond of Columbia, advertising agency executives, and talent agency executives Willard Alexander and Irving (later "Swifty") Lazar. New talent—perhaps, because it was cheap—was welcome. Billy Taylor, Maxine Sullivan, Erroll Garner, and others have told of how they arrived on The Street one night, sat in the next, and were booked immediately.

By 1935, the editor of *Variety*, Abel Green, observed: "West 52nd St., New York, is the capital of the Swing world. The addicts sit around entranced in an ultramodern jazz coma, as the boys cut their didoes at the Onyx Club, Famous Door and the Hickory House."

Songwriter/singer Johnny Mercer provided a partial explanation for Green's comment: "For the influential musicians of the time," he told me, "52nd St. was the focal point of jazz. When they weren't playing, they wanted to listen. . . . And the great names and the new all came to The Street."

Saxophonist Bud Freeman offers a subjective note: "When we wanted to play for ourselves, we went to 52nd St. In those days [the thirties], I was making a busy living, playing with Ray Noble [the Rainbow Room], recording, concerts and films with *Amos 'n' Andy*. But the only time I had fun, musically speaking, was in the clubs on The Street. . . . It really was an es-oteric street, even if some of the joints were owned by questionable people. Jazz was not a paying proposition, as it became for a time after Benny Good-man made it. So 52nd Street clubs—the Onyx, the Door and later Jimmy Ryan's—played an extremely vital role in the history of jazz—almost as important as Harlem, which moved downtown. It was a place where you could let off musical steam."

Trombonist Tommy Dorsey provided active support to Freeman's feeling. He was then working at the Glen Island Casino, off Shore Road in New Rochelle. "It was a drive," said publicist Jack Egan, "but Tommy made it night after night. I drove that old Buick of his. And I can never forget how he would sit outside a club, listen until he could identify the tune and key—McKenzie, Riley and Farley were then playing at the Onyx—and then go marching in playing his horn. What made him do it? After all, he had been playing for hours. I guess that sitting-in permitted a certain kind of freedom, a give-and-take between musicians that was absent when they played from charts. And there was something about The Street, something in the atmo-sphere, I can't find the words. But it was there."

Pianist Billy Taylor, who later played with jazz fiddler Eddie South and bassist Slam Stewart at the Three Deuces, adds: "It was the informality and intimacy of the 52nd St. clubs, as well as the interchange between artist and audience, that gave The Street its character and warm glow and changed the character of American popular music."

Trumpeter Louis Prima was less specific but echoed Jack Egan's senti-ment. After spending a year in the Hollywood club he established and min-gling with the celebrities of the screen, he returned to New York. "I was glad to get back to 52nd Street," he said. "There was something about the Street—I can't find the words. It always reminded me of the old Bourbon Street in New Orleans. But it was more than just music. It was a feeling that it gave you."

52nd Street was a people's street as well as a musicians' oasis. "In those days," Slim Gaillard, author of *Flat Foot Floogie*, has said, "whenever a traveler hit New York, he'd want to know where Times Square was, the prime rib places, the theatres, and 52nd Street. Here was one block where they'd find all the sounds of the day, yesterday, and maybe tomorrow."

"Musicians made 52nd Street," Sam Weiss of the Onyx and Door has said. "They brought the radio crowd, the music publishers, the talent agency execs, the theatre people, the advertising guys—and, finally, the college kids, the society people, the cloak and suitors, and the public. Name musicians made The Street into Glamourville with the help of the columnists."

Apart from glamour, during the thirties and forties The Street enriched popular music with more hit songs, more talented performers, and more re-cordings that any other entertainment center in the country.

To the world of popular music, the world of Tin Pan Alley, it was a gathering place of friendly competition—publishers, recording men, songwriters, arrangers, musicians, bandleaders, managers, and bookers. Out of this "coffee house," "cocktail-and-cigarettes" atmosphere, new songs, styles, and artists were born.

Among the songs that bear a 52nd Street association, one thinks of "Body and Soul," "Until the Real Thing Comes Along," "Flat Foot Floogie (With the Floy Floy)," "No Regrets," "Loch Lomond," "Misty," "Rockin' Chair Lady," "The End of a Love Affair," "Salt Peanuts"—and others.

One of The Street's unforgettable fans, Frank Sinatra, said: "It is Billie Holiday whom I first heard in 52nd Street clubs in the Thirties who was and still remains the greatest single musical influence on me." Lady Day and The Voice (who never appeared on The Street) typify its significance in American entertainment and popular music.

Jonah Jones (1909–   )

Born in Louisville, Kentucky, in October 1909, Robert Elliott "Jonah" Jones is a virtuoso trumpeter who can play soft, sweet, and muted, and loud, driving, and brassy. In his career, he played with many big bands, including Benny Carter, Fletcher Henderson, and Cab Calloway. But his main association during the thirties was with fiddler/vocalist Hezekiah Leroy Gordon Smith, better known as Stuff Smith, with whom he often shared comedy vocals. He made recordings with Stuff, Cab, Teddy Wilson, and Billie Holiday, among others, and under his own name.

Interview with Jonah Jones

When I was a school boy living in Louisville, I was not allowed to go out of the house beyond the gate. My mother could keep an eye on me there. They raised kids differently in those days. Standing at the gate one day when I was ten or eleven years old, I saw this marching band of kids—nine, ten, eleven years old—about thirty-five of them came strutting by, with the shining trombones in front. This was the Booker T. Washington Community Center Band, sponsored by a Ms. Bessie L. Allen, who would give you a horn free and teach you. But you had to rehearse every day after school and all day Sunday.

I don't know why, but when I saw those glistening trombones, I raced back into the house shouting, "I want a trombone! I want a trombone!" My mother said, "Just where do you think that we can get a trombone?" Well, my father knew a trombone player in town who knew about the Community Band, and he told my dad all about it. So I got hold of a horn and just couldn't get a sound out of it. I thought that the more wind you put into it, the more sound would come out. But no sound came out. After Ms. Allen watched me blowing my brains out without any results, she said: "Now, put this mouthpiece in and buzz into it like this—Burrr." I did that and was startled to hear a sound come out. Was I in heaven! Then she asked me to make a sound in the seventh position. I tried, I tried, and I tried. she said: "That's a shame! His arm is too short. But we have another horn here for you." And she gave me an alto horn in E♭. It's the one that goes: ump-TA, ump-TA-TA-TA-TA. I liked that and they put me on it—I was thirteen—but then they switched me to trumpet. There were about fifteen other guys playing trumpet. I wanted to get a fresh, individual sound and play some solos. But she had us play nothing but marches. No jazz. All the Sousa marches. And on Sunday, an overture like *William Tell; 1812; Princess of India; Morning, Noon and Night; Light Calvary*. It made you a great reader.

My first professional gig was with trombonist Wallace Bryant's Band on the Island Queen riverboat. Back in Louisville, I played with John Montague and Clarence Muse. In Cleveland, I joined up in 1928 with Horace Henderson, the brother of Fletcher Henderson, and toured with him until the band broke up in Buffalo. The Jimmie Lunceford Band was playing in Buffalo then, and he was staying in a hotel in the colored section where I was gigging for kicks with a small four-piece band. Lunceford would stop to listen to us at times and, I guess, liked my playing. When Paul Webster quit, I took his chair in the Lunceford Band. That was in 1931. He was a wonderful guy to work with and I stayed with him for about a year. We played colleges twice a week—Rochester University, Cornell, Colgate, Syracuse. The college kids liked big bands. I wasn't making much money and my wife was very unhappy about it.

So I finally quit and went with Stuff Smith at the Little Harlem Club in Buffalo. I liked to drink at the time, and you could drink with Stuff, but not with Lunceford, who was on his way up and a strict disciplinarian. Lunceford did a tremendous amount of rehearsing before he would play a number in public, and he got Sy Oliver to come with original arrangements.

I stayed with Stuff, who was a powerhouse jazz fiddler, for about two years, from 1932 to 1934. We were among the early combos that lit up 52nd Street, like the Spirits of Rhythm, John Kirby, and Louis Prima. But Stuff's big date on The Street was at the Onyx in 1936, right after Riley and Farley hit it big with "The Music Goes 'Round." Between those two Stuff Smith engagements, I worked with Lil Armstrong's big band. She billed me a *King Louis the Second*. I thought that was great. I was doing my own thing because jazz is self-expression. It was a great band, but it didn't last long.

When I quit her, I went with McKinney's Cotton Pickers, a band that got started originally in my home state, Kentucky. Don Redman, who had whipped them into a great swing band, was no longer with them. I stayed with them about six weeks and then went back to Buffalo with Stuff, first at the Little Harlem and then at the Silver Grill.

We stayed at the Onyx for about sixteen months and we had a ball. Joe Helbock, who owned the place, wouldn't give us a day off—not even Sunday. We played seven nights, and the club was packed every single night. We had Cozy Cole on drums. Ben Webster played tenor with us for a while. We enjoyed ourselves. Stuff was a great clown like Fats Waller, as well as a virtuoso violinist. He liked to appear in a batted black stovepipe, shoved far back on his head. I joined him in a derby. Stuff wrote two great novelty numbers, "I'se a Muggin' " and "You'se a Viper," both dealing with marijuana, which was then viewed in a comical and not a criminal light. I did the vocal on "Viper," and Stuff and I killed the crowd with a comical version of "Truckin'."

After sixteen banner months at the Onyx, we went out to California and played at the Famous Door, which was on Vine Street at the time. Jerry Colonna's brother was the owner with another fellow named Parker. While we were in California, I made an album at Capitol, *Jonah Jones and Glen Gray*. Dave Cavanaugh was the A & R man. We played the Traymore for a while and then returned to the Onyx, which was then managed by a guitarist named Carl Kress. It was a new Onyx. The old one had burned down, and Kress brought in the finances to reopen it. All the studio musicians around town would come in to hear us. The thirties were the era of the big bands, but they were also a great period for small jazz combos.

✦ 5 ✦

Your Hit Parade

Your Hit Parade made its debut on coast-to-coast radio on Saturday evening, April 20, 1935, the same year that Benny Goodman was crowned King of Swing and ignited the Swing explosion. It rapidly became one of the most popular shows of the thirties and forties, and it changed the character of the hit-making process in popular song.

There were a number of reasons for its appeal. Until then, the tabulation of song hits was an intramural music business activity, relying largely on lists in *Variety, Billboard,* and "the sheet," whose statistics appeared in a racing paper, *The Enquirer,* little known to the public but avidly read by denizens of the music business as much for its racing charts as its music lists. "The sheet" merely listed the titles of the songs performed on the local New York outlets of the three major networks (WABC, WEAF, WJZ), covering the hours from 5:00 P.M. to 1:00 A.M. on weekdays and all day Sunday. After a time, "the sheet" took the form of a set of mimeographed pages, delivered on subscription to the music publishers, who found it lying on their doorsteps each morning. The first activity in each publishing office was to check the plugs that had come through or missed and to study the standings of competitive songs.

What *Your Hit Parade* did—and notice the use of the pronoun—was to involve the public for the first time in the guessing game of which songs would hit or "bomb" and what song would be No. 1 the following Saturday night. Although no prizes were awarded, the public became so deeply enmeshed that when Frank Sinatra (the featured singer at a later date) paid a visit to FDR, he was asked by the president whether he knew what would be No. 1 the next Saturday.

Sinatra did not know. The order in which songs were to appear was one of the most closely guarded secrets in the entire radio field. For one thing, neither the American Tobacco Company, the show's sponsor, nor Batten, Barton, Durstine, Osborne (BBDO), the ad agency, ever revealed how they compiled their lists. There were general references to performances on the air, sheet music sales, reports of requests to bandleaders, sales of recordings, and plays of disks in jukeboxes. It was comprehensive enough, but also sufficiently vague and private to prevent even an educated guess. Clearly, to compile information of this extensive character would require quite an enormous staff. But apparently, there was no such staff—and the selection of the numbers that appeared on the *Parade* was made by a small, tightly knit cabal. Some of the music business cognoscenti even hazarded the guess that some type of average was struck among the titles appearing in *Billboard*, *Variety*, and "the sheet."

In any event, here is how Ray Charles (not the soulful warbler), who wrote vocal arrangements and rehearsed the singers from 1949 to 1958, described the inner workings of the process: "It was a most family-like operation. The esprit de corps was unbelievable. There would be a luncheon meeting at BBDO each Monday. Mark Warnow, the conductor, the chief writer, the choreographer [they were then on TV], the set designer, costume designer, director, the co-producers, and two representatives of the agency. . . . About midway through lunch, a phone call would come in from the American Tobacco Company giving us the ten [later seven] songs in the survey. After visualizations of the songs were worked out, the sponsor was phoned for approval. "Oh, yes, nothing, but nothing was done without American Tobacco's okay."

Naturally, every publisher tried to break through the veil of secrecy. Being on the *Parade* gave a song a terrific boost, and having advance knowledge would make it possible to capitalize in terms of "hyping" sheet sales, record releases, other plugs, and jukebox exploitation. Publishers made approaches to anybody and everybody connected with the show—ushers, copyists, property men, musicians, arrangers, directors, "gofers," and so on. But the fact is that no one knew—not even the conductor—in what order the chosen song would be programmed. The musicians (who were not expected to talk) rehearsed seven or ten numbers without knowing until the final downbeat which was No. 5, which No. 1, and so on.

Some years later, a novel appeared called *The Hucksters*, and it was widely rumored that the subject of the caricature was George Washington Hill, the dictatorial president of the American Tobacco Company. It was no secret in the business that he personally controlled every facet of the program, including determining the tempi at which numbers were performed. Even Sinatra made no headway when he complained that ballads were being played so fast that it was impossible to make the lyrics intelligible.

Whether or not the music business relied on that tabulated criteria set down by the *Parade*, the fact is that radio performances became the crux of the hit-making process in the thirties, as vaudeville had been previously. In fact, the era became known as that of "The No. 1 Plug"—and that was what top songwriters demanded in placing a song with a publisher. The reference was to a process by which the entire machinery of a company was geared to bunching plugs for a "drive week." Naturally, the commercial coast-to-coast shows were the primary focus, and a drive was set when a number of such shows could be persuaded to plug a song during the same week. But the so-called "day men," pluggers who dealt with the minor daytime shows, and the "night men," who contacted the minor nighttime shows, were all involved in the process—with the aim being to blanket the air waves and rack up the largest number of total plugs possible. No holds were barred—payola, hy-pola, giftola, layola—get the plug! The gambit usually worked in getting the song onto the *Parade*. If it did not, the song was dropped and forgotten.

During the thirties, the *Parade* used as many as thirteen different con-ductors. With few exceptions, they were men with studio experience, such as Al Goodman, Harry Salter, or Harry Sosnick. There were a limited number of big bandleaders like Abe Lyman and Leo Reisman—not the really big names. Obviously, George Washington Hill was determined to create a sound unique to his show, one not to be confused with sounds of the many big bands. And he succeeded, regardless of whether the singers were happy, in creating a sound remembered for its harp glissandi, uptempo pacing, and jaunty, almost happy marching beat.

The initial conductor was young Lennie Hayton, later an MGM conductor and the husband of Lena Horne, who waved the baton for seven months. Most bandleaders lasted for a brief period of several weeks. Ray Sinatra, Frank's distant cousin, occupied the stand for almost two years in 1936–37. The Raymond Scott Quintet, a semi-jazz group, was retained for almost eight months in 1938. Singers also were generally short-lived; at least nineteen were on the show between its inception in 1935 to the end of the decade. The longest lasting seemed to be Lanny Ross, Georgia Gibbs, and Buddy Clark.

In an overall view, the song that registered as the biggest hit of the thir-ties—considering that it made No. 1 for eight weeks—was "My Reverie" (1938), words and adaptation by Larry Clinton from a piece by Claude De-bussy. Clinton and his orchestra made the best-selling record with a vocal by Bea Wain.

Among its closest competitors, with seven No. 1 placements, was "Once in a While" (1937), with words by Bud Green and music by Michael Edwards. It was first introduced as an instrumental under the title "Dancing with You" by Tommy Dorsey and His Orchestra, who also presented the vocal version by Jack Leonard.

Two other songs made No. 1 for seven weeks: "Deep Purple" (1934) and "Over the Rainbow" (1939). The former, with music by Peter De Rose, was originally introduced on the radio by Paul Whiteman and His Orchestra, but the best-selling vocal version, with words by Mitchell Parish, was by Larry Clinton and His Orchestra with a vocal by Bea Wain. The classic "Over the Rainbow" (words by E. Y. Harburg; music by Harold Arlen), as noted before, was introduced by Judy Garland in the film *The Wizard of Oz* and was voted Best Song of the Year by the Motion Picture Academy.

"Until rock and roll," choral director/arranger Charles told me, "the song was the thing. Suddenly, it was the *performance.* Viewers did not want to hear Dorothy Collins singing 'Rock Around the Clock.' They wanted Bill Haley and the Comets. . . . Our audience was middle generation, and they didn't like the music that was coming in. And the kids whose music it was didn't like the people who were performing it."

"Soon," the Rodgers-Hart ballad introduced by Bing Crosby in the film *Mississippi* (1935), made No. 1 for a single week and then was superseded by Warren and Dubin's "Lullaby of Broadway," from one *Gold Diggers of Broadway* (1935).

One of only two songs that held the top spot for five weeks, Irving Berlin's "Cheek to Cheek," was introduced by Fred Astaire and Ginger Rogers in the film musical *Top Hat* (RKO, 1935).

Two songs held the top notch for many weeks: "Chasing Shadows" (No. 1 for five weeks) (music by Abner Silver; words by Benny Davis), while "Red Sails in the Sunset" (four weeks) was a British import (music by Will Grosz; words by Jimmy Kennedy), introduced by Ray Noble and His Orchestra before it was interpolated into *The Provincetown Follies.*

After being on the air for a number of years, the *Parade* developed a novel opening format that remains in the memory of many fans. The show opened cold with an announcer intoning: "With men who know tobacco best, it's Luckies 2 to 1." This was immediately followed by the voice of a tobacco auctioneer calling unidentifiable prices in his mumbo-jumbo and ending with "Sold to American." The rhythmic clicking of a telegrapher's key was duplicated by an announcer chanting: "L–S . . . M–F–T, L–S . . . M–F–T." Another voice: "You said it! Lucky Strike means fine tobacco! So round, so firm, so fully packed . . . so free and easy on the draw!" Once again, the auctioneer sang out in his mumbo-jumbo of prices and ended, "Sold to A-mer . . . i-can!" An ascending harp glissando led the band into the first sixteen bars of "This Is My Lucky Day," played in a brassy fast tempo. Finally came the announcement: "Lucky Strike presents *Your Hit Parade.*"

Tobacco companies began their insidious campaign in the twenties, and by the thirties sponsors were all over the radio networks. Cigarettes in particular were touted as great additives for smart looks, even soignée come-hither looks. The chapter title gives the tobacco object a metaphorical twist. "Love Is Like a Cigarette" first appeared with a melody by Victor Herbert and lyrics by Glen McDonough in *Algeria* in 1908, but the 1936 version (words and music by Jerome Jerome and Richard Byron) achieved a more appealing luster when Duke Ellington recorded it with a vocal by Ivie Anderson. Yet perhaps the more realistic song for *Your Hit Parade* and accompanying BBDO hype, with George Washington Hill's dictatorial presence and operations, the Jerome Kern/Otto Harbach "Smoke Gets in Your Eyes" would seem preferable.

Jack Yellen (1892–1991)

Born July 6, 1892, in Rezeki, Poland, Yellen came to this country in 1897. He was a graduate of the University of Michigan (1915), with a B.A. degree. His career spanned the years from 1913 into the 1950s and involved screenwriting as well as songwriting and publishing. He served as a director of ASCAP from 1951 to 1969, and was among twenty-four outstanding lyricists listed in *The World Almanac* (1988). He was deeply involved with the career of Sophie Tucker, who introduced many of his songs. During Sophie's later years, when she became actively involved in raising money for Israel, Jack Yellen, sans portfolio, wrote the speeches that proved so effective in her fundraising.

Interview with Lucille Yellen

Jack Yellen wrote his first song while attending Central High School in Buffalo. He continued writing while attending the University of Michigan, selling his songs to a Buffalo photographer who moonlighted as a publisher. He was paid in certificates for photographs, which when peddled netted him $5 a song. After a time he collaborated with George D. Cobb, a pianist, to increase his output. A trip to New York proved abortive insofar as his interesting Broadway publishers in their songs.

He continued his collaborating with Cobb after graduating from Michigan, but also worked as a reporter on the *Buffalo Courier*, where he became an assistant to the sports editor. Jack and Cobb finally produced a potential hit in "All Aboard for Dixieland," which was sung by the headliner at Shea's Theatre, Elizabeth Murray, leading them to sell the song for $100 outright (no royalties) to Fred Helf. Appearing in Rudolf Friml's operetta hit, *High Jinks* (1913), Elizabeth Murray made such a hit of "All Aboard for Dixieland" that Remick bought the song for $5,000 plus royalties, in which Yellen and Cobb did not participate. But they soon produced a winner in "Are You from Dixie?," which elicited an advance of $1,000 with royalties from Witmark. Only Yellen received this, for he refused the offer of an outright purchase, which Julius Witmark gave and Cobb accepted.

At the urging of his *Buffalo Courier* boss, Billy Kelley, Jack moved to New York City. While he struggled to advance his career as a songwriter, he plugged songs in Coney Island dance halls, lived in a Tenth Avenue furnished room, and existed on free lunches snagged at counters in saloons. At one point, through Mose Gumble of Witmark, he wrote English lyrics for seven French songs for $50. Time out for World War I.

Back to Buffalo Yellen went, where contact with Marion Healy, who demonstrated songs at Kresge's, led to his meeting Abe Olman, the composer of "Oh Johnny, Oh!" and "Down Among the Sheltering Pines." Olman was then stationed at the Curtis plant, awaiting his Army discharge. Working in Olman's apartment, Yellen and he wrote "Down by the O-Hi-O" and "I'm Waiting for Ships That Never Come In." On his discharge, Olman became a piano player and then general manager at the Chicago publishing house of Fred Forster, who had made it big with "Missouri Waltz." Through Olman, Yellen met Sophie Tucker, who credited her eventual success to Yellen and dedicated both her biographies to him. Tucker took a liking to "Down by the O-Hi-O" and made such a hit with it that it was thereafter performed by Al Jolson, Eddie Cantor, Van & Schenck, Belle Baker, and Ted Lewis's band.

Returning to New York, Jack met Milton Ager, a piano player at Feist Music. Ager had composed in collaboration with George Meyer and Grant Clarke "Everything Is Peaches Down in Georgia" and "Anything Is Nice If It Comes from Dixieland." The first collaboration of Jack and Milton was on some songs for a John Murray Anderson show, *What's in a Name?* (1920). It was not a success. But they were really excited by the next song they wrote, "Lovin' Sam, the Sheik of Alabam." When publishers turned it down, they were motivated by the redhead—meaning Marion Healy—to start their own firm. Thus was born Ager, Yellen and Bornstein in 1922, with Saul Bourne, as he became known, as a business manager.

At the start, they were saved from folding when Grace Hayes sang "Who Cares" in a Broadway musical. Their patron saint was Max Winslow, Irving Berlin's professional manager. Their firm was saved a second time when Van & Schenck introduced their sentimental ballad, "I Wonder What's Become of Sally," at the Palace Theatre. It became a million-copy hit, although it had been written as what Jack called "a counter-seller." This was a type of song that was not plugged professionally but was sold through performances by the girls behind music store counters. He called it an "ear of corn." But when he tried it out on some performers, it had such an effect that he took the train to Philadelphia to audition for Van & Schenck, who were appearing at a vaudeville theatre. Within days after the duo introduced the song at the Palace, the offices of Ager and Yellen were jammed with vaudevillians hungry for a copy.

In 1927, they had "Ain't She Sweet," which was introduced by Paul Ash and His Orchestra at the Oriental Theatre in Chicago. Performed by Lillian Roth, it became the rage of the flappers. Eddie Cantor and Sophie Tucker also helped make it a hit.

Another Buffalo friend, socialite Judge Louis B. Hart, was instrumental in making their show, *Rain or Shine*, starring comedian Joe Cook, a hit in the town about which impresario Morris Guest said: "There are two bad weeks in showbiz: Holy Week and a week in Buffalo." Hart arranged to have the theatre packed with friends from the Buffalo and Saturn Clubs, all attired in formal clothes. There were ovations for Don Voorhees, who conducted the orchestra, and for Joe Cook on his entrance. The show came onto Broadway as a hit at the George M. Cohan Theatre, with influential critic Alexander Woollcott lavish in his praise. Jack attributed its success entirely to Joe Cook, but it had one attractive song in "Forever and Ever."

Jack and Milton Ager did not trek to Hollywood with the advent of the talkies as many Tin Pan Alley songwriters did. But by this time Sophie Tucker, who was scheduled to make *Honky Tonk* at Warner Bros., would not set foot on the Warner lot without Jack. So Jack and Milton went West and wrote "I'm the Last of the Red Hot Mamas" and the other songs she sang in the film. They were not happy with the screenplay, and Warner Bros. was not happy with the finished film. Nevertheless, they received a call from Irving Thalberg at MGM, whose *Broadway Melody* had set a new standard for musicals. He made them a tempting offer, which they accepted only when he agreed that they could publish the songs in their own firm, Ager, Yellen and Bornstein—this even though MGM had by then acquired the music firms of Robbins, Feist and Miller. An unexplained animosity developed between them, which left its mark on the songs they wrote.

When the film, titled *Chasing Rainbows*, was almost completed, Thalberg called Jack and indicated that the director needed another song for a scene that was being added. Jack phoned Milton, who dropped in at the house on his way to the golf course. As he walked into the house without a hello and sat himself at the piano, he asked, "Got a title?" Yellen blurted out "Happy Days Are Here Again," a title that he swears had never entered his mind until that moment. The song was completed in about half an hour, and Jack took a penciled lead-sheet to the studio, where it was played for the producer. It was filmed a day or two later, with a single chorus being sung by a group of doughboys celebrating news of the Armistice.

Although they were anxious to return to New York, two new assignments came to them. MGM had signed Van & Schenck and wanted Jack and Milton to write the score. And John Murray Anderson, who had arrived at Universal

Studios to produce *The King of Jazz*, opted for their services. Two of their songs, "Happy Feet" and "A Bench in the Park," introduced by the Rhythm Boys—the latter also by the Brox Sisters—attracted attention.

Meanwhile, Wall Street took a Humpty-Dumpty fall. On the night of Black Thursday, Irving Tanz, a moon-faced song-plugger, jauntily sauntered into the huge dining room of the Pennsylvania Hotel, where George Olsen and his band were playing. "Here's what you need, George," chuckled the song-plugger as he handed Olsen an orchestration. Glancing at the title, the band-leader hurled the orchestration under the piano. On second thought, he retrieved the sheets, handed them out for the musicians, and told his vocalist to sing without a rehearsal.

As they heard the words, "Happy Days Are Here Again," the dejected diners broke into a roar of laughter. They then rose from the tables, danced over to the bandstand, and derisively chanted the words with the singer. Within a few days, New York's cafés and barrooms were booming with renditions of the song. With the Depression advancing, a newspaper reported that a hotel guest, poised on window ledge, shouted, "Happy days are here again!" and jumped. A popular joke along Broadway was that when a man registered at a hotel, the clerk would ask: "For sleeping or for jumping?"

From the Pennsylvania Hotel, the George Olsen Orchestra trekked out to the coast. Its opening at the Roosevelt Hotel in Hollywood was a gala social event, attended in formal evening attire by studio execs, stars, and directors. When Olsen opened his program with "Happy Days Are Here Again," Irving Thalberg of MGM turned to his entourage of underlings and songwriters with the query: "Now, why can't we have a song like that in our pictures?" Imagine his surprise when one of the writers informed him that it was in fact in an MGM film titled *Chasing Rainbows*, which had been shelved. The cast, which included Bessie Love and Charley King of *Broadway Melody* fame, was quickly reassembled, new sets and costumes were made, and several choruses of the song were added. Nevertheless, the film, a 1930 release, was a bomb. But the song was included in ASCAP's prestigious list, *60 All-Time Hits*.

Stopping at Buffalo on his way back to New York, Jack found that the redhead (Marion Healy) was not only in full charge of Kresge's counter, but that it had become the center of the local professional managers of the country's music publishing companies. Nobody in the music business passed through Buffalo without calling on Marion Healy, and that included top bandleaders like the Lombardos, Glenn Miller, the Dorsey brothers, and Freddy Martin, and hit songwriters like Jimmy McHugh. For suggestions as to what to play in slide presentations came the organists who had become part of the grand movie palaces—Shea's Buffalo, Loew's State, the Great Lakes, and the Hippodrome. Among the organists was Albert Hay Malotte,

later part of the Walt Disney Studios and the composer of the widely performed "The Lord's Prayer" (1935).

By the time he was on his way to London in 1930 at Sophie Tucker's
behest, Jack was no longer collaborating with Milton Ager. He wrote the lyrics
for *Follow a Star* with a British composer engaged by the producers. "It was
a lovely show," he said, "but not good enough. Neither were the songs. But
Soph—as everybody in London called her—was wonderful. The British idol-
ized her far more than Americans did. On opening night, the boxes were filled
with nobility and royalty; after the show, mounted policemen had to clear a
path from the stage door to her car."

Another so-so show followed, except that Jack was co-producer with comic
Lou Holtz, who starred in *You Said It*. Together they wrote the book and
lyrics for which Harold Arlen composed the music. It was Arlen's first full
score, and it contained "Sweet and Hot," which was introduced with a catchy
Slavic accent by Lyda Roberti, a pretty Polish blonde, and recorded by Arlen,
who had a good singing voice, with Red Nichols and His Orchestra. When
You Said It, a collegiate musical—they were in vogue then—closed after a
twenty-one-week run, Yellen left the music publishing firm he had founded
with Milton Ager. He took one copyright with him, "My Yiddishe Momme,"
which Sophie Tucker had made into an international favorite and which had
a special personal meaning for him.

Hurting like the rest of the world as a result of the stock market crash,
Jack returned to Buffalo, stuck with a mortgage foreclosure that turned out
to be a farm near Springville and remained there in seclusion until a phone
call from George White in Hollywood brought him back to the coast to write
the score for *Scandals* on the William Fox lot.

George White was an amazing character. Born in Toronto, he ran away
from home at the age of ten, traveled to New York via freight trains, learned
to dance in Bowery saloons, played in burlesque, headlined in vaudeville,
and, with money borrowed from gamblers and loan sharks, presented his
revue, *George White's Scandals*—conceived, created, and produced, as the
billboards modestly proclaimed, by George White. Choice seats for his opening sold at $200 a pair, and within three years he was a multimillionaire.
The first *Scandals* came in 1919 and the last in 1939. From 1919 through
1927, there was an annual production. Skipping 1928, there were *Scandals*
in 1929, 1931, and 1935, the peak years being between 1926 and 1931.

White had a reputation for being tough, arrogant, and ruthless. If men
hated him, women adored him, for he was young, dark, and handsome. He
had a phenomenal gift for discovering talent—his "finds" included Ann
Pennington, Willie Howard, Helen Morgan, Harry Richman, Alice Faye,
Winnie Lightner, Lou Holtz, Tommy Patricola, Jack Rose, Lester Allen,
and Bert Lahr. In addition to making stars of these, he started George

Gershwin on his Broadway career, and helped make De Sylva, Brown, and Henderson the most successful team of songwriters in popular music. The opportunity to write with Ray Henderson motivated Jack Yellen to accept White's offer.

The picture was in trouble from the start and never fully recovered, even though Rudy Vallee was its star. Alice Faye, a chorus girl who made the gossip columns because of her romance with the Yale crooner, became the leading lady when the British star scheduled for the role turned it down after reading the script. When Yellen's contract as songwriter expired, he was hired to work on the book at double his salary.

Yellen had hardly begun work on the *Scandals* book when he had a call from Winnie Sheehan, who came from Buffalo, had been a star reporter on the *New York World*, and was now bossman of 20th Century Fox. Sheehan needed a few funny scenes for Stepin Fechit in his production of *David Harum*. A week's work led to a five-year six-figure contract for Jack as a screenwriter.

After a brief return to New York for the opening of George White's *Scandals*, Jack went back to Hollywood, where Darryl Zanuck was in charge. Zanuck asked Jack to take on a young chap, formerly his secretary, Milton Sperling. They crafted the screenplay for *Sing, Baby, Sing*—the title song with a melody by Lew Pollack—and Alice Faye and Adolphe Menjou made it a box-office smash in 1936. It was the first of a series of screen hits that included *Pigskin Parade*, with Jack Haley, Judy Garland, and Betty Grable, and *Little Miss Broadway*, with Shirley Temple, Jimmy Durante, and a dancer, later a U.S. senator, named George Murphy (1938).

Jack Yellen returned to the bright lights of Broadway with Ed Wynn's *Boys and Girls Together* (1939) and the *George White's Scandals of 1939*, continuing as show song lyric-writer into the forties.

Walter Donaldson (1893–1947)

Born in Brooklyn in 1893 to a piano-playing mother, Donaldson died in Santa Monica in 1947. Although his most fertile period was in the twenties, when he composed "My Buddy," "Yes, Sir! That's My Baby," "At Sundown," "My Blue Heaven," and the hit songs for the Broadway musical *Makin' Whoopee*, which included the emotive torch ballad "Love Me or Leave Me." He was extremely active on the Hollywood scene all through the thirties and forties. In the thirties, he produced two of the era's biggest ballad hits in "Little White Lies" and "You're Driving Me Crazy," both introduced and popularized by Guy Lombardo and His Royal Canadians.

Interview with Ellen Donaldson

I've always thought it was hard to define Dad in the thirties without noting (briefly) the past—the early decades of wonder, delirious growth, fervent partriotism; the arrival of millions of immigrants; the *strenuousness* (all the energy and ambitions and dreams); the accompanying music (whether syncopated or three-quarter time); crossing the Brooklyn Bridge as a kid; the dynamic that was New York City (always a musical city).

His father was Scottish, his mother Irish. Ten brothers and sisters, one brother his twin; aunts, uncles, nephews, nieces, cousins—they were a large, warm, close family, music lovers all. His mother, a classically trained pianist, taught piano, taught *him*, played the organ in the neighborhood church.

He began (tentatively) writing songs in 1909, and had his first three *phenomenal* song hits in 1915. From that year forward the creative momentum didn't stop. There was solid musical achievement and fabulous success. He was in the Army during World War I, and after that lived in a sophisticated city (New York) that he knew well and adored with his family, close friends, and countless acquaintances. He felt a sense of "community" and camaraderie in the music world of Tin Pan Alley, and he had many enthusiasms. Pretty women, the theatre, golf (he was known to be a superb golfer), horses (he had a near-fatal passion for the racetrack), baseball, football, Notre Dame, jazz, the circus (with all the nieces and nephews), trains, parties, Florida, and his work. There was always a fascination with people, with the teeming life in the streets, and with the bright restlessness, the hard-edged gaiety (and general madness) that was in the twenties. Along with "Oh, Baby!" and "Yes, Sir! That's My Baby" he rightly sensed a need for "My Blue Heaven" too.

Throughout all this, paradoxically, he adhered to the self-imposed rigorous work schedule that would continue during his life. He was highly disciplined and his musical output was prodigious. He is acknowledged to be one of the most prolific (and gifted) songwriters of the era. Also through his life, and *particularly throughout the brutal Depression years (thirties)*, he was consistently generous in his gifts to family.

His home was New York City (and/or Brooklyn with his family). The axis he moved in didn't include California until 1930.

1930—He wrote "Cottage in the Country, That's the Thing" for the Ziegfeld show *Simple Simon*, and "Little White Lies." He came to Hollywood with Gus Kahn for the Samuel Goldwyn film *Whoopee*. Many people originally associated with the stage production had come West to do the film: Ziegfeld, Eddie Cantor, Seymour Felix (the Ziegfeld choreographer and a lifelong close pal of Dad's), and many original cast members. Seymour would be replaced by a newcomer named Busby Berkeley, who was making his film debut. For the film Dad and Gus wrote "My Baby Just Cares for Me" and "A Girl Friend of a Boy Friend of Mine." The best-known songs are the above-mentioned, "Sweet Jennie Lee," and "My Man from Caroline." He ended the year in a flourish with "You're Driving Me Crazy."

Dad entertained *no* thoughts of moving to the West Coast. He was a city boy, a true New Yorker. Although the music business was moving West and many of his friends in the music community were making the move permanent (and it was all rather entertaining), he felt for years that it was "just temporary, then we'll go back to New York." Accordingly, he simply refused to buy a home here until 1939. Even then he was doubtful. (In 1930, he wrote seventeen songs.)

1931—This was a most difficult year for Dad. It began with the death (in January) of his elder brother, and, barely a week later, the death of his beloved twin brother, his confidant and closest pal—both died of pneumonia. Dad was inconsolable for months; he, who had written daily, consistently, since the early 1910s, wrote nothing at all for almost six months. He stayed close to the family and children, traveling between New York and Pennsylvania, where his twin brother's family lived. The first song he wrote after the tragedies was "Without That Gal," recorded by Gene Austin. Then, among other songs, a jazz number called "Nobody Love No Baby Like My Baby Loves Me"; "Hello Beautiful!," recorded by Maurice Chevalier; "An Ev'ning in Carolina" (widely recorded by dance bands). For the *Ziegfeld Follies of 1931*, whose main writers were Gordon and Revel, he wrote "I'm with You," for Helen Morgan. That year he wrote twenty songs.

1932—New York—Los Angeles—New York—mulling over a move. (He wrote eleven songs that year.)

1933—Dad moved West. He rented a home in Beverly Hills and wrote some songs for MGM and Universal Pictures, notably "Dancing in the Moonlight," "You've Got Everything" (both with Gus Kahn) for *The Prizefighter and the Lady* (MGM), and "Only Yesterday" (his own music and lyrics) for the Universal film of the same title starring Margaret Sullavan. Golf continued throughout the thirties to be a *great* enthusiasm. He played often with Gus Kahn and other friends. And, of course, horseracing. He had discovered the fun of the charming resort-hotel and racetrack in Agua Caliente in Mexico, a popular place in those days. (He wrote twelve songs that year.)

1934—Dad had met Mother in late 1933. Love blossomed, and a madly romantic courtship led to marriage in the autumn of '34, in Agua Caliente. For her he wrote "A Thousand Good Nights" and many other songs. It was a quieter time, one of deep contentment. (Dad wrote thirty-three songs that year, including "Sleepy Head" and "Riptide.")

1935—A sublimely happy year for the Donaldsons personally and professionally. Their firstborn (a daughter) arrived midsummer, and Dad flashed baby pictures all over town. He worked with Harold Adamson as lyricist on songs for *The Great Ziegfeld*. The film was choreographed by his old friend Seymour Felix, and the screenplay was written by another old friend, the madcap William McGuire (who, incidentally, would be my godfather). Hal and Dad also wrote "Tender Is the Night" for the film *Here Comes the Band*. (He wrote nine songs that year.)

1936—The Great Ziegfeld opened and was a great success, winning several Oscars. Songwriters associated with the film were Irving Berlin, Con Conrad, Herb Magidson, Buddy De Sylva, Joseph Meyer, George Gershwin. Dad also wrote "Did I Remember," with lyrics by Harold Adamson, which brought him an Academy Award nomination for the film *Suzy*, starring Cary Grant and Jean Harlow. And again, with Hal as lyricist, "Can't We Fall in Love" for the film *His Brother's Wife*. Toward the end of the year he began writing with Bob Wright and Chet Forrest as lyricists and they brought forth, among other songs, "I'd Be Lost Without You" for the film *Sinner Takes All* and "Blow That Horn" for *After the Thin Man*, starring William Powell and Myrna Loy. (Twenty-one songs that year.)

1937—Dad wrote throughout the year with Bob Wright and Chet Forrest. Some glorious songs came out of this collaboration, many, unfortunately, unheard (which must have driven him crazy at times). Wright and Forrest are marvelous men—kind, witty—and they had a great rapport with Dad and Mother. They wrote "The Horse with the Dreamy Eyes" and "Saratoga" for the film *Saratoga*, starring Clark Gable and Jean Harlow. And, notably, among others, "You've Got a Certain Something," "Let Me Day Dream," "Maybe It's the Moon," and then "You're Setting Me on Fire" for the film *Madam X*. (Thirteen songs that year.)

1938—This was another really difficult year. Eddie and Bernice Mannix were very close friends of Dad and Mother. Actually, it was through the Mannixes that they met. Bernice Mannix was killed in '39 in a tragic car accident, which was a crushing blow. She had been my mother's closest friend. Eddie, Dad and Mother, Spencer Tracy, and other of her closest friends and family accompanied her body back to Boston by train for her burial there. Also, at this point, Dad was no longer working at MGM, and money was excruciatingly short. (Dad had made a lot of money; Dad had *spent* a lot of money.) Moderately bright spots: I was born in spring of that year, and Dad began working with Johnny Mercer. (Twelve songs written that year.)

1939—The Donaldson/Mercer collaboration brought forth "Cuckoo in the Clock," "Gotta Get Some Shut-Eye," and "Smarty Pants," among other songs. Dad wrote music and lyrics for "I'm Fit to Be Tied" for the film *That's Right, You're Wrong*, starring Kay Kyser (eleven songs that year). And the Donaldsons (finally) bought a wonderful house in Santa Monica, a block (and a hill) away from the beach, and prepared to settle in.

◦ 6 ◦

The Big Band Boom

"When Benny Goodman opened at the Paramount Theatre in the winter of 1936," according to a story in the *Saturday Evening Post*, "six hundred people had already been waiting outside an hour. At Six O'Clock, there were 3,000 of them, mostly high school kids from the Bronx and Brooklyn and Staten Island. . . . At 7:30 the West 47th Street precinct police station ordered Sergeant Harry Moore to saddle up and proceed with ten mounted men to the scene. . . .

"On the sergeant's advice, the management opened the theatre at Eight O'Clock, for by this time Mr. Goodman's fans were multiplying by the minute, pouring out of the Times Square subway exits like bees from a smoked hive. Fifty-five ushers, called for special duty, marshaled 3,634 of them inside before the fire department ordered the doors closed. Outside, about 2,000 disappointed youngsters were massed out into the street, paralyzing early morning traffic."

After the band played its first number, "Satan Takes a Holiday," "the children began to dance in the aisles, trampling ushers. There were policemen in front of the bandstand, but some of the kids got by them and up on the stage. They did the Shag, Lindy Hop, the Big Apple—all the leaping Harlem dances—while Goodman grinned and dodged them. . . .

"No other band of this quality," the *Saturday Evening Post* article noted, "had ever had such popular acceptance. In the past year and a half, it has sold more records, played longer runs and scored higher ratings than any band of its kind in the history of American popular music. . . . By the time the Paramount engagement was over, Goodman had smashed everyone's previous attendance record. . . . If any one musician brought along the Swing age, it was Benny Goodman."

The Paramount panic—it antedated the so-called "first" Paramount panic involving Frank Sinatra by eight years—was a confirmation of what had happened, though it was hardly anticipated, at the Palomar Ballroom in Los Angeles in August of 1935. Here, the Goodman band made its initial splash after a disastrous tour that started at the Hotel Roosevelt in Manhattan, where Guy Lombardo was an established favorite. Before the Roosevelt date, the band had attained a degree of recognition as one of three featured on NBC's *Let's Dance* program, a show sponsored by the National Biscuit Company to introduce a new cookie. It was employees of the biscuit company who attended an audition and voted on the bands to be presented on the air. Xavier Cugat was chosen for the Latin sound. Kel Murray was selected to play sweet balladry. And by one vote, Goodman won out over competitors as the Swing band. Premiering on December 1, 1934, with each band performing for half an hour, *Let's Dance* was heard on fifty-three stations on coast-to-coast radio three times a week, from 10:30 P.M. to 1:30 A.M. Eastern time.

By the spring of 1935, the band seemed ripe for a tour, and the Roosevelt—a curious choice—was picked for its opening date. It was fired after one night when patrons and even the waiters complained that the music was too loud. So-so stands in other cities were climaxed by a brush-off at the Elitch Gardens in Denver. The band that arrived in the film capital for its Palomar date was quite dispirited. Throwing caution to the wind, Goodman programmed his most challenging Fletcher Henderson arrangements. To his amazement, the audience responded with unrestrained enthusiasm. Goodman was doubtless unaware that the Los Angeles youngsters had become acquainted with the band as a result of the *Let's Dance* broadcasts, which were heard on the Coast in prime time. The Palomar stand was a blockbuster and became the band's launching pad—and the Swing Era's inaugural as well. It led to a date in Goodman's hometown, Chicago, where an appearance at the Congress Hotel, slated for three to six weeks, stretched for seven record-breaking months.

By then Goodman was being hailed as the King of Swing. There followed sold-out stands at the Hotel Pennsylvania in Manhattan (fourteen weeks), at the Paramount Theatre, and a first for jazz and swing bands, at the venerable home of classicism, Carnegie Hall, on January 16, 1938.

Mel Powell, Goodman's pianist/arranger in the early forties, then later a professor of composition at the California Institute of the Arts, recalls his excitement at hearing the band at the Paramount: "The first jazz group I ever saw was the Benny Goodman band on Broadway. I was thirteen. Lloyd (who got me interested in jazz) and I sat in the first row, and the movie with show was *Maid of Cadiz*. We saw it five times. I never heard anything so ecstatic as this music, and yet so gleaming and crystalline in its precision. Teddy Wilson's pianism in particular astonished me. And when Lionel Hampton lost one of his mallets and it flew off the stage and landed in my lap, it was almost too much."

Even while the band was bombing at the Roosevelt, it made some outstanding recordings, using Fletcher Henderson arrangements of "King Porter Stomp," "Blue Skies," and "Sometimes I'm Happy." Before Teddy Wilson appeared on stage with the Benny Goodman Trio, it cut a group of superlative sides: "Body and Soul," "After You've Gone," "Someday Sweetheart," and "Who."

These Trio sides came about, reports have it, as the result of a party at the home of Red Norvo and Mildred Bailey (then married) when Goodman and drummer Gene Krupa held an impromptu session with Wilson. John Hammond, the brilliant record producer and talent scout, had been urging Goodman to break the color line by hiring Wilson, which he did first with the Trio and later, with Lionel Hampton added, in the Quartet.

During the Congress Hotel booking, the band recorded one of its best-selling records in "Stompin' at the Savoy," written and arranged by Edgar Sampson, although three additional names appear on the writer credits: Benny Goodman, Chick Webb (music), Andy Razaf (words). Other legendary disks include "One O'Clock Jump," "Let's Dance" (which became his theme), and, in the early 1940s, "Why Don't You Do Right," with a memorable Peggy Lee vocal. Two best-selling records have been voted into NARA's *Hall of Fame* records: "And the Angels Sing," with a vocal by Martha Tilton and a high-flying trumpet solo by Ziggy Elman; and "Sing, Sing, Sing," featuring Krupa on drums, written and originally recorded by Louis Prima.

To assess the explosive character of the Goodman band's emergence, one must be aware that dance bands were a feature of American entertainment from the time that King Oliver, Louis Armstrong, the Original Dixieland Jazz Band, the New Orleans Rhythm Kings, and other jazz groups made their appearance in the 1910s. In 1917, the ODJB created a furor with its playing at Reisenweber's in Manhattan and making the first jazz recordings.

Before long, the flapper was on the scene, kicking her heels, flapping her short skirts, and flipping her bobbed hair to such uptempo dances as the Charleston, Black Bottom, and Varsity Drag. These were performed at first by small combos of five to seven musicians—Clarence Williams's Blue Five, the Original Memphis Five, and so on—playing New Orleans polyphony or two-beat Dixieland.

Through the twenties and into the thirties, there was a mushrooming of bands, prompting *The New Yorker's* jazz critic, Whitney Balliett, later to observe that "having a big band was a disease of the time." Playing for dining and dancing as well as commercial radio shows and the vaudeville theatres were the orchestras of Isham Jones, Vincent Lopez, Ben Bernie, Abe Lyman, Fred Waring and His Pennsylvanians, Guy Lombardo and His Royal Canadians (who boasted of "The Sweetest Music This Side of Heaven"), and, of course, the leviathan band of Paul Whiteman. These accounted for the hit songs of the twenties and thirties.

More significant than these to the turn that dance music took in the mid-thirties were the black bands of Duke Ellington, Bennie Moten's Kansas City Orchestra, Cab Calloway, Louis Armstrong, Benny Carter, and Count Basie. The most influential of this group was that of Fletcher Henderson, who was playing Roseland Ballroom in the early twenties and developing with the assistance of his virtuoso sideman, Don Redman, the style that became known as Swing.

"By 1926 Fletcher Henderson," Marshall Stearns has observed, "had a strictly swing band of eleven jazzmen. Before the twenties were over, black bands led by Chick Webb, Earl Hines, Cecil Scott, William McKinney, Charlie Johnson, Luis Russell and the Duke were all playing in a style in which the whole band swung together. And before 1935, when Goodman arrived, these bands were joined by Cab Calloway, Jimmie Lunceford, Teddy Hill, Les Hite, Andy Kirk, Don Redman and, especially Bennie Moten."

What this brief survey of the dance band scene indicates is that the sound and style given whirlwind currency by Goodman were germinating for a number of years before his rise. In fact, at least one band anticipated the Goodman genre as early as 1930, using call-and-response between brass and reed choirs as well as a riff style of arranging. Its appearance on the stage of the New York Paramount in the spring of 1935 inaugurated the theatre's name-band policy. It was also the first band to be featured on the radio commercial series, *The Camel Caravan*.

A mid-twenties offshoot of one of Jean Goldkette's splinter groups, this band was originally known as the Orange Blossoms in its Detroit venue. It acquired its name by accident when it played a palace-type hotel club in Toronto, built to receive the visiting Prince of Wales. While the band was well received, the Casa Loma Club failed, and the band simply adopted its name. After gigging around Detroit, it played its first New York engagement at the Roseland Ballroom, immediately eliciting a recording contract from Okeh Records.

With Gene Gifford as its arranger, it cut "hot" numbers for Okeh and, as the first band to work for two labels, danceable numbers for Brunswick. Original compositions helped anticipate the Swing Era: numbers like "Casa

Loma Stomp," "White Jazz," and "Black Jazz." Scoring its greatest success in the pre-Goodman era, 1930 to 1935, it made a strong appeal to college youngsters through a contrasting use of tempi: following a very fast number with a slow ballad, played at a much slower tempo than any other band would attempt. It made limited use of freewheeling hot solos, emphasizing precision in its handling of arrangements. (Benny Goodman was much impressed by the element of precision, which later figured greatly in his own band style.)

Although handsome Glen Gray, born Glen Gray (Spike) Knoblaugh in Illinois in 1906, was the leader of the band (which functioned as a cooperative), he did not front it until early 1937. It used as its theme the beautiful ballad "Was I to Blame for Falling in Love with You?" (words and music by Chester Conn, Victor Young, and Gus Kahn), and later, after 1933, "Smoke Rings" (words by Ned Washington; music by H. Eugene Gifford). Its biggest record, recorded in 1939, was "Sunrise Serenade," with the flipside "No Name Jive." In his book *The Big Bands*, George T. Simon observes: "More than any other single musical organization, the Casa Loma set the stage for the big band era." [The Casa Loma Band lured this jazz/swing buff into the Colonnades of the Essex House on Central Park South night after night.–Ed.]

Another band frequently cited as a Goodman precursor is that of the Dorsey Brothers, who ostensibly were playing swinging arrangements in the late twenties and early thirties. Having gigged around, made recordings, and played on the radio with different bands, the brothers—Jimmy on clarinet and Tommy on trombone—established their own band early in 1934. A group of fellow college musicians who heard them in Waltham, Massachusetts, were completely bowled over. George T. Simon recalls: "It was a stupendous, solidly swinging band that impressed that night—much more solid and much more swinging than Glen Gray and the Casa Loma Orchestra, which had been *the* outfit among collegians." Instead of the usual brass complement of three trumpets and two trombones, the eleven-piece group had one trumpet and three trombones. Two of the sliphorns were played by Tommy Dorsey and Glenn Miller, the latter being responsible for many of the arrangements and undoubtedly the "novel" instrumentation. Using repeated riffs, Miller also exploited swinging rhythmic interludes and fadeouts, the latter a feature of his own orchestra. By May 15, the band opened for the summer season at the popular and much-sought-after booking at the Glen Island Casino in New Rochelle, New York.

The brothers, however, did not get along. Tommy was critical of Jimmy's "excessive" drinking, while Jimmy insisted on needling his hot-tempered brother. Finally, one night in June, after Tommy gave the downbeat on a tune called "I'll Never Say Never Again" and Jimmy objected to the tempo, Tommy packed up his horn and walked off the stage and out of the band.

It was not long before Tommy took over the band of a friend, Joe Haymes, playing "hotel swing" at Manhattan's McAlpin Hotel, and proceeded to develop, in George T. Simon's words, "the greatest all-around dance band of them all." After recording some nondescript sides for RCA Victor in September 1936, the band made its New York debut at the Blue Room in the Hotel Lincoln. Seeking to enhance the band's quality, Tommy added such outstanding musicians as Bunny Berigan, trumpet; drummer Dave Tough; tenorman Bud Freeman; guitarist Carmen Mastren; and, from a local band led by Bert Block, flaxen-haired Axel Stordahl (later Sinatra's arranger/conductor) and vocalist Jack Leonard, whom Sinatra succeeded in the Dorsey Band.

Leonard remained with Dorsey for almost four years, recording many notable sides, the best-known of which was "Marie." (When Sinatra, then singing with Harry James, auditioned for Dorsey in Chicago, he had to sing "Marie" à la Jack Leonard.) The "Marie" disk, recorded in January 1938, set a pattern that Dorsey followed in a number of other best-sellers—"East of the Sun," "Yearning," and "Who," among others. It was a matter of switching the riff technique from instruments to voices. Leonard sang the melody in a sustained style against rhythmic background riffs vocalized by members of the band or, later, the Pied Pipers. Incidentally, the formula was one that Dorsey borrowed from a black band, Doc Wheeler's Sunset Royal Orchestra, that he heard at Nixon's Grand Theatre in Philadelphia. (Tommy indicated in a June 1938 *Metronome* article that he traded eight arrangements for Wheeler's "Marie.") The coupling to "Marie" was "Song of India," done in "Marie" style, and a best-seller that prompted adaptations of classical melodies; each featured a brilliant solo by Bunny Berigan.

Most big bands tried to establish an identity through their themes. Only a limited number had a distinctive sound, like Charlie Barnet, whose band was called "the blackest white band of all" by Duke Ellington.

The comparatively short-lived band of Glenn Miller was one of the few with an identifiable sound. Organized by Miller in 1937, it caught on in the spring of 1939 and was disbanded in September 1942 when Miller, having been turned down by the Navy, accepted a commission in the Army Air Force. But in those three short years it became one of the country's most popular dance bands, competing with or surpassing Benny Goodman and Artie Shaw. Its music had an aura of romanticism that endeared it to the youngsters of the day.

The Miller Sound began to take shape in the Ramor Ballroom in Boston in the fall of 1937, when the clarinet lead for the reed section began to be heard on coast-to-coast broadcasts. Originally, Miller's arranging device involved a trumpet doubling melody an octave above the tenor sax. When Pee Wee Erwin left the band, the difficulty of finding a trumpeter who could play the high notes led to the substitution of the clarinet. Voila! The Miller Sound.

The possibility that the sound may have evolved as a result of Miller's studies with Russian émigré composer/theorist Joseph Schillinger is not to be dismissed. A curious phenomenon of the Swing Era was the interest of many name bandleaders in Schillinger's unorthodox theories. George Gershwin was one of the first to become involved with Schillinger's mathematical approach to music. Oscar Levant early followed Gershwin. And, in time, the musicians and bandleaders who were using graph papers in their studies included, among others, Will Bradley, Vernon Duke, Paul Lavalle, Lyn Murray, and Leith Stevens. Other swingsters who came for consultation were Tommy Dorsey and Benny Goodman. In considering Schillinger's possible influence on the Miller Sound, one must bear in mind that "Moonlight Serenade," Miller's theme, was originally written by him as an exercise for his studies.

Another staunch advocate of the Russian composer/theorist was *Pins and Needles* composer Harold Rome, who lamented, "One of my great regrets is that Joseph Schillinger died before I had a chance really to study with him."

When I suggested that he could pursue study of the Schillinger System, a mathematical approach to musical composition embodied in twelve volumes of which I was the co-editor, Rome replied: "It's not the same thing at all. He was an incredible man. He had a magnetism that's indescribable. Anyway, I did learn a lot and I'm very thankful to him. I studied with him for about nine months. I was there at the hospital in 1943 when he was dying of cancer, ready to give blood."

Returning to the Glenn Miller early saga, we note that the band endured difficult times before it achieved its renown, for in January 1938 Glenn considered giving it up. However, late in 1938 after he switched from Brunswick Records to Victor, he cut his biggest record until then, "Sunrise Serenade," backed with "Moonlight Serenade," the latter his own composition. The real turning point in the band's future came in March 1939, when Glenn received word that the band was to be the summer replacement at the vitally important Glen Island Casino. The news immediately brought a booking at the popular Frank Dailey's Meadowbrook in New Jersey. Thereafter, the Miller band, with its eight-man brass choir—the first in big bands—broke attendance records wherever it played.

Of the black big bands that powered the rise of swing, one of the most influential was that of Jimmie Lunceford. A Bachelor of Music graduate of Fisk University, Lunceford formed a band in 1929 partly from students he had taught at a Memphis High School. By 1934, he was playing at the Lafayette Theatre in Harlem, and in the following year became the featured band at the Cotton Club. Although he was master of many instruments, including all the saxes, guitar, trombone, and flute, he seldom performed.

Perhaps because of his academic background, he was a demanding leader who rehearsed his men so strenuously that absolute precision in performance became an earmark of the Lunceford sound. Goodman's own demand for precision is said to have stemmed from his admiration of Lunceford, whose band also won plaudits for its showmanship, imitated by Glenn Miller. The Lunceford trumpets would tilt their horns together and wave their derby mutes synchronously in front of them. The trombones would point their horns toward the ceiling and shoot out their slides in unison. After trumpeter/vocalist Sy Oliver joined the band, his colorful arrangements added an infectious two-beat rhythmic pulse that appealed to dancers and made Oliver one of the most imitated arrangers of the thirties.

Widespread touring, including a tour of Scandinavia in February 1937, plus numerous recordings for Victor, Decca, Vocalion, and Columbia, helped develop a virtually international reputation for the band. His hits included Cliff Friend's novelty, "The Merry-Go-Round Broke Down" (1937); " 'Tain't What You Do" (1939), a jump tune by Sy Oliver and James Young; "Blues in the Night" (1941), a film tune by Harold Arlen and Johnny Mercer; and the band's theme, "Rhythm Is Our Business."

The band reached its peak in 1940, with its achievement given recognition at a big band shindig held in Madison Square Garden November 18, 1940. Twenty-eight bands performed, including Benny Goodman, Glenn Miller, Count Basie, Glen Gray, Guy Lombardo, Les Brown, and Sammy Kaye. Each band was supposed to play a fifteen-minute segment. All did except Lunceford, whose band created pandemonium, accompanied by repeated shouts of "More!" Well-known disc jockey Martin Block, acting as Master of Ceremonies, could not quiet the crowd of 6,000 until Lunceford agreed to play additional numbers.

Among the men who led big bands were a few who were distinctive showmen. One thinks of Ben Bernie ("Yowsah"), Kay Kyser as the Professor of his College of Musical Knowledge, Ted Lewis ("Is Everybody Happy?"), Shep Field and his musical straw creating "Rippling Rhythm" sounds. There were instrumentalists like Gene Krupa, Lionel Hampton, Dizzy Gillespie, Fats Waller, Art Tatum, Buddy Rich, Harry James, and others whose performances were dazzling displays of showmanship. It was partly his exaggerated zoot suit getup but mostly his singing of a song that established Cab Calloway as one of the era's stellar showmen. Leading the Missourians at the Cotton Club in 1931, he delivered "Minnie the Moocher," of which he was co-author, with such joyful zest that overnight he became known as the Hi-De-Ho Man ("Hi-De-Ho" was the song's subtitle). But Calloway was much more than a zany performer. By the late thirties he led a highly respected big band. Later, he demonstrated his histrionic abilities, performing the Sportin' Life role in the Gershwin opera *Porgy and Bess.*

In his *Story of Jazz*, Marshall W. Stearns lists the following as black bands that played "in a style in which the whole band sung together": Chick Webb, Earl Hines, Cecil Scott, William McKinney, Charlie Johnson, Luis Russell, and Duke Ellington. All of these functioned during the twenties. Stearns adds the following who performed before Goodman arrived in 1935: Cab Calloway, Jimmie Lunceford, Teddy Hill, Les Hite, Andy Kirk, Don Redman, and Bennie Moten. According to Stearns, "This music was swinging, relaxed, powerful, but for the most part unheard." Unheard because, with few exceptions, they were not booked on the commercial coast-to-coast shows or in major hotel dining rooms.

The Bennie Moten band metamorphosed after a time into the Count Basie Band. When Willard Alexander, the MCA booker, flew down to Kansas City in 1937 to sign Count Basie at the urging of John Hammond and Benny Goodman, he tried also to sign Andy Kirk. Basie was playing at the Reno Club and Kirk at a nearby spot. But Kirk had already been signed by the enterprising agent Joe Glaser. These two signings suggest how vital Kansas City was in the development of jazz and swing.

Basie's first Eastern booking was at the Roseland Ballroom, followed by an appearance at the Paramount Theatre, by which time the beauteous Billie Holiday was singing with the band. But it was not until Basie played the Famous Door on 52nd Street in the summer of 1937 and was heard over a national hookup that the band attained the recognition its powerhouse music warranted.

Soon after the band began to record for Decca, delivering such well-known sides as "One O'Clock Jump," its theme; "Jumpin' at the Woodside"; and "Sent for You Yesterday" (with a sock vocal by "Mr. Five-by-Five," Jimmy Rushing).

One of the most important figures to emerge from the Basie band was tenor saxist Lester Young, later known as the Father of the Cool School. Young was flippant and unpredictable then, and he was fired at one point by Basie for missing a record date. No reference to the Basie band would be complete without mention of Basie's unique piano style and sound (splink/splank).

Without sacrificing the robust bluesiness of his style, Basie was able in his later years to work with pop/jazz artists like Tony Bennett and Frank Sinatra. And who can forget his scintillating version of Vernon Duke's evocative "April in Paris," a Top 3 song in 1933, and a smash for Basie—with its memorable "One more time" tag—in the late fifties.

That highly combustible Basie period of the fifties included a Norman Granz booking into the Dunes in Las Vegas with blues shouter Joe Williams, who later settled in the burgeoning desert entertainment center. Also on the bill with Basie was "Lady Day" in latter-year Billie Holiday singing and stylistic form. It was a fortnight to remember.

And so we come to the thirties era's most distinguished bandleader, songwriter, composer, arranger, and pianist—not to mention bon vivant. Three years before the 1935 swing explosion, the Duke wrote "It Don't Mean a Thing If It Ain't Got That Swing," perhaps the first use of the term in a pop tune, but Ellington had been swinging as far back as the early twenties when he played the Hollywood Club, later the Kentucky Club, with Sonny Greer on drums and Elmer Snowden as leader. The Washingtonians, into which this group coalesced in 1924, came under the leadership of the Duke. It made an impressive tour of New England until it finally settled at the Cotton Club in December 1927 for a five-year run. Broadcasts from the club gave it national renown that led to appearances in Hollywood and on Broadway.

By 1930, after bringing crowds uptown to the swank Cotton Club for three years, Ellington scored his first pop hit, "Mood Indigo," making its appearance at first as an instrumental title, "Dreamy Melody." He followed this with the elegant "Sophisticated Lady," lyricized by Mitchell Parish; "In a Sentimental Mood"; "Solitude"; "Prelude to a Kiss"; and "I Let a Song Go Out of My Heart," a Cotton Club hit in 1938. Even though these were cast in the standard 32-bar song form, they had a distinctive harmonic, bluesy quality that was the Duke's unique stamp.

Already in the Ellington book were his written and recorded "Creole Love Call," "Black and Tan Fantasy," and "The Mooch," among other compositions such as "Rockin' in Rhythm," and collaborating with smooth trombonist Juan Tizol on "Caravan" in 1936.

Not too much attention was paid to the distinctive character of these songs. They were clearly not products of Tin Pan Alley, and, although they were steeped in the harmonies of blues and jazz, they were singularly Ellington. There was no period in his career when he did not have an orchestra, regardless of whether they had engagements, and it was the sounds, textures, timbres, harmonies, and melodic turns of the orchestra that gave his songs their unique quality.

In the forties, superlative lyricist Bob Russell helped make best-sellers of melodies that became known as "Do Nothin' Till You Hear from Me" and "Don't Get Around Much Anymore," "New World A-Comin'," and "In the Beginning God." Those who were strong advocates of his swing/jazz work, like John Hammond, felt that Ellington was deserting his roots. But these works as well as scores he did for several films helped bring him worldwide fame as a composer, and not merely as a songwriter. Yet through this entire period, right up to his death in 1974, he maintained his band, causing many to feel that the ensemble, not the piano, was really his instrument.

From 1935 to 1946, midtown Manhattan, not unlike the main stems of other big cities, was a swinging extravaganza, with hotel showrooms and grills, ballrooms, theatres, and night clubs resounding to the beat of the big bands.

Starting at the Lexington Grill on Lexington Avenue, you could hop to the bounce of Bob Crosby and His Dixieland Bob Cats. Then over to the Hotel Commodore's Palm Room on 42nd Street, where the Sweethearts of Swing, Mildred Bailey and Red Norvo, held forth. Nearby, there were the Moonlight Terrace of the Biltmore, with Horace Heidt and His Musical Knights, and the Grill Room of the Roosevelt, with Guy Lombardo and His Royal Canadians.

Going west you could catch Glenn Miller and His Orchestra at the Paradise Restaurant. Benny Goodman was at the Manhattan Room of the Hotel Pennsylvania. Jimmy Dorsey, with Bob Eberly and Helen O'Connell, was at the Terrace Room of the New Yorker. Artie Shaw and Helen Forrest were in the Blue Room of the Hotel Lincoln, and Les Brown was in the Green Room of the Hotel Edison.

Tommy Dorsey and his band or Lionel Hampton and his vibes might be at the Paramount; Xavier Cugat could be heard with his Latin swing at the Strand; and Jimmie Lunceford might be at Loew's State.

If you wanted to travel uptown, you could catch Chick Webb and Ella Fitzgerald at the Savoy. Duke Ellington graduated from "Jungle" music at the Cotton Club to the New Midtown Cotton Club, where Cab Calloway later held forth.

Or if you were on the West Coast, there was Ted Fiorito at the Beverly Wilshire, Jimmy Grier at the Biltmore Grill, Les Hite at the Café International in Culver City, Ozzie and Harriet Nelson at the Victor Hugo in Beverly Hills, Garwood Van at the Hollywood Trocadero, and Freddy Martin at the Cocoanut Grove of the Ambassador.

The rise of swing brought major changes in the publishing business as well as in the country's popular music. Whereas the music publishers and songwriters had once wooed the vaudevillians, wining and dining them, financing their trips across country (paying for scenery, costumes, etc.), and "cutting them in" on royalties and song credits, now the bandleaders became the focus of their attentions.

As one examines the list of song hits, it is obvious that more songs were introduced and popularized by bands than solo singers. "Payola," covert and overt, like putting their names on song anthologies and paying an overriding royalty, was now aimed at the men who gave the downbeat.

When a name band opened at one of the city's major hotels, publishers fell over themselves, vying for upfront tables (where they would be seen by the leader) and filling them with notable guests who might attract the batoneer to them. The routines of the song-pluggers altered as they spent their evenings going from hotel grill to ballroom, traveling out to the Glen Island Casino in Westchester, or Frank Daily's Meadowbrook in New Jersey. And the record labels vied with each other in signing the bands that drew the crowds and made the hits.

Out of this syndrome a whole new lingo developed. "Rocking-chair hit" meant a song that had made it on its own and allowed the publisher to sit in his chair and rock. "Curve" was a promised plug that did not come through. "Fish hooks in his pocket" referred to the individual whose hand remained in his pocket when the check arrived. "Sheet-shot" meant a plug that was not commercial and had a small listening audience. "He'd take a hot stove" was lingo for a person who would take an open bribe.

Naturally, dance styles changed. Instead of the Charleston, Black Bottom, and Varsity Drag, favorites of the flappers, the youngsters of the thirties found appeal in the Shag, Big Apple (which originated in North Carolina), Suzy Q, Continental, Carioca, Truckin', Yam, Posin', and (from England) the Lambeth Walk. At the Savoy Ballroom in Harlem, the Lindy Hop superseded the widely performed Charleston.

♦ 7 ♦

"I Got Rhythm"
(1930)

Between shows at the Brooklyn Paramount—four singing stints a day, alternating with presentations of the film—she traveled by subway to the Gershwin penthouse apartment at 33 Riverside Drive to an audition, arranged by producer Vinton Freedley, with George Gershwin himself at the piano, with brother Ira listening in. She sang Walter Donaldson's "Little White Lies" and Jimmy McHugh's "Exactly Like You." A few days later, producers Freedley and Aarons invited Ethel Merman to their office and signed a contract for her appearance in *Girl Crazy* at $375 a week. Al Siegel, who had been her regular accompanist, was also signed for the show, the Gershwins' second musical of the year, following the pathbreaking *Strike Up the Band*.

During rehearsals, Lou Irwin, her manager, arranged for an appearance at the Palace—the realization of a dream for Ethel Agnes Zimmerman, the name she acquired at birth in Astoria, Long Island, and shortened, not without her German Lutheran father's opposition. Until her appearance in *Girl Crazy*, Ethel had been working as a full-time secretary and filling engagements at clubs and theatres that sometimes made it necessary for her to catch up on sleep on the job. At one point, Irwin got her a contract with Warner Bros. films. Although she received $200 a week for several months, the only use the movie company made of her was in a long-forgotten short. Nevertheless, all the gigs at hardly impressive locations spread word of the girl who sang with a verve and volume that led Vinton Freedley to make a trip to the Brooklyn Paramount to hear her.

Her appearance at the Palace did not go unnoticed. On September 15, 1930, a reviewer wrote in the *New York Times*: "Miss Merman's torch singing premiere turns out to be an auspicious event in lyric celebration of the broken Broadway heart and promises well for her debut later in the season on the musical comedy stage."

Girl Crazy had its New York premiere at 52nd Street's Alvin Theatre on October 14, 1930. With the cream of New York society and the entertainment world attending, Gershwin himself conducted the pit orchestra for the opening performance. In the pit was the Red Nichols Band, plus such distinguished jazz instrumentalists as Benny Goodman, Glenn Miller, Jack Teagarden, Gene Krupa, and Tommy Dorsey.

"As soon as I sang 'Sam and Delilah,' I knew I was in," Ethel told her biographer. "Immediately afterward she had an even greater number," Bob Thomas wrote. "She gazed down with assurance at Al Siegel, who had left a hospital bed to accompany her on opening night, and began 'I Got Rhythm.' When she launched her long note in the second chorus (while the orchestra played through half the chorus), the Alvin Theatre reverberated. 'It was,' Ira Gershwin observed, 'a no-nonsense voice that would reach not only standees but ticket takers in the lobby.' Ethel had to perform encore after encore before the first act curtain could descend."

Gershwin himself was the first to acknowledge her achievement. "He hurried out of the orchestra pit," Bob Thomas wrote, "and dashed up three flights of stairs to Ethel's dressing room. He swung open the door and exclaimed, 'Ethel, you've done it!' Then he uttered the line that Merman quoted for the rest of her life, 'Never but never go near a singing teacher.' "

The following day's reviews were such that when she lunched with Gershwin at his apartment, with all the papers spread out on the floor, he exclaimed: "They loved my songs, the show's a hit and you're a sensation!"

Robert Coleman's comment in the *Daily Mirror* was typical of the day's reviews. "The big surprise of the evening was Ethel Merman, a young and talented songstress with a peculiar delivery who tied the proceedings up in knots. A graduate of night clubs and motion picture theatres, this girl bids fair to become the toast of Broadway." And she did overnight emerge as the Queen of Broadway, despite the presence in the cast of sparkling Ginger Rogers, who was also making her Broadway debut, and whose numbers included the lilting ballad "But Not for Me" and the classic "Embraceable You."

Opening night of *Girl Crazy* marked the terminus of the professional relationship between Ethel and Al Siegel, who was taken out of the theatre on a stretcher at the end of the first act. Later, Ethel and manager Irwin visited Siegel in the hospital—he was suffering from tuberculosis—and offered to have him write new arrangements of the *Girl Crazy* songs for the night club appearances. When he asked for 33 percent of all her future earnings, Ethel severed their relationship, continuing to pay him 25 percent of her income during the period that their contract was still in force. The relationship between the two remained strained through the years; Al and his supporters, including columnist Walter Winchell, kept claiming that it was he who shaped the famous Merman style. Ethel's reaction was always couched in language whose color matched the volume of her voice.

Girl Crazy was followed by Cole Porter's *Anything Goes* (1934), "a thundering good song and dance show," in Brooks Atkinson's view, "crammed with hits." Although Merman scored with "You're the Top" and "Blow, Gabriel, Blow," it was "I Get a Kick Out of You," a number that initially posed problems, that became the gem of the show. It was her inventive handling of the syllable "rif" in the word "terrific'ly," extending its duration, that, in Ethel's words, "killed the people and helped make the song the hit of a show filled with outstanding musical numbers." Maurice Zolotow confirms that the extended hold, also practiced by Sinatra, who is sometimes credited with devising it, "knocked the audience totally unprepared for a 'Loop.' "

A favorite with such top composers as Berlin, Porter, and Gershwin, Merman lent her brassy singing and zestful personality to *Du Barry Was a Lady* (1939), *Panama Hattie* (1940), *Annie Get Your Gun* (1946), *Call Me Madam* (1950), and *Gypsy* (1959). Her singing was always on the nose, even if it sometimes seemed too theatrical, and the clarity of her diction coupled with the dynamics of her delivery gave song lyrics a full hearing. But those qualities never resulted in a hit recording for Merman (1909–1974). She was the absolute proof, not unlike beauteous Lena Horne, that there is an incomprehensible and inescapable gap between theatrical and disk appeal.

The night after Merman stunned theatregoers, there was new excitement on Broadway. *Three's a Crowd* opened with Clifton Webb, Fred Allen, and Libby Holman at the Selwyn. The three, who had scored in the first *Little Show* (1927), were bypassed by the second, affording canny producer Max Gordon an opportunity to sign them as well as composer Arthur Schwartz and lyricist Howard Dietz. *Three's a Crowd* was to chalk up 271 performances, one less than *Girl Crazy*.

From it, Elspeth Holtzman (1906–1971), better known as Libby Holman, became the scintillating star who had begun to twinkle with her rendition of "Moanin' Low" in the first *Little Show*. Her new ear-arresting vehicle was "Body and Soul" (music by John Green; words by Edward Heyman, Robert Sour, Frank Eyton), a torch ballad hit of 1930 that became an even bigger hit at the end of the decade as the result of a jazz record by tenor-saxist Coleman Hawkins.

Slotting the song in the revue became a problem. As Holman tells it: "In Philadelphia I first did *Body and Soul* on my knees. On a pulley. The stage was totally dark. I sang, 'I'm lost in the dark.' Boom! A spot hit my face. I

sang the next line: 'Where is the spark for my love?' The pulley jerked forward. They turned on the tiny footlights. I sang the next line. Another jerk!
It was awful. The damn thing was making such a racket nobody could hear
me. I really got sick over it. They tried putting the song in different places in
the show. They got Johnny Green to arrange and conduct it. Nothing worked.
I even hung up a sign on my dressing room door: TWO's COMPANY—ONE
GOT SICK."

What saved that day was an accidental meeting in Pennsylvania Station
of Howard Dietz and Ralph Rainger, composer-arranger of "Moanin' Low."
Dietz virtually shanghaied Rainger onto the train to Philadelphia, where he
worked all through the night on a new arrangement. And overnight, "Body
and Soul," as sung by Libby Holman and danced by Clifton Webb and Tamara Geva, became the towering hit of the show, although Holman also
introduced the romantic parting-with-a-soldier ballad, "Something to Remember You By" (music by Arthur Schwartz; words by Howard Dietz).

The following year (1931), Libby married Zachary Smith Reynolds, heir
to the titanic tobacco company fortune, whose death by shooting a year later
led to her being charged with murder. Though she was cleared, the sensa-
tionalism of the trial played havoc with her career. She did appear in *Revenge
with Music* (1934), introducing the melodious "You and the Night and the
Music" (music by Arthur Schwartz; words by Howard Dietz); also in Cole
Porter's *You Never Know* (1938). But the magic was gone for Holman. In the
early forties, she worked in a duo with handsome black folksinger Josh
White—who magnetized the ladies by singing with a lit cigarette resting on
his ear—later appearing in concert in a program titled "Blues, Ballads and
Sin Songs." In 1971, she locked herself in her car parked in her Stamford,
Connecticut, garage, turned on the ignition, and died from the inhalation of
carbon monoxide fumes.

Ethel Merman was the show singer par excellence. Libby Holman was a
distinctive interpreter of white sultry blues. Neither swung. But Mildred Bailey (1907–1951), who sang with Paul Whiteman, did swing even in slow
ballads as well as uptempo songs. A sister of Al Rinker of Whiteman's Rhythm
Boys, Mildred joined the orchestra in 1930 when it was in Hollywood to star
in the film *King of Jazz*. The band had actually arrived at Universal Studios
in June 1929 in the period when the studios had at least fifty musicals scheduled for production. In the rush to capitalize on Warner Bros.' success with
The Jazz Singer, Universal was planning to make *King of Jazz* not only all-
talking, all-singing, and all-dancing, but all-color as well. It faced a "small"
problem: it had no script, a problem whose solution took so many months
that the film was not finished until March 1930.

The film lent an air of authority to the title with which Whiteman had
been increasingly vested by the media since the Aeolian Hall concert at which
he had introduced Gershwin's *Rhapsody in Blue* in 1924. Since then, he and

his orchestra had grown in prestige not only as the outstanding dance band of the day but as the purveyor of what was referred to as "symphonic jazz." Employing a larger complement of musicians than most of his competitors, he attracted some of the best jazz-oriented players. By 1928, his band boasted such stellar improvising instrumentalists as Bix Beiderbecke, Frankie Trumbauer, Jimmy and Tommy Dorsey, Eddie Lang, Joe Venuti, and Red Nichols, among others. In addition to Ferde Grofé, who had arranged *Rhapsody in Blue*, Whiteman used Bill Challis, an arranger who had obviously studied the work of Fletcher Henderson (for whom he later wrote arrangements) and who provided stimulating background for the improvisers.

King of Jazz contained a mishmash of songs, mostly by Milton Ager and Jack Yellen, yielding only the hit "It Happened in Monterey," written by Mabel Wayne and Billy Rose. There were no jazz songs as such, or even the hits that Whiteman had created on disk. Hollywood was simply exploiting the popularity of the Rhythm Boys (lead singer, Bing Crosby) and especially Whiteman, whose title was, of course, a misnomer. The true kings of jazz were the black innovators like Count Basie, Duke Ellington, Fletcher Henderson, Chick Webb, and so on, who were then as little in evidence on the screen as on commercial network radio shows.

Universal Pictures worked at making a mammoth event of the film, booking Gershwin himself to play his *Rhapsody* with Whiteman at the New York premiere. The two were together again—and the hope was that the exultant reception of the twenties would be duplicated. It was not. The film received lukewarm notices, and Whiteman, who was well received, plus Technicolor, failed to make the picture a box-office success. There was some reason to believe that audiences were also reacting to a glut of all-star, plotless revues. Indeed, Universal's own scathing exposé of the futility of war in *All Quiet on the Western Front* was then drawing capacity crowds. In Whiteman's absence from Broadway, too, a new favorite singer had become popular—Rudy Vallee, who was playing to standing-room-only audiences at the Brooklyn Paramount. By then the Depression was visible in New York—and box-office receipts dropped so badly that the Roxy eliminated the stage show after one week and kept the film running for another.

During the thirties, Whiteman starred in a series of popular radio network shows: *The Old Gold Hour* (1929–30); *The Kraft Music Hall* (1933–35), often with Al Jolson; and *Chesterfield Time* (1937–39). He also appeared in the spectacular Hippodrome musical *Jumbo* (1935), where he made his entrance on a large white horse. The animal's lack of alimentary control at one performance led a reviewer to exclaim, "A critic, too!" Whiteman continued to employ musicians of a jazz persuasion—Bunny Berigan, Jack Teagarden, Miff Mole, Frank Signorelli, among others—and his choice of singers was oriented toward the bluesy, rhythm-styled vocalists Red McKenzie, Johnny

Mercer, Jack Teagarden, and Mildred Bailey. He had a larger perspective than most of his confreres, commissioning extended compositions in an American classical form from Dana Suesse (*Blue Moonlight*, 1930), Eastwood Lane, John Alden Carpenter, Leo Sowerby, Deems Taylor, and others.

When Whiteman hired Mildred Bailey, she became the first female vocalist to sing with a name band. A week after he heard her at her home in the Hollywood Hills, he presented her on his Old Gold show, singing "Moanin' Low": salary $75 a week. Within a year, Whiteman, who was known to pay his musicians well, was handing her a weekly check of $1,250. When the band was working at the Edgewater Beach Hotel in Chicago, Mildred introduced Hoagy Carmichael's "Rockin' Chair" on the radio show and scored such a sensation that the song became her theme; she was thereafter known as the Rockin' Chair Lady. She remained with Whiteman until 1933, except for an interval in 1932. Severely injured in an automobile accident, she was compelled to remain inactive for an extended period. It was then that she put on the weight that gave her the plump figure she sported for the rest of her days. For three years, between 1936 and 1939, she worked in a band with her husband, the brilliant jazz xylophonist Red Norvo, during which they were featured as Mr. and Mrs. Swing. She joined Benny Goodman on the radio and on records in 1939. Although she was active throughout the forties, the path of her career, interrupted by illnesses, was on a downward grade.

"Mildred Bailey and Connee Boswell," historian-critic Henry Pleasants has written, "were the first white singers, male or female, to absorb and master the blues, or rather the early jazz idiom of the black music of the 1920s. Mildred Bailey was singing bluesy jazz and swing when the rest of white Americans had hardly got beyond the Charleston."

Connie Boswell (1912–1976) was one of three New Orleans sisters who made their radio debut on station KFWB in Los Angeles in 1930 and came to be regarded as the leading vocal trio of the period 1931 to 1935. In addition to singing, Martha played piano, Vet violin, and Connie cello. Their style was jazz inflected—they grew up in the Crescent City when jazz was being born—and their backing on disk was by top jazzmen like the Dorsey Brothers, trumpeter Bunny Berigan, guitarist Eddie Lang, clarinetist Benny Goodman, and fiddler Joe Venuti. They appeared regularly on the *Chesterfield Quarter-Hour* (1931–33). Their most famous record was their collaboration with Bing Crosby on "Life Is Just a Bowl of Cherries," an anti-Depression song by Lew Brown and Ray Henderson, introduced by Ethel Merman in *George White's Scandals* (1931). They were featured in a number of films, including *The Big Broadcast of 1932*. In 1935, the group dissolved when Martha and Vet got married.

Despite a severe physical handicap as a result of polio in her infancy, a condition later aggravated by a fall, Connie pursued an active solo career, changing her name to Connee in the forties. She appeared on the top radio shows of the thirties and forties, including *The Bing Crosby Show*, *The Kraft Music Hall*, and *The Camel Caravan*. In a long list of solo records, her biggest hit was "Lullaby of the Leaves" (music by Bernice Petkere; words by Joe Young), which she recorded with Victor Young's Orchestra and that remained in *Variety's* Top Ten for five months. She also made recordings with such jazzmen as Red Nichols, Woody Herman, and Bob Crosby—all this while working in a wheelchair.

Both the Paul Whiteman Orchestra and the Guy Lombardo Band started in the twenties. Unlike Whiteman, Lombardo played a commercially appealing type of dance music that kept it performing in the nation's top spots for over forty years.

With four brothers as the basic unit—Lebert on lead trumpet, Victor on baritone sax, Carmen as lead altoist, and Guy as leader—he had studied fiddle but seldom if ever played it—the Royal Canadians (as they called themselves) came out of Canada and Cleveland to settle in the Grill Room of the Hotel Roosevelt in 1929, where they continued to occupy the bandstand (with occasional hiatuses) into the 1960s. Stressing melody, simple harmonies, and moderate tempi, the band hyped its sound "The Sweetest Music This Side of Heaven." Detractors referred to Guy as the King of Corn, pointing to the twin tinkling pianos, the cloyingly sweet sound of Carmen Lombardo's alto, and the cornball ending with a cymbal shot. But despite the stringencies that struck the music business and other bands, the Lombardo Orchestra was never out of work.

Inside the music business, the band was among the most popular. There was an area behind the Roosevelt bandstand, used when the Grill became crowded, where the members of the band generally relaxed at tables during the "Take 5"s. Their accessibility made for an easy camaraderie between publishers, song-pluggers, songwriters, and the bandsmen. Guy, Carmen, vocalist Kenny Gardner, and one or two others usually occupied a round table in the far corner of the room. At least once a week, song-pluggers could approach the group—a kind of administrative committee—with new material. The Lombardos were very businesslike, and there was no hanky-panky, no cut-ins, no under-the-table deals. They would examine the lead-sheets and tentatively accept or reject a new song. By the following week, a song-plugger learned whether the song had passed a more careful scrutiny and would be arranged—and a week or two later would be advised when it would be introduced in the Grill Room, on the air, or both, thus making it possible for the publisher to bunch plugs for impact and recognition on the all-important *Your Hit Parade*. Few bands operated in this simple, straightforward manner. It is no wonder that the Lombardo Band is said to have introduced as many as 275 new songs, accounting for more song hits than any other band.

During the thirties, it sold a million records of Irving Berlin's "Easter Parade" (repeating the feat again in 1947), and it helped make a No. 1 ballad of "Little White Lies," written for it by Walter Donaldson. Its recording of "Penny Serenade," a 1938 English import, became the No. 1 jukebox hit, and kept the song in the Top Ten of *Your Hit Parade* for ten weeks.

Although he was involved with a number of top radio shows, Guy Lombardo became widely known as a result of playing the band's theme, "Auld Lang Syne," on radio and then TV each New Year's Eve as millions watched the New Year make its entrance to the descent of a lighted globe from the top of the Times Square Tower. A genial, relaxed, and friendly man, he had a strange hobby: speeedboat racing. In 1946, he won the sport's highest prize, the Gold Cup, with his giant speedboat, Tempo VI. To many historians, his is the most commercially successful dance band of all time.

In 1930, Ruth Etting starred in the Rodgers and Hart musical *Simple Simon* and turned "Ten Cents a Dance," a song that had little or nothing to do with the story and was written for another member of the cast, into the show's high point. The touching evocation of the travail of a dime-a-dance ballroom hostess, it was sung by Etting seated on a piano, attached to a bicycle pedaled by comic Ed Wynn. By 1930, Etting had established herself as one of the prime interpreters of popular song with such hits as "I'll Get By" (music by Fred E. Ahlert; words by Roy Turk) and "Love Me or Leave Me" (music by Walter Donaldson; words by Gus Kahn). The latter song, which seemed a commentary on her ugly marriage to a mobster, became the title of her 1955 screen biography, with James Cagney playing the mobster husband and Doris Day playing Ruth.

There were three men who helped enrich popular music in the thirties: Rudy Vallee, who came from Vermont; Maurice Chevalier, an enchanting Parisian; and Harry Richman, who hailed from Cincinnati.

Hubert Pryor Vallee (1901–1986), better known as Rudy Vallee, was educated first at the University of Maine but mainly at Yale, where he played sax with the Yale Collegians. Arriving in New York in the late twenties, he early began attracting crowds to the Heigh-Ho Club, where he performed with his Connecticut Yankees, a name chosen after the Rodgers and Hart musical *A Connecticut Yankee*. A New England Yankee, he took New York society and the "glitterati" by storm between 1929 and 1931. The media contributed by referring to him as the Vagabond Lover, the title of a film in which he starred in 1929. That year he became the host of an NBC network show for Fleischmann Yeast—the first program aired during the week of the stock market crash—which developed quickly into a top-rated variety show. His theme song was "My Time Is Your Time," a song he had heard in London in 1925 and first played in the dining hall at Yale University; it became the title of his autobiography, written with Gil McKean in 1962. Through his radio broadcasts and recordings, he helped create hits of "I'm Dancing with Tears in My Eyes" (music by Joe Burke; words by Al Dubin), "When Your Hair Has Turned to Silver" (music by Peter De Rose; words by Charles Tobias), and "The Stein Song" (music by E. A. Fenstead; words by Lincoln Concord)—all in 1930.

In his club appearances, he used a megaphone to amplify a thin, nasal voice—he was one of the earliest crooners—but its novelty made it an audience grabber. Later, he claimed to have introduced electrical amplification of music into public performances. "It sounds like a real Goldberg contraption," he told Paul Whiteman, "but it works. I borrowed an old carbon mike from NBC, hooked up a homemade amplifier with some radios, and I've got a sort of electronic megaphone. I had the legs sawed off the radios so they don't look so strange."

Although the Depression had begun to have a strong effect, Vallee carried over some of the themes and moods of the flippant twenties. He cultivated the fascination of the public with the college scene, not only by reviving and popularizing the University of Maine's "Stein Song," Amherst College's prom song, "Deep Night" (his first recording), and Yale University's famous "Whiffenpoof Song," but also by co-writing "Betty Co-Ed" with J. Paul Fogarty. The following year (1931), he recorded "Life Is Just a Bowl of Cherries," with its frivolity and cynicism now serving, perhaps, as an antidepressant.

While the riots caused by Frank Sinatra and Benny Goodman at the New York Paramount have received extensive coverage, it is sometimes forgotten that a Vallee riot anticipated these others by at least fifteen years. Appearing at Keith's 81st Street Theatre with his Connecticut Yankees in February 1929, he created such a furor that the police had to be summoned to quiet the unruly and excited crowd. When he moved from the Heigh-Ho Club to the Versailles on East 60th Street, his popularity was such that its name was changed to the Villa Vallee. To increase its access to his broadcasts and recordings, the publishing house of Leo Feist, Inc., put him on a weekly retainer as a consultant.

What the megaphone was to Rudy Vallee, a straw hat was to Maurice Chevalier (1888–1972). But to that hat he added the charm, Gallic pronunciation, and jaunty air that made him an audience rouser for decades. Coming from Paris music halls where he was a great favorite, he burst on the American scene in 1929 and 1930 in three early Paramount movie musicals—the biggest star to grace those early experiments in sound. He was the sole star of *Innocents of Paris*, whose songs by Richard Whiting and Leo Robin included the lilting "Louise." In *The Love Parade*, a musical directed by the famed Ernest Lubitsch, he starred with Jeanette MacDonald long before the teaming of Jeanette with Nelson Eddy. And in *The Big Pond*, he co-starred with Claudette Colbert, popularizing "This Is My Lucky Day" by De Sylva, Brown, and Henderson, and "You Brought a New Kind of Love to Me" (music by Pierre Norman Connor and Sammy Fain; words by Irving Kahal). It was Sammy Fain's first movie song. In time, Chevalier appeared in more than twenty-five films, with *Gigi* (1958) as the high point of a notable career.

In 1930, under the auspices of Charles Dillingham, he began a series of one-man Broadway appearances—the first also involved Eleanor Powell and Duke Ellington—that found audiences clamoring for him in 1932, 1947, 1948, 1955, and as late as 1963. Although he recorded and sang many French and American songs, the Chevalier name immediately conjures up at least two: "Louise" and "Mimi" (music by Richard Rodgers; words by Lorenz Hart), which he sang in the Rouben Mamoulian film musical *Love Me Tonight* (1932), regarded as the best collaboration of Chevalier and Jeanette Mac-Donald. And who can forget the elegant charm of the duet with Hermione Gingold in *Gigi*'s "I Remember It Well," when he muffed every detail of a date they were nostalgically recalling.

Like Chevalier, he used a straw hat (or top hat) plus a cane. He lisped, but he was debonair, projected an air of sophistication, and sang in a stentorian style that appealed to the ladies and made him one of the topflight stage entertainers of the twenties and thirties. Stardom came to Harry Reichman (1895–1972), better known as Harry Richman, in *George White's Scandals* of 1926. "The Birth of the Blues," by De Sylva, Brown, and Henderson, as sung dramatically by Richman, abetted by two sets of girls, was a hit and soon became a standard. His career peaked in the thirties when he appeared in four Broadway shows—*International Revue*, *Ziegfeld Follies of 1931*, *George White's Music Hall Varieties*, and *Say When*; also four musical films—*Puttin' on the Ritz*, *The Music Goes 'Round*, *Stars Over Arizona*, and an English film, *Kickin' the Moon Around*. He was also playing top venues like the London Palladium and the Café de Paris (reportedly at the highest figure paid a performer), and starring on his own major network radio show for Conoco (1934–35).

In 1930, he played a key role in popularizing four sterling songs. In *Lew Leslie's International Revue* they were "Exactly Like You" and "On the Sunny Side of the Street," both by Jimmy McHugh (music) and Dorothy Fields (words). On "Exactly Like You," Richman sang opposite the pert Gertrude Lawrence. A song that came out of Tin Pan Alley, "Walkin' My Baby Back Home" (music by Roy Turk; words by Fred E. Ahlert), became intimately identified with him, more so than his other hits with the exception of "Puttin' on the Ritz." Richman starred in the Universal film of the title, and Irving Berlin was able to capitalize on Richman's style in the song—dapper, sophisticated, debonair. The following year (1931), he helped popularize "I Love a Parade" (music by Harold Arlen; words by Ted Koehler), introduced at the Cotton Club by the effervescent Cab Calloway.

In his autobiography, Richman characterizes "the high point of his life" as not a show, not a song, not even his overpowering love affair with Clara Bow—the "It" girl, who informed him she had married Rex Bell when he called to describe their wedding plans—but his round-trip crossing of the Atlantic Ocean in his own plane. He had previously set two airplane records in an outdated Sikorsky amphibian, one for altitude (flying 19,000 feet) and another for speed. Flying with Dick Merrill, he did not quite make England's Croydon Field as the result of a storm but was forced to land at a village not too distant. When they arrived at Croydon the next morning—after their equipment was repaired—they were greeted by a huge crowd that included Maurice Chevalier. Richman called his autobiography, written with Richard Gehman, *A Hell of a Life*. It must have been, since he earned and spent over $13 million.

Charley Patton (1887–1934) never appeared in a night club, a theatre, or a film, and when he got drunk, he was arrested. But he did make records and, through them, helped develop a vital type of music known as Mississippi Delta Blues. He was one of Paramount Records' leading artists from 1929 until his death in 1934, although the titles of his songs are little known. This is largely the result of his "writing" and singing about local and personal events: the flood of 1927 in "High Water Everywhere," his being jailed for drunkenness in "High Sheriff Blues," and other such episodes. But he occupied the same position in the Mississippi Delta of the twenties and early thirties as Elvis Presley later did in the fifties rock scene. Like Elvis, Patton was a showman whose antics made him an in-demand performer on plantations, in country dance halls, at picnics, and at Saturday night whiskey balls. Playing the guitar behind his back or over his head, twirling and tapping it, and dancing as he sang gave him a big following. His large repertoire embraced church songs, knife songs, old-time dance numbers, and popular country tunes of the day, all sung in a hoarse, chesty growl of a voice, loud enough to dominate noisy carousers. That he was a commanding figure is evident from the following he attracted among Delta bluesmen, a group that included in varying degrees Son House (his principal heir) and Howlin' Wolf (who literally sat at his feet)—bluesmen whose work led to the evolution of Chicago electric, ensemble blues from Mississippi down-home blues.

"They run me from Will Dockery's [the plantation where he worked]," he sings in "34 Blues," interweaving his own economic difficulties with those of the Depression scourge, which had "women and children flaggin' freight trains for rides." In "High Sheriff Blues" he intones: "Thirty days seem like years in a jailhouse where there is no booze. . . . It takes boozy booze, Lord, to carry me through." His songs have the emotive intensity of life lived, which gives the blues, and good songs, their power.

In 1930, the music business was in a state of flux, if not confusion, with the woes of the Depression exacerbated by the rise of two new powerful media: the radio in the home and the talkies on the screen. Both dealt shattering blows to what had been the industry's major medium of exposure, vaudeville. With the death in March of E. G. Albee, vaudeville lost its greatest champion. (Top music publisher Leo Feist died in June.) Nevertheless, there was talk in the business and in the trade papers about reviving vaudeville. But RKO closed ten offices in March, and other booking agencies followed suit.

Pit musicians were hurt by the talkies as shows were postponed or folded. *Billboard* reported in May 1930: "Broadway Slump Continues as Eight Shows Fold." The Hollywood studios intensified the crisis on the New York scene, singing a golden siren song to Gotham's hit songwriters. There was a steady flow from East to West until a glut of talkies and a dwindling box office reversed the flow.

Hollywood's main competition was the Broadway theatre, on whose pool of songwriters it drew extensively until it developed its own core. In 1930, the Gershwins produced six hits, including "I Got Rhythm," "Embraceable You," and "I've Got a Crush on You," in *Girl Crazy* and *Strike Up the Band*. Rodgers and Hart created the torchy "Ten Cents a Dance" and "Dancing on the Ceiling" for *Simple Simon*. Cole Porter's piano and typewriter brought forth "risqué" "Love for Sale," from *The New Yorker*, and from *Wake Up and Dream*, "What Is This Thing Called Love?" To the *International Revue*, Jimmy McHugh and Dorothy Fields contributed "Exactly Like You" and "On the Sunny Side of the Street." Harold Arlen had his first stage hit in "Get Happy" in the short-lived *9:15 Revue*. *Three's a Crowd* introduced the classic "Body and Soul" and Arthur Schwartz and Howard Dietz's "Something to Remember You By."

Film hits of 1930 came from the pens of Tin Pan Alley songwriters. "Three Little Words" in the film *Check and Double Check* was part of the first movie score by Harry Ruby and Bert Kalmar, while "You Brought a New Kind of Love to Me" was Sammy Fain's first movie song. "My Baby Just Cares for Me" was written especially for the film version of *Whoopee*, which Walter Donaldson and Gus Kahn had originally composed for the Broadway stage in 1928.

The biggest pop hit of 1930, vying in popularity with the unconsciously ironic "Happy Days Are Here Again," was "Little White Lies" by Walter Donaldson (1893–1947), a tune that Lombardo made a best-seller. Another Donaldson gem of 1930 was "You're Driving Me Crazy," for which he wrote both the music and words, attracting two such disparate exponents as Carmen Lombardo and Louis Armstrong, who each rendered appealing but contrasting vocals. The song was interpolated in Vincent Youman's score of *Smiles*, which contained one of Youmans's imperishable hits, "Time on My Hands."

In the pantheon reserved for only the greatest of popular songs, "Star Dust" will likely be forever enshrined. Hoagland Howard Carmichael, better known as Hoagy Carmichael (1899–1982), wrote the song in 1927 as a flippant fox-trot for piano, but Victor Young arranged it in slower time for an Isham Jones Brunswick recording. Then, after the tune was given a memorable lyric by Mitchell Parish and was then sung by such diverse voices as Bing Crosby and Louis Armstrong, and when Artie Shaw's memorable record treatment hit the jazz constituency, "Star Dust" was on its way to becoming one of the most-recorded and performed songs. Hoagy Carmichael was a latecomer to the film musical, contributing a little-known song to the movie version of *Anything Goes* in 1936. The son of a woman who played for silent movies in Bloomington, Indiana, he was a ragtime buff who drew inspiration from the Wolverines and especially the great Bix Beiderbecke, with whom he was good friends. He composed "Riverboat Shuffle" and "Washboard Blues" (1925) under their influence. In 1930, he produced two notable songs, both introduced originally by Mildred Bailey. "Rockin' Chair" became her theme. The other song, "Georgia on My Mind" (words by Stuart Correll), did not reach its peak popularity until the 1960s, when the "Father of Soul," Ray Charles, produced a Gold Record and won Grammys for his disk as Best Rock and Roll Recording of 1960 and Best Vocal Performance. Although Charles faced criticism from the more militant members of the black community, his many performances, as well as the prestige of the awards, led the state of Georgia to adopt the number as its official State Song. Beginning in the mid-forties, Carmichael himself appeared in films in character roles, including the movie version of Ernest Hemingway's *To Have and Have Not*. He wrote two autobiographies, *Sometimes I Wonder* and *The Stardust Road*.

Despite the California Gold Rush, a number of songwriters preferred to rely on the Broadway theatre and the song-plugging machinery of the New York publishers to generate hits. Among these were Fred Ahlert, Roy Turk, Peter De Rose, and Charles Tobias.

By the time he scored his first big hit of the thirties, Fred E. Ahlert (1892–1953) had composed "I'll Get By" (1928) and "Mean to Me" (1929), both Ruth Etting favorites. The year 1930 brought "Walkin' My Baby Back Home," with words by Roy Turk (1892–1934), his longtime lyricist. Harry Richman, who introduced and popularized the lively ballad, is listed as a collaborator. It attained its greatest popularity in the early fifties when disks by "weeper" Johnny Ray and Nat King Cole, of the pristine diction, made it a best-selling revival.

Ahlert was educated at CCNY and Fordham Law School, which doubtless worked to his advantage when, having served on the Board of Directors of ASCAP for twenty years, he was elected President of the Society (1948–50), succeeding composer Deems Taylor. Before he began writing songs professionally, he worked as an arranger at Waterson, Berlin and Snyder, and in a similar capacity for Fred Waring's Glee Club.

The year 1931 saw an upsurge of interest in Latin songs. Typical was the first Cuban hit to stir attention to the Rumba, "Mama Inez" (words by L. Wolfe Gilbert), which furnished English lyrics to "Ay! Mamá-Inés" (music by Eliseo Grenet). "Mama" was introduced in the United States, in a broadcast by Enrique Madriguera from the Biltmore Hotel in New York. Madriguera's Orchestra waxed it for Columbia. Xavier Cugat's popularity played a significant role during the thirties and beyond by simplifying the original Latin-American rhythm.

Kay Swift (1897–1993)

I was born in New York City in 1905 [1897, according to the *Guinness Encyclopedia of Popular Music*]. My family was very musical. My father, Samuel Swift, was a music critic for a number of newspapers, and my mother, Ellen Faulkner Swift, played the piano. I had one brother, Samuel Swift, Jr., and he was musical, too. I was just five years old when I began to invent musical things. I began studying the piano at the age of seven and continued with the instrument under the tutelage of a Mrs. Tapper for ten years. By that time I was teaching the piano; I had, in fact, been teaching for several years, acquiring students who could not fit into Mrs. Tapper's busy schedule. I pursued further study at the Institute of Musical Art. I went to private school for my academic training. My parents, though they were people of modest income, were wonderful. They spared no expense in providing for my growth. I'm very grateful even now.

I began playing popular music while I was involved with the classics. I didn't see that it made any difference if it was popular or classic so long as it was good. The songs of Irving Berlin were early favorites. Between times, I got married and had three daughters. My husband, James P. Warburg, was a 1917 Phi Beta Kappa graduate of Harvard and was related to the famous banking families of the Loebs, Schiffs, and Warburgs. He became my collaborator toward the end of the thirties.

For a period of two years, I worked as staff composer of the Radio City Music Hall and as assistant director of entertainment. Al Silverman, who changed his name to Al Stillman at the suggestion of George Gershwin, collaborated on the lyrics.

I was also the rehearsal pianist for a number of Broadway shows, including Richard Rodgers's *A Connecticut Yankee*. This experience made me want to have a show of my own.

I met Jascha Heifetz, the great violinist, through a cello player with whom I gave some concerts and toured. She was a wonderful cellist, and it was also through her that I met George Gershwin at my mother's home. In the spring of 1925, my husband and I gave a party for Heifetz to which Marie Rosanoff, then of the Musical Art Quartet, brought Gershwin. I recall that George played the piano, as he always did so magnificently at parties, but sprang suddenly from the bench, announced, "I have to go to Europe," and was off like a gust of wind. I met him again several months later at the home of Walter Damrosch, the conductor, and I believe it was at the time when his *Concerto in F* had its premiere.

I knew and admired Gershwin's music before I met him. I pride myself on being one who early heard the spark of genius in his work. We became very good friends and occasionally played piano duets together. When Simon & Schuster published *The Gershwin Songbook*, containing piano transcriptions of his playing of some of his great hits, I had the honor of having the book dedicated to me.

But that came several years before *Porgy and Bess* was produced in 1935. There was such pressure to get the work ready for the opening at the Alvin Theatre that I assisted in copying some of the parts of the orchestration.

My own career took a leap forward in 1929 with the presentation of the first *Little Show*. My husband, who used the pseudonym Paul James, and I wrote "Can't We Be Friends?," which was sung by Libby Holman, the sensation of the show.

The following year, my husband and I had our own show. *Fine and Dandy* starred the comedian Joe Cook, and he had a tremendous hit in the title song. The country was in the doldrums with the effects of the Depression, and we tried to lift the spirits of people.

After George's death, I was able with his brother Ira's cooperation to finish some of George's unfinished songs. We took one melody from his notebooks and wrote "The Dawn of a New Day," which was used as the theme of the World's Fair in New York in 1939. Later, we drew a number of tunes from George's notebook and created a complete score for the film *The Shocking Miss Pilgrim*, including the hit "For You, For Me, For Evermore."

George left us when he was only thirty-eight years old. But the legacy of the music he left will never die.

Medley 1930

Despite the ominous rumblings of disaster, a front-page *New York Times* story was headed: "General Price Rise Made 1929 Stock Trading Moderately Bullish for 1930." There were songs, of course, that sought to lighten the gloom descending on the American economic scene; among others were "Get Happy," by Harold Arlen and "On the Sunny Side of the Street" (music by Jimmy McHugh; words by Dorothy Fields), which promised "gold dust at your feet."

With more than thirty musicals and revues playing on Broadway, the impact of the Depression had yet to be felt on the theatre. Only one show—*Strike Up the Band*—took a realistic turn and dealt satirically with the problem of war and international diplomacy. As the first show to open in the thirties, it accidentally struck a keynote for the new type of sociological musical and the driving big band rhythms of the era.

The year 1930 added an impressive number of hits to the catalogue of popular music: "Embraceable You" by the Gershwins, "What Is This Thing Called Love?" by Cole Porter, "Something to Remember You By" by Arthur Schwartz, "Cheerful Little Earful" by Harry Warren, "Fine and Dandy" by Kay Swift, "Exactly Like You" by Jimmy McHugh, "Memories of You" by Eubie Blake, "I'm Only Human After All" by Vernon Duke, and "Get Happy" by Harold Arlen, among others.

Film musicals added such memorable melodies as "My Future Just Passed" and "Beyond the Blue Horizon" by Richard Whiting, "My Baby Just Cares for Me" by Walter Donaldson, "Three Little Words" by Kalmar and Ruby, "You Brought a New Kind of Love to Me" by Sammy Fain and Irving Kahal, "Puttin' on the Ritz" by Irving Berlin, "The Moon Is Low" by Nacio Herb Brown, and "I'm Yours" by John Green.

The shortages created by the Depression did not affect the production of hits.

❧ 8 ❧

"Where the Blue of the Night Meets the Gold of the Day"
(1931)

When the shooting of *The King of Jazz* was completed, Paul Whiteman summarily fired the Rhythm Boys. For some time, "Pops," as he was known among musicians, had been dissatisfied with the youthful shenanigans of the trio, especially those of Bing Crosby (1903–1977), who fooled around, frequently was too tired to sing, and drank too much. In his autobiography, *Call Me Lucky*, Bing admitted: "With the coming of fame, we became regular callers at Agua Caliente. Since we had Sunday off, we'd go there occasionally for a weekend. What with driving about 150 miles each way and playing roulette, golf and the races and belting a little tequila around, come Tuesday when I stood or swayed up front of the microphones, my pipes were gone."

When they were fired, the Rhythm Boys had been with Whiteman for three and a half years, adding a zingy touch of vocalism and producing some highly successful recordings—notably the swinging "Mississippi Mud" (words by James Cavanaugh; music by Harry Barris, one of the trio), in which they were backed by the Dorsey Brothers and the gemlike sounds of Bix Beiderbecke's trumpet. The trio had no difficulty in finding new employment. Gus Arnheim (1897–1955), whose orchestra occupied the bandstand of the Cocoanut Grove, was quite pleased to snatch them up.

During their tenure with Arnheim, Crosby began doing solo vocals. A ballad by Harry Barris and Gordon Clifford, "I Surrender, Dear," was the starting point, with audiences reacting so strongly that Bing recorded the song on January 19, 1931, with the Gus Arnheim Orchestra. The record's massive sales led to the making of a short film, which brought Crosby a CBS radio contract. Although it was initially a sustaining program, it soon attracted sponsors—Cremo cigars, Woodbury soap, and Chesterfield cigarettes. It marked the beginning of the fabulous forty-year career, during which the man with the receding hairline and jug ears—"A camera pointed at you," said Fox's casting director to him, "would make you look like a taxi with both doors open"—climbed to the top rung of all the media of entertainment.

During his career, first with Brunswick, and after 1934 with Decca, he recorded 2,600 titles, accounting by 1975 for an aggregate of sales of over 400 million disks. Twenty-two were gold records, selling over a million each, and his version of Irving Berlin's "White Christmas" became the top-selling single of all time. By 1968, it had established a world record for the sales of a single disk (30 million), and by 1970 it reached the astronomical figure of 90 million.

Crosby began appearing in films in 1932—*Going Hollywood* and *The Big Broadcast*—and, one year later, was ranked among the ten top box-office stars. He eventually performed in more than forty films, many of them involving straight dramatic roles and some comedies, like the very popular Road series he made with Bob Hope and Dorothy Lamour.

Having established his prominence on radio through the *Chesterfield Show*, he switched from CBS to NBC in 1936 to become the genial host of the prestigious *Kraft Music Hall*, a post he occupied for ten years. In 1946, he parted company with NBC because he wanted his show taped to avoid repeat broadcast for West Coast listeners. ABC was quite ready to hire him on any basis, and on October 1, 1947, he appeared on the air with the first magnetically taped radio show.

There is no way of characterizing him, save as an entertainment colossus. Those who have tried to analyze his appeal and popularity conclude that it was the easy identification that the average man could make with him. "Bing Crosby has been the antihero or nonhero," Henry Pleasants observes, "the ordinary, middle-class, middle city (Tacoma and Spokane) American male, whose only outstanding attribute initially was his ears."

Crosby himself did not disagree. In his autobiography, he writes: "I think that every man who sees one of my movies, or listens to one of my records or who hears me on the radio, believes firmly that he sings as well as I do, especially when he's in the bathroom shower." But he adds perceptively, "It's no kick for him to believe this because I have none of the mannerisms of a trained singer, and I have very little voice. If I've achieved any success as a warbler, it's because I've managed to keep the kind of naturalness in my style, my phrasing and my mannerisms which any Joe Doakes possesses."

But this easy explanation entails significant esthetic concepts. For one thing, his "naturalness" of style was helped by the development of the radio microphone. It was possible for him, as it was not for Al Jolson or the early Rudy Vallee and his megaphone, to stop singing *at* you and to sing *to* you. This is precisely what crooners like Perry Como, Frank Sinatra, and later Nat King Cole and others did. And there is another important esthetic factor implicit in Crosby's statement. "When I'm asked to describe what I do," Crosby states, "I say, 'I'm not a singer, I'm a phraser.' That means that I don't think of a song in terms of notes, I try to think of what it purports to say lyrically."

By way of emphasis, Crosby worked at projecting his "naturalness" even in his general demeanor. He dressed casually, sometimes donning a boatman's cap; he smoked a pipe; his hobbies were those of Joe Average—golf, hunting, and the racetrack; and he made no secret that his hair was thinning and that he wore a toupee. Nor did he balk at being typed "The Groaner," the "Gentile Cantor," or the "Boo-Boo-Boo Man."

Let us not overstate the case of "naturalness" so that we overlook his musical attributes: a rich, mellow baritone voice, even if its range was limited; precise diction; and a rhythmic feeling for jazz, with which he had grown up, coupled with a talent for melodic invention. His singing was buoyant, relaxed, uninhibited, and without artistic pretense.

This lack of inhibition is, perhaps, what accounts for the amazing variety of the material Crosby recorded—and sang well. In his choice of songs, he exhibited a degree of versatility approached by virtually no other vocalist. In 1932, he gave currency to the Depression song, "Brother, Can You Spare a Dime?" He did a group of Western and cowboy ballads, including Billy Hill's "The Last Roundup" and "Empty Saddles" as well as Joseph Carey's "Sierra Sue." He sang Hawaiian songs—"Sweet Leilani" in the film *Waikiki Wedding* won an Oscar and became the first of his Gold Records. He sang Irish songs like "Galway Bay" and "Too-ra-loo-ra-loo-ra" in the film *Going My Way*. He made a hit of an exotic Maori song, "Now Is the Hour." And he was a master of nostalgic seasonal songs, selling a million records of "I'll Be Home for Christmas" and transforming Berlin's "White Christmas" into the year's Oscar winner as well as a worldwide favorite. Perhaps he was able to present all these with appeal and authority because, as Henry Pleasants suggests, "His most original contribution was the lowering of the voice, not so much in pitch as in intensity, to a conversational level."

Inside the music business, a publisher who landed a Crosby record felt that he had a "rocking chair hit"—he could sit back in his chair and rock while the public gobbled up massive quantities of his record and the sheet music.

Amos 'n' Andy, opening to the theme of "The Perfect Song" by Clarence Lucas, was unquestionably the biggest radio comedy of the thirties. In the area of musical variety shows, Crosby, whose theme was "Where the Blue of the Night Meets the Gold of the Day," faced his strongest competition in Kate Smith, whose theme was "When the Moon Comes Over the Mountain" by Harry Woods, Howard Johnson, and, of course, Kate Smith. Although she did appear at the Palace Theatre, in a Broadway musical *(Honeymoon Lane)*, and in several films *(The Big Broadcast of 1932* among others), Kate's size and weight militated against her making it in these visual media. Her popularity was the product of her radio show and, to a lesser degree, her records.

Born in Greenville, Virginia, in 1909 (d. 1986), Kathryn Elizabeth Smith was about to quit the entertainment field when Ted Collins, a Columbia Records executive, took over her management and guided her career skillfully during a long association. Premiering her 15-minute radio show in May 1931, her "Hello, everybody!" became quickly known, as did her cognomen, Songbird of the South. Her opening program included "Dream a Little Dream of Me" (words by Gus Kahn; music by Wilbur Schwandt, Fabian Andre)—later a favorite of another weighty lady, Mama Cass Elliott; "By the River Sainte Marie" (music by Harry Warren; words by Edgar Leslie); and "Please Don't Talk About Me When I'm Gone" (music by Sam H. Stept; words by Sidney Clare). Although her sustainer faced the competition of the very popular *Amos 'n' Andy* show, in less than a month she had a sponsor in Palmer cigars. By 1936, she was the hostess of *The A & P Bandwagon*, a variety show, followed soon by the daytime *Kate Smith Hour* and the weekly *Kate Smith Hour*.

"Dream a Little Dream of Me" was a hit record for Kate in 1931; later, in 1936, she scored on disk with the Billy Mayhew ballad "It's a Sin to Tell a Lie," revived in 1955 by Something Smith and the Redheads. Kate Smith's greatest claim to fame was, of course, her introduction and popularization of Irving Berlin's inspiring anthem, "God Bless America." Radio listeners were treated to the premiere of a song that would become a patriotic classic. For her Armistice Day program—the last peacetime Armistice Day prior to World War II—Kate Smith asked Irving Berlin to write an appropriate song. Unable to create one that satisfied him, Berlin dug down into his files and came up with a patriotic ballad he had written in 1918 for his soldier show, *Yip, Yip, Yaphank*, but kept out of the score. It was, of course, "God Bless America." If one broadcast can make a song, Kate's presentation did—or, at least, it launched the ballad, so that in a national poll in the late fifties it placed second to the national anthem as the nation's favorite patriotic song.

The year following Kate's introduction, it was the theme song at the presidential nominating conventions of both political parties. Its impact may have derived from the events of the day. It was about the time that Hitler invaded Poland (September 1), England and France declared war on Germany (September 3), and FDR proclaimed a limited State of Emergency (September 8). Although the world was then not yet aware, it was the beginning of World

War II. Refusing to capitalize on patriotism, Berlin arranged for all proceeds of the song to go to Boy and Girl Scouts of America. By the early 1980s more than $1 million had been received by the Scouts. It is said that Berlin considered "God Bless America" among his five best songs, along with "Always," "Easter Parade," "There's No Business Like Show Business," and "White Christmas."

Kate Smith continued to appear on radio through the fifties and also had three television series. Upon the death of Ted Collins, she retired in 1964, returning for occasional guest appearances on TV variety shows.

One of the most talked about novelty songs of 1931 was "Minnie the Moocher," written by a man known the world over as the scattin' Hi-De-Ho Man. Performing with his band at Harlem's Cotton Club, Cab Calloway (1907–1994) introduced "Minnie the Moocher" (words and music by Cab Calloway, Irving Mills, and Clarence Gaskill), juggling the scattin' syllables like hot verbal coals. It stunned audiences so that Cab was drafted to perform the novelty in the film *The Big Broadcast* (1932), replete with frenetic gyrations. By then, Minnie was so famous that Harold Arlen and Ted Koehler, whose "I Love a Parade" Cab had introduced at the Cotton Club, wrote "Minnie the Moocher's Wedding Day," which Cab also debuted at the club.

In his autobiography, *Of Minnie the Moocher and Me* (1976), he wrote of a period when he was the halftime entertainer at basketball games; he was just fourteen and was out on the large gymnasium floor with only an upright piano: "It was a ball, me just swinging and swaying, with my hair flopping down on my forehead and my arms stretched out, singing my heart out. There's no feeling like that for me in the world. I don't care what the setting is, you just put me in front of a mike, with a little instrumental support and a crowd, and I will perform. I love it."

But there is much more to Cab Calloway than the fame that came through "Minnie the Moocher." For one thing, he has a rich, robust tenor voice that inspired singers like Billy Eckstine and led to his starring when he was sixty years old in an all-black production of *Hello, Dolly* on Broadway. (He made his debut on the Broadway stage in 1929, singing the Fats Waller hit "Ain't Misbehavin' " in the revue *Hot Chocolates*.) For another, it is said that his style of ribald comedy and comical singing became the inspiration for the George Gershwin character Sportin' Life in *Porgy and Bess*; although he did not play the role in the original production, Calloway was Sportin' Life in a revival in the fifties.

Add to these accomplishments his many years as a successful bandleader and one who was favored by musicians because of his concern for their financial security. In fact, he began as a bandleader in Chicago's heyday in the twenties, bringing the Alabamians to New York's Savoy Ballroom. Unfortunately they bombed because, as he later explained, they played "Dipsy-Doodle" midwest jazz, a combination of Dixieland and 1920s Chicago Swing. But soon he was leading the Missourians, who became the Cotton Club band. When Duke Ellington caught Cab at the Cotton, he arranged for him to headline at the Paramount. It led to a radio network hiring him for a coast-to-coast show, making him the first black to break the network color barrier. During the thirties and forties, he fronted a band that has been widely praised because of its illustrious jazz personnel, among whom was trumpeter Dizzy Gillespie, who was fired for hitting Cab with a spitball—a widely reported but unconfirmed tale. While Cab's disk of "Minnie the Moocher" never went Gold, he did sell a million of "Jumpin' Jive," a dance disk that was popular during World War II.

Despite his multiple talents and extensive achievements, unquestionably the image of Cab Calloway that remains with us is well described by writer Leslie Gourse: "He was the master of overkill in language as well as in his clothing and rollicking performances, with a lock of black hair falling in his eyes. Television audiences remember him mostly for his manic renditions of novelty tunes and hyped and hokey blues, his swoops around the octaves, his growls and falsetto yowling, and, perhaps most of all, for his individualistic scat words 'Hi-de-ho'." Cab's last film was *The Cotton Club* (1991).

In 1931, the United States purchased the Virgin Islands from Denmark for $25 million. Rockefeller Center began raising its skyscraper towers in mid-town Manhattan with the erection of the RKO Building on Sixth Avenue, later renamed Avenue of the Americas. The George Washington Bridge, connecting upper Manhattan with New Jersey, was completed. The 47-story Waldorf-Astoria Hotel shot up on Park Avenue. And the Empire State Building was opened as the world's tallest structure. Considering these gigantic projects—a carryover of the expansive twenties—one would hardly believe that the country was in the midst of a worldwide Depression.

The music business felt the impact. Sheet music sales cascaded downward, with hits selling between 250,000 and 500,000 instead of a million, as they had in the twenties. An English import by Ray Noble, James Campbell, and Reg Connelly, "Goodnight, Sweetheart," attracted the interest of Rudy Vallee, who recorded it and performed it frequently on the radio. It was also featured in the 1931 edition of Earl Carroll's *Vanities*. On the basis of sheet sales, it would appear to have finished as the top song of the year.

The 1931 song that many regard as bigger than "Goodnight, Sweetheart" was "The Peanut Vendor." It too was an import, but from Cuba, where it was known as "El Manisero." Written by Moisés Simón, the composer also of "Marta," it was discovered by Herbert E. Marks, the son of music publisher Edward B. Marks, while on his honeymoon in Cuba. The first English lyrics written to it apparently did not work out. But a new set by L. Wolfe Gilbert, also responsible for the English lyrics to "Marta," in collaboration with Marion Sunshine, led to its introduction at the Palace Theatre by Cuban bandleader Dan Azpiazu, who was Ms. Sunshine's husband. It was soon recorded by Paul Whiteman, Guy Lombardo, and Xavier Cugat, whose disks and performances turned it into an enormous hit. That it was one of the first rumbas to attract American dancers added to its popularity.

The Latin sound was potent enough so that it received recognition in a film title. The theme of *Cuban Love Song* (music by Jimmy McHugh and Herbert Stothart; words by Dorothy Fields) was introduced by Lawrence Tibbett, who harmonized with himself, appearing on the screen as a soldier singing with the image of his ghost. Composer McHugh worked out the sequence by having Tibbett overdub a harmony track to his solo. Because overdubbing, popularized by Les Paul in the early fifties, was then unknown, this was doubtless the first instance of a multiple recording.

"Cuban Love Song" was among the songs of 1931 included by *Variety* in its *Fifty-Year Hit Parade*. The others were "When It's Sleepy Time Down South," a bluesy ballad by three Los Angelinos (Leon and Otis René and Clarence Muse) that became known through Louis Armstrong's performances and recording; "Sweet and Lovely," popularized by Russ Columbo and Bing Crosby and performed at Hollywood's Cocoanut Grove by bandleader Gus Arnheim, one of the writers, and Jules Lemare and Harry Tobias; and "Penthouse Serenade," an instrumental by Will Jason and Val Burton.

As a title, "Life Is Just a Bowl of Cherries" (music by Ray Henderson; words by Lew Brown) possessed a flippancy and cynicism that was more appropriate to the twenties than the thirties. And it was belted out by Ethel Merman in *George White's Scandals of 1931*. But in the gloomy atmosphere of the Depression years, it assumed the character of an "uplift" song. This was the spirit that pervaded the Bing Crosby–Boswell Sisters disk. Incidentally, they recorded it as part of a two-sided 12-inch version in *The Scandals*, one of the earliest instances of the presentation on disk of a complete Broadway musical. "Smile, Darn Ya, Smile" (music by Max Rich; words by Charles O'Flynn and Jack Meskill) was a more direct attempt to raise the outlook of folks—"Things are never as black as they are painted." The theme song of Fred Allen's radio show, it went to become No. 3 in the spring of 1931.

Two composers came through with great standards, but found the initial period tough sledding. John Green, who had already produced "Body and Soul," published "Out of Nowhere" himself, with his collaborator Edward Heyman, even though it was introduced by Guy Lombardo and became a Bing Crosby solo hit recording.

Vincent Youmans, an established composer, suffered through the travail of two flop shows—*Through the Years* and *Smiles*—but he gave us the magnificent title tune of the former (words by Edward Heyman) and the magnificent "Time on My Hands" in the latter, later the theme of radio's *Chase and Sanborn Hour* (words by Harold Adamson and Mack Gordon).

For Harry Warren, as for Harold Arlen, the thirties marked the beginning of a prodigiously productive career. In 1931, Warren scored with "I Found a Million Dollar Baby (in a Five and Ten Cent Store)" (words by Mort Dixon and Billy Rose), and featured in the Billy Rose revue *Crazy Quilt*. A second Warren hit that year was "You're My Everything" (words by Mort Dixon and Joe Young), featured in Ed Wynn's *The Laugh Parade*.

Parades in general were the subject of the hit introduced by Cab Calloway in the Cotton Club. The inside stories that are sometimes told about songs don't always ring true. But there is no reason to question that "I Love a Parade" was written by Helen and Ted Koehler simply while they were taking a walk and trying to energize their pace with a song. It started with Helen humming a tune, Koehler adding a phrase, Helen extending her initial set of notes, Koehler chiming in with words—and by the end of the walk, they had "I Love a Parade."

It became a standard, as did "All of Me" (music by Gerald Marks; words by Seymour Simons). Neither initially shook up the music scene or seemed headed for the long life and performances that they secured.

Although the Broadway theatre of 1931 was short on audiences and new musicals, it contributed a memorable number of hit songs to the catalogue of popular music. Two shows that were richest in this respect were the Gershwins' *Of Thee I Sing*—"Love Is Sweeping the Country," "Who Cares?," and the sprightly title song—and the brilliant Schwartz-Dietz revue, *The Band Wagon*—"New Sun in the Sky," "High and Low," "I Love Louisa," and the brooding "Dancing in the Dark."

Then there were two romantic operetta hits from Kern's *The Cat and the Fiddle*—"She Didn't Say Yes, She Didn't Say No" and "The Night Was Made for Love"—and the anti-Depression song "I've Got Five Dollars" in Rodgers and Hart's *America's Sweetheart*.

A number of 1931 songs started their climb to popularity slowly and had to wait years before they blossomed as hits. Herman Hupfeld's "As Time Goes By" was introduced by Frances Williams in the movie *Everybody's Welcome*. A Rudy Vallee recording helped give it only moderate acceptance. But in 1942 when it was used as the impassioned romantic theme of the World War II film *Casablanca*, underscoring the love of Humphrey Bogart and Ingrid Bergman that was sacrificed to wartime exigencies, it zoomed in popularity and became a worldwide standard. Vallee's record was re-released—

there was a recording ban at the time—and became a best-seller. Now, no one can hear "As Time Goes By" without recalling the heartbreaking dramatic scenes between Bogart and Bergman in the film.

"Heartaches" (music by Al Hoffman; words by John Klenner) was another song whose popularity did not skyrocket until 1947. In 1931, it was introduced by Guy Lombardo and His Royal Canadians and recorded by Ted Weems and His Orchestra, the band that lured Perry Como from the barberchair. Nothing really exciting happened until a disc jockey on Station WBT in North Carolina (Kurt Webster) chanced to find the Weems disk in the station library, was enchanted by Elmo Tanner's whistling chorus, and began playing it on the air. Record shops were suddenly swamped with orders, forcing Decca hurriedly to put the master back on the presses. It stayed at No. 1 on *Your Hit Parade* for a dozen weeks, much later became the No. 3 *Hit Parade* song of the year 1947.

A third song whose day on the charts did not come until fifteen years after it appeared was "Prisoner of Love" (music by Russ Columbo and Clarence Gaskill; words by Leo Robin). It was introduced in 1931 by Russ Columbo, the ill-fated singer accidentally shot to death by a friend when the friend struck a match on a supposedly unloaded antique pistol serving as a paperweight on his desk. The ardent ballad made no real impact until it was recorded by another crooner, Perry Como, in 1946. It then achieved such popularity that it finished No. 3 in the year's Top Ten. A second period of best-selling popularity followed when it was revived in 1963 by Soul Brother James Brown and His Famous Flames.

More than a quarter of a century elapsed before "Love Letters in the Sand" became one of the biggest hits of the day. Appearing originally as a poem in a *Daily Mirror* column, the words so impressed composer J. Fred Coots that he asked permission of columnists Nick and Charles Kenny to set them to music. Russ Columbo made the first recording, while orchestra leader George Hill played it repeatedly on his broadcasts, eventually adopting it as his theme (as sung by vocalist Dolly Dawn). But in 1957 it attained its majority when Pat Boone sang it in the film *Bernadine* and recorded it. Despite the rock 'n' roll influence of the period, the song sold over one million copies, emerging as the biggest hit of 1956.

The so-called Night Club Era did not come into existence until the repeal of Prohibition in December 1933 made it possible for more affluent speakeasies to become legitimate clubs. But wealthy and influential Americans like Tallulah Bankhead, novelist F. Scott Fitzgerald, songwriter Cole Porter, Mayor Jimmy Walker, and others frequented clubs outside the United States to imbibe, be entertained, and while away dusk-to-dawn hours. Perhaps the best known if not the most popular of these was Bricktop's in Paris, which flourished during the Prohibition era. In November 1931, despite the ominous economic situation, the red-headed black entertainer known as Bricktop (she was christened Beatrice Queen Victoria Louise Virginia Smith) decided to expand her operation and opened a larger nitery at 66 Rue Pigalle. It was a symphony in black and red with exquisite lighting by one of the most creative theatre light-men. As her first performer, Bricktop hired a woman who later became famous on New York's 52nd Street. Mabel Mercer, who was born in New Staffordshire, England, of a white mother and black musician father, was then singing soprano, hardly the type of voice for a night club. But Bricktop was impressed by her manner and retained her at what was then a high price—200 francs. Mabel had charisma and became extremely popular, but, according to Bricktop, "she didn't make her reputation singing, that's for sure." The unique Mercer style of delivering a song, a style that brought crowds to Tony's and the veneration of the more sophisticated songwriters like Alec Wilder and Bart Howard, came later.

The Tobias Brothers

They call themselves The Royal Family of Tin Pan Alley, and they support the claim by producing a long list containing songs by the three brothers, Harry, Charles, and Henry, by the wives of Harry and Charles, and by songs of Harry and Charles—a total of eight songwriters. Included are important copyrights like "Born Too Late" by Fred Tobias and the songs of Charles Tobias, whose hits include "When Your Hair Has Turned to Silver," "Don't Sit Under the Apple Tree," "The Old Lamplighter," and the filla-ga-dusha song.

The three major figures of the family did not do very many songs together, but did produce the smash, "Miss You." Charles Tobias, who died in 1970, was posthumously elected to the Songwriters Hall of Fame, and Harry Tobias was inducted in March 1983. Henry Tobias is the co-author of *The Borscht Circuit* and author of *Music in My Heart, Borscht in My Blood*.

Los Angeles Mayor Bradley proclaimed May 7, 1984, "Tobias Brothers Day."

Interview with Harry Tobias (1895–1994)

I am the oldest of the Tobias Brothers, born in 1895. Charley was the second. Then came Nat. Then Henry and Hilton. Five brothers. Three of us are left. Charley is gone; he died in 1970. He was very versatile and wrote with many, many writers. I'm very proud of him. As a boy, my idols were Ty Cobb in baseball, Eddie Cantor (who was married to my cousin Ida) in show business, and Irving Berlin, whose "Alexander's Ragtime Band" inspired me to write songs.

From 1911, when my first song was published—I had to buy 200 copies from the World War I publisher—I struggled to make it as a songwriter. I had entertained 40,000 troops with my buddy Abe Olman, who wrote "Oh Johnny, Oh!" and throughout the twenties I peddled Chevrolets. My big break came in 1929 with "Miss You," which I wrote with brothers Charles and Henry, and which was introduced and recorded by Rudy Vallee.

In 1930, I had a number of hits. "It's a Lonesome Old Town," which I wrote with the late Charley Kisco, became Ben Bernie's theme. He introduced it at the College Inn in Chicago and used it until he passed away. Between songs, he played it and used it on all of his commercials. Bernie popularized it so that it was recorded by dozens of singers, including Sinatra, Lena Horne, Nat Cole and many, many others. It's one of my most-recorded songs, along with "Miss You," "Sweet and Lovely," and "Sail Along Silv'ry Moon." Bing recorded most of my songs. I wrote "At Your Command" with his partner, Harry Barris, and Bing was in on the song, which he introduced at the Cocoanut Grove in 1931. The Grove was then the biggest thing here in Hollywood, and I had a dozen songs that got started here. Gus Arnheim and His Band, with whom Bing sang, had a coast-to-coast hookup.

My No. 1 song right now is "Sail Along, Silv'ry Moon," which I wrote with Percy Wenrich, who wrote "Put on Your Old Grey Bonnet" and "When You Wore a Tulip." Bing Crosby recorded it in 1937; Billy Vaughn revived it in 1958.

Dolly, a very beautiful gal, was Percy Wenrich's wife. They were very big vaudevillians—Wenrich at the piano and Dolly doing the vocals. They performed all over the country. I used to run into them on Hollywood Boulevard. Years ago, in the early thirties, Hollywood Boulevard was like Fifth Avenue in New York. On Sundays, everybody walked along, looking at the windows. I loved Wenrich's music, and one day when I bumped into them, I suggested we do a song together. We kept meeting and talking about writing a song for a couple of months. Then, at last, he did come with his wife and played me this little melody of "Sail Along." I wrote it up and it caught on.

When I first came out to Hollywood, the young punks used to kid me about writing only with the old-timers. And I would say: "Listen, kids, I adore their music and I love their melodies. To me, they're an inspiration. When I get an opportunity to work with them I do, whether they're old or not." Charles N. Daniels wrote under the names of Neil Moret and Jules Lemare. He used Lemare on "Sweet and Lovely" in 1931, and we cut in Gus Arnheim. He plugged it coast-to-coast with his band from the Cocoanut Grove and made it very popular. It's still popular all over the world. Bing also plugged it, as did Russ Columbo.

"No Regrets" came in 1936. I wrote it with Roy Ingraham, who used to have a band at the Hotel Paramount in New York City. His brother, Herbert

Ingraham, used to be the Irving Berlin of Tin Pan Alley. He wrote some beautiful songs, words, and music. Sherman Clay, out of San Francisco, took "No Regrets" when they opened an office in New York. It was one of their first plug tunes. The Casa Loma Band introduced it. Tommy Dorsey made one of the earliest records. I am told that Frances Faye made a big thing of it at the Yacht Club on 52nd Street. Judy Holliday plugged it. The most recent record was by Phoebe Snow on Columbia. "No Regrets" made the Lucky Strike *Hit Parade* and was on it for more than ten weeks.

The publishers I mostly worked with were Robbins, Feist, and Miller, especially Robbins, who had a large plugging staff out here. They used to attend rehearsals of the Gus Arnheim band. As soon as they heard a new song, they'd grab it. That's what happened with "What Is It?," a song I wrote with Harry Barris. "Put Your Arms Around Me" was another one that Robbins picked up when they heard Bing rehearsing it with Arnheim. [Tobias sings it in good voice, despite his years.] I had a song called "I'm Gonna Get You" that Dick Powers and Arthur Freed put out when they got into the publishing business. They cut in Arnheim, who introduced it, and gave us a $1,000 advance. And those were the days of the lousiest Depression that we ever had.

In between I wrote quite a number of picture songs for little films and big. I had songs in fifty or sixty pictures. Thanksgiving '87 will be my fifty-seventh year in Hollywood. I arrived the night before Thanksgiving in 1929 with my brother Henry in a four-cylinder Chevrolet. It was the worst time in the world to try to break through—right after the big stock market crash. [He chuckles.] It took us two to three weeks to make the trip.

Henry had to go back because he was a great social director in the Borscht Belt, a great guy in putting on shows. He put on about a dozen tributes for me out there.

Interview with Henry Tobias (19??–19??)

The thirties were very active years for the Tobias brothers. My brother Harry had his biggest songs during the Depression years. And he didn't make the kind of money he could have on songs like "Sweet and Lovely," "It's a Lonesome Old Town," and "Sail Along, Silv'ry Moon." In the thirties, the Tobiases were riding high with these as well as "Miss You."

Around 1939, Moe Jaffe came to me with the title "If I Had My Life to Live Over." After we finished the song, we brought it to Larry Vincent, who was a piano player at a Covington, Kentucky, night club, across the river from Cincinnati. He was making records for a small label, some of them what are known as "party" records with risqué material. Somehow, he got our song recorded with strings, and then, through a friend in Brooklyn, he had our record placed in jukeboxes. His was a corny version, but it caught on. The first artist to record the song after Vincent was Kate Smith. But there were disks also by Buddy Clark, Guy Mitchell, and Bob Eberly. Later on, Eddy Arnold did it and made it popular in Nashville. The most recent recording is by Lou Rawls on Capitol. He was the first to do it as a fox-trot and uptempo.

We had to put Larry Vincent's name on the song because he was responsible for starting the whole thing. He was a cut-in. To me, that's a dirty word, and I don't believe in it. But it's part of life and part of the music business. There's a difference between "payola" and "cut-in." Payola refers to payment given to a disc jockey to play a song on the air. Cut-ins are usually artists responsible for making a song popular. We gave Rudy Vallee a piece of "Miss You." When it was revived eleven years later, we went to him and he agreed to relinguish the 25 percent share he had been collecting.

I signed "If I Had My Life to Live Over" to Moe Jaffe's firm. He was partners then with Paul Knapp in General Music. Later, Paul suggested that we buy out Larry Vincent's share, which we did. So I own 50 percent of the publishing rights. When the renewals came up seven or eight years ago, I was able to recapture my share as a writer.

My first job in the music business was Mills Music. I wrote "Katinka" (1926) with Ben Russell for Feist. I met Billy Rose at Mills and wrote "Pretty Little Thing" with him. Billy gave me a chance to write a show, which ran for six months at the Shubert Theatre. It was called *Padlocks of 1927*, with Texas Guinan. In addition to lyricist Ballard MacDonald, who was the main writer, Billy hired three unknown melody writers. The obvious reason was that he didn't have to pay box-office money. To me, it was a big thing, at the age of nineteen or twenty, to have a show at the Shubert Theatre. That led to my meeting Max Dreyfus, who published all the big show writers like Gershwin, Kern, Porter, and others. Dreyfus said to me: "You have a gift for melody and you can write popular music. But you lack the musical education to write shows in which you have to be able to write ballets and more sophisticated material."

I am self-taught and learned what I did about music from working with other writers. So I gave up the idea of writing shows.

Now, just about this time, Billy Rose was getting married to Fanny Brice. I attended their wedding at City Hall in New York, officiated by Mayor Jimmy Walker. It was a strange union, but Billy was a climber and she was a wonderful gal, with money and a reputation. I went to have breakfast with them at a hotel on Madison Avenue. As she was standing at the stove, she said; "Isn't it wonderful cooking breakfast for the one I love." And Billy, who was a champion shorthand writer—he was a secretary to Charles Schwab—scribbled something in those crazy ciphers. He thought "Cooking Breakfast for the One I Love" was a great title and he gave me an opening line. After I wrote a melody, he kept pushing me to rewrite. He was a perfectionist, and he wanted the release changed. He thought I was lazy, and I couldn't make him see that a melody has to come naturally to me. I don't like to labor over a thing. Anyway, Fanny Brice recorded it and sang it in a picture, *Be Yourself* (1931).

Not too long ago, when I was reading Leonard Feather's jazz column in the *Los Angeles Times*, in a review of a pianist, Maria Muldare, I noticed the title "Cooking Breakfast for the One I Love." I don't know that much about jazz pianists, though I was wild about the playing of Art Tatum. I had no idea of how big an artist she was, but I started collecting royalties from all over the world. She may not be that well known here, except in some jazz circles, but abroad she seems to be a giant.

I forgot to mention a curious development with regard to "If I Had My Life to Live Over." When a picture came out with Bette Davis and Joan Crawford called *Whatever Happened to Baby Jane?*, my brother-in-law phoned me and urged me to see it. He said there was a song in it that had the exact melody of "If I Had My Life to Live Over," note for note. Sure enough, there was a song called "I've Written a Letter to Danny" with my melody. It was credited to Frank DeVol, who is a wonderful guy and was musical director. When I got in touch with him, he explained that he had been asked to write a corny melody, and he produced what he thought was an original. Reputable writers don't steal melodies, and DeVol was a reputable writer. Anyway, a lawyer's letter was sent to 20th Century–Fox, and we settled for a lump sum. More important, we got half the publishing rights for all over the world. And the story did not end with this film. When Bette Midler made the picture based on the life of Janis Joplin, *The Rose*, she sang "I've Written a Letter to Danny."

You may know that in 1929 when most songwriters were returning to New York from Hollywood, my brother Harry and I drove out to the coast in an old broken-down Chevrolet. He decided to stay, and he did quite well. But I went back to the Borscht Belt, where I served as a social director at Totem Lodge in the Catskills, starting in 1927. I was at Totem on and off into the 1970s. I tried Grossinger's one year, but found it too demanding.

Incidentally, I played the piano for three of the biggest stars of vaudeville: Eddie Cantor, George Jessel, and, believe it or not, Mae West. The Tobias family comes from Worcester, Massachusetts. When I was twelve, we moved to the Bronx, and a piano became part of the household. I never took lessons. To break into the music business, I took a job as a shipping clerk in the office of Joe Davis, a small music publisher. At Mills Music, I got a job as a piano-player, rehearsing singers who came in to learn our songs. I don't know why but Mae West took a liking to me, and she asked Jack Mills to let me go on the road with her. She had a small five-piece combo working with her. I wrote my first song, "Katinka," published by Leo Feist when I was twenty-one.

I was not nearly as active a songwriter as my brothers, Charley and Harry. But there have been eight songwriters in the Tobias family.

Gerald Marks (1900–1997)

The following was written by Gerald Marks, with the note, "Here 'tis, with plenty of tongue in cheek! . . . I can't be too serious about it. Besides, it'll give your audience a chuckle or two."

Interview with Gerald Marks

HELP COMETH YOUR WAY, the way
being the route to a
successful Tin Pan Alley
career, or SHORT-CUTS TO TIN
PAN ALLEY SUCCESS
> Words and Music by
> Gerald Marks

ROUTE A—throw your clothes out the window and write a hit. I wrote a few songs with Al Bryan, who had a clutch of hits for many, many years—"Peg o' My Heart," "I Didn't Raise My Boy to Be a Soldier," et al., et al., et al. He had a habit when he entered his apartment of immediately divesting himself of all his garments. Whenever I wrote with him in his apartment he paced the floor bare-assed, tossing me lines to fit my tunes. Discussing a lyric with him, I concentrated on the ceiling, pretending I was inhaling inspiration from the spirits above the seventh circle. This saved me from staring at different aspects of his naked torso as he kept whirling around the room to toss me a phrase. Writing with a writer of multiple hits requires that you exhibit no shock at anything—at anything!

ROUTE B—memorize the phrase "I love you"; that sanctified trio is sacred in the lyricist's lexicon, but the writer standing in front of you has had min-imal success with those three little words. When I use the phrase it sounds like a prayer for destruction. Years ago I had a smash in the *Scandals* with a song called "You're the One, You Beautiful Son-of-a-Gun," but you will not find "I love you" in the song.

ROUTE C—though you have but a modicum of talent, don't despair. The four-letter word "luck" is a most important ingredient in the career we're discussing. I can unequivocally testify that the following is the true and tried way to songwriting success: You must be born in Saginaw, Michigan, and not learn until some thirty years later who your father was. During your formative years your mother, a widow of course, supplies food for the table by doing drawn-work, her income in the neighborhood of two to three dollars per week. Music is in your blood, but your mother cannot afford the fifteen cents once a week for piano lessons, so naturally, at eight years of age, you figure the puzzle out for yourself. And inasmuch as she also cannot afford the dime for a piece of sheet music, you start to scribble tunes so you'll have something to play. Right? Right. Now, in Saginaw it doesn't take long for the story to travel that you are a genius. . . . Ten or twelve years later you collaborate on a song called "All of Me" with Seymour Simons, a highly respected, recognized professional, and you hop on the bus to New York, manuscript in pocket, and peddle it up and down the Great White Way, where it is turned down cold by every damned publisher on the street.

Now, here's where that word "luck" enters for the first time. You have returned to Michigan to tell Simons the sad news of the turn-downs, after which you take a solemn oath to commit suicide, when, lo and behold, you and Simons meet Belle Baker, a top vaudeville star, who falls in love with your song and sings it one night on a local New York radio station, from where it takes off to the Fiji Islands, Outer Mongolia, Lapland, and the island of Corsica, among other important towns, where natives by the millions buy copies of your sheet music. Your song, thank Demeter, the goddess of bread, does not diminish in sales for well over half a century.

Then, to keep up your membership in the Heavenly Order of Geniuses, you write another song turned down by every publisher, called "Is It True What They Say About Dixie?," although you have never been south. You still don't believe in luck, kid? Well, wake up and smell the coffee. The only one who likes this ditty is a guy—excuse me—the biggest musical comedy star ever—Al Jolson—the prime singer of southern songs. He introduces it for you one night on radio, and, whammo, it sells copies in Madagascar, North and South Dakota, Luxembourg—in fact, it sold so many copies the printer retired to Florida.

Demeter, bless her, still has her fingers in your hair, and you compose twenty-two songs on the subject of safety, one of which, through one accident after another, finally finds its way to kids in the lower grades—title: "Sing a Song of Safety"—all over the map.

Your genius is now so well publicized that naturally you are appointed to the most prestigious ASCAP Board of Directors, where you burrow in for some ten years. And not only that: ASCAP discovers that you speak English and sends you to somewhere between three and four hundred colleges in all the states, to lecture on the background of the pop music business and profession. Modesty to one side, I must acknowledge that one of the universities—in its greatest hour of wisdom—the University of Charleston—presents you with an honorary Doctorate of Humane Letters, and the list of other honors becomes in time too long to enumerate. From then on much of your time is taken up by acknowledging encomiums of praise on innumerable plagues bestowed upon you, with time out for taking bows . . .

Can anyone with a few grains of common sense afford to pass up such an ennobling career?

Oh, yes, you asked about education, formal, that is. Forget it! You arrange to drop out of Saginaw High School and join a mind-reading act. Does one need a heavier dose of education than that?

Please don't write.

Medley 1931

As of 1988, the only 1931 recording voted into NARAS's Hall of Fame was Duke Ellington's own Victor disk of his "Mood Indigo."

DeSylva, Brown and Henderson, who had built a songwriting-publishing colossus during the five-year period from 1926, dissolved in 1931 when Buddy DeSylva decided to settle in Hollywood and devote himself to film work.

Mildred Bailey introduced what became her theme, "Ol' Rockin' Chair Got Me," during a Paul Whiteman broadcast from the Edgewater Beach Hotel in Chicago. Also in 1931, Whiteman introduced Ferde Grofé's *Grand Canyon Suite* in Chicago's Studebaker show.

On August 7, 1931, Charles Chaplin premiered his new film *City Lights*, puzzling, startling, and/or enraging the movie colony by eschewing sound. Near-riots ensued in some cities over his failure to talk. The same month, the "voice" of another genius, Leon "Bix" Beiderbecke, was permanently silenced when he died of pneumonia. "The Young Man with a Horn," as he came to be known as the result of a novel based gently on his life, was just twenty-eight years old.

Gangster Jack "Legs" Diamond, who acquired his cognomen because he was so successful in outrunning his competitors, failed to escape a hail of bullets in an Albany, New York, boardinghouse on December 18, 1931.

"The Star-Spangled Banner" was declared the national anthem on March 3, 1931, beating out "America the Beautiful."

During the gang wars of the twenties, frequently waged inside the speakeasies, mobsters generally avoided endangering musicians. The original Lindy's restaurant, hangout of the Brill Building songwriting enclave, was curbed by the hold-up boys. But the new Lindy's at 50th Street and Broadway (northwest corner) was held up in 1931 shortly after its opening.

⚡ 9 ⚡

"Brother, Can You Spare a Dime?"
(1932)

"This radio business is not for Jolie," he announced at the close of his last show for Chevrolet in 1932. And he seized the mike and threw it to the floor. "It's a sad day when Jolie needs a mike to sing into." Jolie was, of course, Al Jolson (1886–1950), the hit-maker *par excellence* of the 1910s and 1920s, a singer who needed applause and a live audience like a diabetic needs insulin. Having disposed of the microphone, Jolie proceeded to sing to the studio audience without it. He had been singing to audiences since 1911, when he inaugurated Sunday night concerts at New York's Winter Garden. About them, compadre Eddie Cantor observed: "Many's the night he'd look at the audience about a quarter of eleven and say, 'The girls . . . have some songs and dances, but they've worked pretty hard tonight, let's let them go home, huh? I'll stay here as long as you want . . . ' and he'd send everybody home while he stood there maybe another hour, singing, clowning, giving the audience the time of its life—and having the time of his own!"

Jolson's personal rejection of the microphone was more than a gesture: it really was a symbolic act, semaphore of the death of vaudeville and, as we have already observed with such singers as Crosby and Vallee, the birth of the electronic age in popular music. Jolie was hardly at the end of his career. In 1943, when he was in ill health, he cut the sound tracks for *The Jolson Story* and *Jolson Sings Again*, two mighty box-office films in which Larry Parks lip-synched the songs that Jolson had sung and made famous. They rejuvenated a career that he pursued actively—especially on U.S.O. tours—

105

until a heart attack felled him in a San Francisco hotel room on October 23, 1950.

The year 1932 brought *42nd Street*, a film that helped rejuvenate the movie industry, initiated a film musical renaissance, and became the model for a new series of musicals.

The Warner Bros. film had more than its share of pluses. It starred a new attractive song-and-dance team, Dick Powell and Ruby Keeler, with a strong supporting cast. It had the terpsichorean and camera genius of Busby Berkeley, whose massive dance routines became an industry legend. And then it had a scintillating score by Harry Warren and Al Dubin that included such perennial melodies as "Shuffle Off to Buffalo" (introduced by Ginger Rogers and Una Merkel), "You're Getting To Be a Habit with Me" (sung by Bebe Daniels), and "Young and Healthy." Warren and Dubin were soon recognized as the top movie songwriting team of the thirties. The story was the old Cinderella scenario, so popular in the twenties, except that it had a backstage setting in which the awkward beginner turned into a star. In a time when people were frantic about the future, it brought a welcome sense of hope and optimism.

Both Warren (1893–1981) and Dubin (1891–1945) came to *42nd Street* with impressive track records. As composer, Warren had such hits as "Rose of the Rio Grande" (1922), his first; "I Love My Baby (My Baby Loves Me)" (with Ross Gorman, 1915); "Would You Like to Take a Walk" and "Cheerful Little Earful" from the Broadway revue *Sweet and Low* (1930); and "By the River Sainte Marie" from Billy Rose's *Crazy Quilt* (1931).

Dubin, who became the first lyricist to be given a studio contract, also had an impressive catalogue of hits: "A Cup of Coffee, a Sandwich and You" from *Charlot's Revue of 1926* (1925); "Tiptoe Through the Tulips" and "Painting the Clouds with Sunshine" from the film *Gold Diggers of Broadway*; and "I'm Dancing with Tears in My Eyes" from *Hold Everything* (1932).

When Warren stepped off the train and entered the Warner lot, Darryl Zanuck assigned him to Dubin. In some ways, the two resembled Rodgers and Hart, with Dubin operating as the erratic member of the team. Unable to control his appetite for food, fun, and play, he was overweight and unpredictable.

"He was a terrific eater," Warren told Max Wilk. "Weighed about 300 pounds. He'd disappear on me. Carried a little stub of pencil, wrote lyrics on scrap paper. I'd write a tune and hand him a lead-sheet and then I'd never hear a word. All of a sudden, he'd come back and he'd have the lyric. Once he brought in 'Shuffle Off to Buffalo' on the back of a menu from a San Francisco restaurant."

From *42nd Street*, Warren and Dubin went on to create a rich catalogue of standards, writing the score for *Gold Diggers of 1933*.

The Gold Diggers series all used the same scenario—a group of girls in search of rich husbands. What distinguished the films were the Warren-Dubin songs and Busby Berkeley's prodigious use of massive casts in stupendous dance routines. "We're in the Money," introduced in 1933 by Ginger Rogers, attired in a costume made of silver dollars and supported by a huge chorus, became known as "The Gold Diggers' Song." (It was one of the uplift songs of the era, bidding good-bye to "Old Man Depression" and promising no more breadlines, no more money problems.) That year, Warren and Dubin produced a hit in "The Boulevard of Broken Dreams," introduced in *Moulin Rouge* by Tullio Carmurati.

Al Dubin died in 1945 in his early fifties, with "Feudin' and Fightin'," a comic hillbilly number he wrote with Burton Lane, caught in a battle between the producers of *Laffing Room Only*, an Olsen and Johnson musical extravaganza, and ASCAP. It was not until 1947 that composer Burton Lane was able to acquire the broadcasting rights and arrange for the song to be introduced by Dorothy Shay. A performance on the Bing Crosby Show led to a Columbia recording that helped make the song a posthumous 1947 hit for Dubin.

Harry Warren had begun working with other lyricists even before Dubin's death—and in 1938 he scored two hits with Johnny Mercer. "Jeepers Creepers," an Academy Award nominee, was introduced by Louis Armstrong in the film musical *Going Places* and climbed to No. 1 on *Your Hit Parade* in 1939 for a five-week run. "You Must Have Been a Beautiful Baby" was debuted by Dick Powell in *Hard to Get* for a three-week stay at No. 1. (A 1961 revival by Bobby Darrin resulted in a best-selling disk for him.)

Mercer's introduction into the movie business came in 1932–33 through Paul Whiteman. The portly conductor was then holding a series of contests called *Pontiac Youth of America*. "I won the one held in New York," the late Johnny Mercer once told me, "which entitled me to sing on one of his weekly radio programs. That's when I first met Mildred Bailey and Red Norvo. They could see that I was scared to death, and they both went out of their way to boost my confidence. About a year later, Whiteman hired me as a band vocalist. I got to know the Rockin' Chair Lady and Red pretty well. Theirs was a great musical partnership. Their marriage had its funny and sad moments."

From 1942 to 1945, Warren collaborated mainly with lyricist Mack Gordon (1904–1959), producing at least one Oscar winner in "You'll Never Know" in 1943. Written for the film musical *Hello, Frisco, Hello*, it was sung by Alice Faye. But it was Dick Haymes and the Song Spinners who produced a record that made it a gold hit. Other Mack Gordon collaborations included "Chattanooga Choo Choo," the top song of 1941 featured in the film *Sun Valley Serenade* in which Glenn Miller and His Orchestra performed with ice-skating star Sonja Henie. By February 10, 1942, when RCA Victor presented Miller with the first gold disk (a gold-lacquered facsimile) on the Chesterfield radio show, his Bluebird disk had passed the million mark. In 1942, Warren and Gordon hit with "I've Got a Gal in Kalamazoo," written for the film *Orchestra Wives*, which also proved a million seller for Glenn Miller. In 1943, they scored with "I Had the Craziest Dream," which was introduced by Harry James and His Orchestra with a vocal by Helen Forrest and became a million seller. In 1944, their ballad "My Heart Tells Me" was introduced in the film musical *Sweet Rosie O'Grady* by Betty Grable, then the GIs' favorite pin-up girl, and, the following year, Dick Haymes introduced "The More I See You" in the film *Billy Rose's Diamond Horseshoe*.

In 1945, working once again with Johnny Mercer, Warren produced the novelty rhythm song "On the Atchinson, Topeka, and the Santa Fe." It was performed by Judy Garland, Ray Bolger, and a trainful of Harvey Girls in the MGM film *The Harvey Girls* and became the year's Academy Award winner, assisted in its climb to popularity by a recording made by Johnny Mercer and the Pied Pipers. Warren was skillful in incorporating an imitation of a train whistle in the melody. As late as 1953, the Warren melodic genius found expression in an offbeat ballad, "That's Amoré," which he co-wrote with Jack Brooks for *The Caddy*, a film starring Dean Martin and Jerry Lewis. It became an Academy Award nominee. With it, Dean Martin, giving it an Italianate flair, achieved his first gold record, selling more than four million in the next decade.

In the course of his Hollywood career, Warren worked at virtually all the major studios—Warner Bros., MGM, Paramount, and Fox. Although he died in Los Angeles in 1981, after living there almost fifty years, he told Max Wilk he never had a feeling of permanence about the place. Additionally, he was bothered by most producers' lack of musical taste and judgment—he excluded Louis B. Mayer from this group—and the low esteem in which most songwriters were held.

"I don't know exactly what it was," he said, "all that hostility toward us songwriters. Maybe it was because most of the time you were making more dough than the producer, and he sort of resented that. He knew he needed you—that probably made him hate your guts all the more. The only guy that really gave us respect was Arthur Freed. He'd been a songwriter himself and he knew. Hired the best people he could get, took big chances on young talent."

Considering the number of hits he wrote, it is astounding how little known Harry Warren is to the general public—of his day as well as ours. What is more common is the public's lack of awareness of lyric writers. This is doubtless true partly because most songs are associated with the composer rather than the lyricist, with the possible exception of word-makers who are part of a team like Rodgers and Hart, Lerner and Loewe, Kalmar and Ruby, among others.

Certainly E. Y. (Yip) Harburg (1898–1981) deserves to be better known, considering the number of significant songs for which he wrote the words in the thirties and forties. As a boy, to avoid the gang wars on Manhattan's East Side where he grew up, he joined a literary dramatic club at the Henry Street Settlement. He went to Townsend Harris High School for bright boys—the four-year course was completed in three—and earned a B.S. at City College, which then charged no tuition, but required a high secondary school average. He earned his way by working as a lighter of streetlamps at $3.06 a week. He had a three- or four-mile route and would light the lamps at dusk, then get up before dawn to extinguish them. Although he was writing light verse and seeing it in print (but receiving no money) in FPA's famous "Conning Tower" in *The World* newspaper, he felt writing was not the way to earn a livelihood and went into the electrical supply business. He hated it. Whatever the Depression did to others, it was his savior. It bankrupted the business and motivated him to get in touch with Ira Gershwin. They had sat near each other at City College and together written a column for the college newspaper—"Yip and Gersh." Ira introduced him to Jay Gorney (1896–1990), and one of the first songs they wrote was the legendary "Brother, Can You Spare a Dime?" The song, sometimes regarded as the leitmotif of the Depression, was first heard in the 1932 revue *Americana*.

"I didn't make it a maudlin lyric of a guy begging," he told Max Wilk. "I made it into a commentary. . . . It was about the fellow who works, the fellow who builds, who makes the railroads and the houses—and he's left empty-handed. How come? How did this happen? . . . This is a man proud of what he's done, but bewildered that this country with its dream could do this to him."

Jay Gorney tells an amusing story about the song: "Several years later, when I'd come back from Hollywood, Lee Shubert sent for me and said, 'What I wanted to ask you, do you have another song like "Mister, Will You Give Me Ten Cents?" ' But his brother J. J. never shared Lee's enthusiasm. Whenever anyone mentioned the song he'd say, 'I don't like it. It's too morbid.' "

If Harburg's comment impresses one with the analytical character of his thinking, it is a sound conclusion. He was a man with a philosophical and political outlook, as his lyrics for *Bloomer Girl* (1944), a show about women's rights, and his work as a co-writer of *Finian's Rainbow* (1947), a left-wing fantasy about black and white relationships in the South, would indicate. "They [the Hollywood producers] were all frightened of my ideas, but they all liked me. All of them, even Louis Mayer. . . . They couldn't connect me with conspirational things, somehow. They always thought of me as living in a fairyland world of leprechauns and rainbows. . . . I'd joke with them, I'd kid them, I'd quote George Bernard Shaw. But in the end it wasn't so funny— I was blacklisted."

Harburg was, nonetheless, one of the top lyricists of the thirties (and the forties), with a long, impressive list of hit songs. In the same year that he wrote "Brother, Can You Spare a Dime?," he composed the charming "April in Paris" with Vernon Duke (1903–1969). He had met Duke (né Vladimir Dukelsky) through George Gershwin. Their first collaboration, including Ira Gershwin on the lyrics, brought "I'm Only Human After All," which was introduced in *The Garrick Gaieties of 1930*. Later, they wrote "What Is There To Say?" and "I Like the Likes of You" for the *Ziegfeld Follies of 1934*, the former introduced by Jane Froman and Everett Marshall.

But "April in Paris" had "a very special quality," as Harburg said. "First of all, it captures Paris in a way that only French people have been able to do—and then it's not simply about being in love in Paris, but about *wanting* to be in love anywhere." What is, perhaps, almost unbelievable is that Harburg had never been to Europe and surely not to Paris. He wrote the nostalgically brilliant lyric by visiting travel agencies and studying brochures about Paris.

Although the song initially aroused little interest, it did enchant a number of critics. H. T. Parker of Boston wrote: " 'April in Paris' is worthy, in place and kind, of that city in spring. There is a catch in the throat from it—if one has too many memories."

In 1932, Harburg, collaborating on the lyric with Billy Rose to a tune by Harold Arlen, wrote "If You Believed in Me." It appeared in a nonmusical play, *The Great Magoo*, as a recurring theme. When the play flopped, Harburg reworked the lyric, altering the title to "It's Only a Paper Moon," which was interpolated in the Paramount film *Take a Chance* (1933) and sung by June Knight and Charles "Buddy" Rogers, later Mary Pickford's husband. It became a record best-seller both for the Mills Brothers (Decca) and Nat Cole (Capitol), captivating the public with its poetic concept that nothing is make-believe so long as someone believes in it—not even a paper moon hanging over a cardboard tree.

For *Life Begins at 8:40* (1934), Harburg wrote "Let's Take a Walk Around the Block" and "You're a Builder-Upper," collaborating with Ira Gershwin on the lyrics to melodies by Harold Arlen. The latter song was introduced by Ray Bolger and Dixie Dunbar. Although he produced many hits in the forties, the high point of Harburg's career came in 1939 with *The Wizard of Oz*.

There is no decade from the turn of the century into the sixties in which Irving Berlin (1888–1989) did not produce hits—and few years in which he did not contribute to the permanent repertoire of American popular music. In 1932, he placed at least four romantic ballads on best-seller charts. "How Deep Is the Ocean?," whose publication (we are told) he delayed for several years, questioning its quality, was popularized by Bing Crosby and then went on to be part of a series of films: *Alexander's Ragtime Band* (20th Century–Fox, 1938); *Blue Skies* (MGM, 1946), in which it was also sung by Bing; and *Meet Danny Wilson* (Universal, 1952), where Frank Sinatra gave it his romantic interpretation.

"Let's Have Another Cup of Coffee" was part of the score Berlin wrote for the anti-Depression musical *Face the Music*. Sung by Katherine Carrington and J. Harold Murray as they dined at the Automat, it became a theme song of the Depression for its chin-up positives. It was Rudy Vallee, both on disk and on his radio show, who made a hit of "Say It Isn't So," developing an audience that pushed the song to No. 3 among the top hits of 1932. With "Soft Lights and Sweet Music" Berlin bettered his record on "Say It Isn't So" and achieved the top song of the year. Featured in *Face the Music*, it was introduced by the duo who presented "Let's Have Another Cup of Coffee."

In contrast to Berlin's massive output, Dana Suesse (1911–1987), one of the few successful female songwriters, produced a limited number of hits. Her original interest was in the classics, and extensive piano study led to her playing her own *Jazz Concerto* in Carnegie Hall in 1932 with Paul Whiteman and his symphony orchestra. But she was not too successful in promoting her classical compositions. Thus, she turned to popular music, collaborating mostly with Edward Heyman (1907–1981), one of the lyricists of "Body and Soul."

Suesse's first song hit came in 1932 when "Have You Forgotten the Thrill" was adapted from her instrumental *Syncopated Love Song*. In 1932, Heyman wrote "My Silent Love" to a melody adapted from her instrumental *Jazz Nocturne*, and it became so popular that more than twenty-five years later it was revived in separate recordings by Eydie Gormé and Julie London. In the *Ziegfeld Follies of 1934*, Suesse was represented by "You Oughta Be in Pictures," again with lyrics by Edward Heyman, which was sung by Jane Froman. "The Night Is Young and You're So Beautiful" brought Dana Suesse into a collaboration with Billy Rose and Irving Kahal, who wrote the words. It was introduced in a unique theatre in the round at Billy Rose's Casa

Mañana, a club he opened in Fort Worth, Texas, during the Frontier Days celebration in 1936.

Unquestionably, Dana Suesse would have derived greater satisfaction if a single work from her extensive catalogue of "symphonic" works—titles like *Concerto in A for Piano and Orchestra, American Nocturne, Afternoon of a Black Faun, Concerto in Rhythm*—achieved the acceptance of her few hit songs.

Doubtless, the strangest song hit of 1932 was Cole Porter's "Night and Day," introduced in *Gay Divorce* by Fred Astaire, working for the first time without his sister Adele, who had left Fred to marry a British lord. His leading lady was Claire Luce. It was said that Porter kept the range of the song narrow because of Astaire's limited voice. But Porter also indicated that the inspiration for the weird melody came from a native tune he had heard in Morocco involving the Muslim summons to prayer. The shift from a minor-sounding opening to a major key middle was hardly a novelty. However, instead of adhering to the then-standard form of 32 bars with a sequence of AABA, Porter extended his melody to 48 bars. The popularity of the song was instantaneous, and its appeal was so great, that *Gay Divorce* was known after a time as the "Night and Day" show.

Medley 1932

It was in 1932 that the first mention of the word "Swing" came in a song—a Duke Ellington original. Like many Ellington songs, it started as an instrumental melody. Publisher Irving Mills later added the lyric—"It Don't Mean a Thing If It Ain't Got That Swing," foreshadowing the turn that popular music would take after 1935.

Although the election of FDR to the presidency and the impending repeal of the Prohibition Act suggested that the Speakeasy Era was on the way out, 1932 bore the scars of the violent twenties. Early in the year, a gangster was slain in a crowded West 51st Street club. Nobody moved to apprehend the killers and amid charges of corruption, Jimmy Walker resigned as Mayor of New York City. Even the elegant 21 Club was raided by IRS agents, who came up empty-handed because of the club's intricate system for disposing of illicit evidence. The flow of illegal liquor continued unchecked, although revenue agents padlocked and destroyed clubs, totally unable to cope with the 32,000 speakeasies that sprang from the 15,000 saloons shuttered by Prohibition.

Although it became world famous as a jazz club in its 52nd Street location, Kelly's Stable had its beginnings at 145 West 51st Street, opening in a new addition to the Hotel Victoria, across the street from the stage entrance to the Roxy Theatre. The barbershop located in this addition became a hangout for songwriters and publishers because the most powerful columnist of the time, Walter Winchell, came there daily to be shaved before departing on his rounds of the city's clubs, showrooms, and backstages.

With marijuana regarded as a "harmless" craze, it figured in semi-humorous songs like "Smokin' Reefers" by Howard Dietz and Arthur Schwartz in the 1932 revue *Flying Colors*. In jazz, Don Redman's "Chant of the Weed" became a classic instrumental.

Radio City Music Hall, one of the first giant movie palaces, with 6,200 seats, opened in mid-Manhattan on December 27, 1932. Songwriter Dorothy Fields was featured in the stage show singing "Hey Young Fella, Close Your Old Umbrella," accompanied by collaborator-pianist Jimmy McHugh. Columnist Frank Sullivan initiated his annual Christmas poem, greeting hundreds of New Yorkers and friends by name—a practice he continued in *The New Yorker* each Yuletide until 1974. And columnist Walter Winchell launched his radio news program on December 4, 1932.

Collaborators Al Dubin, Larry Hart, and Harry Woods, among others, have all commented on the fact that after they had been given a melody to lyricize, they would take the lead-sheet and disappear for indeterminate periods of time. They never explained their absences, but they always reappeared, usually with a hit lyric.

That was true of Harry MacGregor Woods, the writer of "Try a Little Tenderness," a poignant ballad written in 1932 with two Englishmen, Jimmy Campbell and Reg Connelly—and probably his best song. Woods (1896–1970), born in Massachusetts, educated at Harvard, and tutored musically by his mother, managed a very successful career as a songwriter (writing music and words), although he had no fingers on his left hand. His first big hit, "When the Red, Red Robin Comes Bob, Bob, Bobbin' Along," came in 1926, followed by "I'm Looking Over a Four Leaf Clover" (1927), "River Stay Away From My Door" (1931), and "When the Moon Comes Over the Mountain" (1931).

⚡ 10 ⚡

"Who's Afraid of the Big Bad Wolf?"
(1933)

It was just a cute ditty in an animated Disney cartoon, *The Three Little Pigs*. But in the atmosphere of 1933, "Who's Afraid of the Big Bad Wolf?," by Frank E. Churchill (1901–1942) and Ann Ronell (1908–1993), took on overtones in which the Wolf became a symbol of the Depression itself. This was the year that FDR was inaugurated as president and delivered his famous speech: "We have nothing to fear but fear itself." "Who's Afraid of the Big Bad Wolf?" was almost a song analogue of the sentiment. It somehow took color from all the moves that FDR made to uplift the dying economy: the establishment of various agencies like the AAA and NIRA to assist farmers and workers with loans and credit; the ballyhoo about a New Deal and the Brain Trust in Washington; the repeal of Prohibition; and the friendly and optimistic fireside chats.

It became a rallying song for a people set to latch onto anything as a spirit raiser. Of comparable impact were the images of energy, jubilation, and fun that two elegant dancers projected from the screen. Fred Astaire and Ginger Rogers became dance partners when Dorothy Jordan, who was scheduled to dance with Astaire, married the picture's executive producer and dropped out of *Flying Down to Rio*. This led to a series of nine brilliant dance musicals. More than any other personalities of the thirties, it was Astaire and Rogers— with their high-spirited dancing and dynamic personalities—who heightened the morale of the American people.

Astaire's dancing was a highwater mark in American popular culture and the *New York Times* described him as a Dancing Man Who Also Sang Up a Storm, quoting an exchange with Bing Crosby:

> Fred dismissed his singing as very roughly in the same class as Bing's dancing, to which Bing replied graciously: "I consider this high praise because I think Fred sings very well indeed. He has a remarkable ear for intonation, a great sense of rhythm, and what is more important, he has great style—delivery, phrasing, but most of all presence. All of these Fred has in abundance."

The bluesy "Stormy Weather"—"keeps raining all the time"—traded in on the gloom, the *Sturm und Drang* of the dismal years of the thirties. Written by Harold Arlen and Ted Koehler for Cab Calloway to introduce in a Cotton Club revue, it was given instead to Ethel Waters (1896–1977) as a song more suitable for a female vocalist. In actuality, the song was already popular when it was heard at the Cotton Club, for Leo Reisman and His Orchestra had quickly recorded it, with Harold Arlen himself doing the vocal. One of the biggest hits of the year, despite its joyless sentiment, it became an Ethel Waters standard and later a Lena Horne perennial.

The impact of the Depression—more specifically of the rise of Hitler who was made Chancellor of the Third Reich in January 1933—was felt in *Let 'Em Eat Cake*. The same group who accounted for *Of Thee I Sing*—libretto by George S. Kaufman and Morrie Ryskind and songs by the Gershwins—also created the satirical musical.

"The smiling satire of the original [*Of Thee I Sing*]," Gerald Bordman observes, "gave way to what the *Times*' Brooks Atkinson termed a 'bitter, hysterical mood.' The horror of the Depression and/or the fascist movements in Italy and Germany had thrown both authors and audience slightly off balance." (If they were off balance, they anticipated a novel with a similar theme, *It Can't Happen Here* by Sinclair Lewis.) The show lasted for only twelve weeks, but it did include a hit in "Mine." Introduced by William Gaxton and Lois Moran, it used a contrapuntal device in which a distinctive countermelody was sung against the main melody.

Although popular music and country music—the latter was then still known as hillbilly—existed as separate streams, as far apart as New York and Nashville, one songwriter seemed able to cross over. He did not write country music so much as cowboy and western ballads. Billy Hill (1899–1940) was born and died in Boston, Massachusetts, but as a youth had worked as a cowboy and traveled throughout the West playing violin and piano in dance halls; he reportedly led the first dance band that played in Salt Lake City.

When he began writing in New York, his songs had a western flavor. It is said that he sold some of his early pieces outright for a few dollars and received no recognition as writer. His first hit came in 1933, a cowboy ballad titled "The Last Round-up," introduced at the Paramount Theatre on Broadway by Joe Morrison. Both Bing Crosby and Roy Rogers recorded it, with *Variety* reporting that by 1935 it had sold 650,000 disks. It was interpolated in the *Ziegfeld Follies of 1934* not only by Don Ross but by Willie and Eugene Howard, who did a comic takeoff. (Later, Roy Rogers, who is said to have gotten a movie contract as a result of his "Last Round-up" recording, used it in the 1945 film *Don't Fence Me In*.)

In 1933, Billy Hill also wrote "The Old Spinning Wheel," which became the radio theme song of child singer Mary Small. Before the year was out, he wrote "Wagon Wheels" in collaboration with Peter De Rose. It was recorded by George Olsen and His Orchestra, and made the Top Ten, rising to become the No. 1 song for three weeks. It was featured in the *Ziegfeld Follies of 1934* together with "The Last Round-up."

Peter De Rose also collaborated on "The Oregon Trail" (1935), composing the music to Billy Hill's words. In 1935, Hill, working with Daniel Richman and Ted Fiorito, wrote "Alone at a Table for Two," which was recorded and introduced by Ted Fiorito and His Orchestra. That year he also provided Ozzie Nelson and Harriet Hilliard with two songs, one titled "Lights Out" and the other, "Put on an Old Pair of Shoes." The latter was a collaboration with Dedette Lee Hill.

The year 1936 brought a number of bigger songs from Hill's pen. "Empty Saddles," written to a poem by J. Keirn Brennan, was introduced by Bing Crosby in *Rhythm on the Range*, and it made No. 1 on *Your Hit Parade* for one week. Shep Fields and His Orchestra made a hit of Hill's "In the Chapel in the Moonlight," more of a torch song than a western or cowboy ballad. The tale of a broken romance became a standard that sold a million records for Kitty Kallen in 1954 and a best-selling disk for Dean Martin in 1967. A song of lesser import but representing a change of pace for Billy Hill was "The Glory of Love," featured in *Guess Who's Coming to Dinner*, a 1967 film starring Sidney Poitier, Katharine Hepburn, and Spencer Tracy.

Although Hill continued writing until the year he died (1940), the spark that ignited his early work was gone and his efforts to experiment with songs outside the cowboy and western tradition seemed to fail.

Two of the most prolific writers of movie musicals in the thirties were Mack Gordon (1904–1959), who came from Warsaw, Poland, and Harry Revel (1905–1958), who hailed from London, England. Gordon, who arrived in the United States at an early age, grew up in Brooklyn and the Bronx and worked as a boy soprano in minstrel shows and a comedian-singer in vaudeville. Harry Revel, who was a self-taught pianist, studied at London's Guild-hall School of Music. At fifteen, he toured Europe with an orchestra and began composing for musical productions in Paris, Copenhagen, Vienna, Berlin, and Rome. The reputation he acquired yielded nothing when he arrived in the United States in 1929. It was only when the two came together that, after scoring unsuccessfully for several Broadway shows, they began producing hit songs—and this happened not in New York but in Hollywood, where they settled in 1933.

That year they produced their first film hit, "Did You Ever See a Dream Walking?," introduced by Jack Haley in *Sitting Pretty*. By the time it made No. 1 in 1934—a spot it occupied for five weeks—they had two other film hits: "Stay As Sweet As You Are," sung to the top of the charts by Lanny Ross (known as Troubadour of the Moon) in *College Rhythm*, and "With My Eyes Wide Open I'm Dreaming," introduced in *Shoot the Works* by Jack Oakie and Dorothy Dell. (It would later become Patti Page's first million seller in 1949.) In the next five years they turned out the scores for at least thirty films and wrote an enormous number of songs for top artists like Bing Crosby, Alice Faye, Tony Martin, and Shirley Temple, among others.

A song introduced by Bing Crosby in *Two for Tonight* (1935), and popularized by him on a Decca disk, led Gordon and Revel to initiate a plagiarism suit. They claimed that the basic melody of their ballad, "Without a Word of Warning," had been appropriated in a song titled "Lady of Love." The defendant countered their claim by asserting and demonstrating that his own melody had been derived partly from Johann Strauss's *Die Fledermaus* and partly from Victor Herbert's *Sweethearts*. What they did not seem to realize—although their attorneys should have known better—is that musicologists have seldom failed to find analogues for so-called "new" strains of melody in old compositions. There are several musicologists with an encyclopedic knowledge of ancient, medieval, and public domain works who serve the music industry in defeating plagiarism suits. The Gordon and Revel suit was thrown out of court.

Perhaps the earliest team producing scores for movie musicals was that of Arthur Freed (1894–1972) and Nacio Herb Brown (1896–1964). Freed was originally a vaudevillian and writer of café revue material, while Brown was a tailor and realtor operating in the movie colony, sometimes performing on the piano. As the co-writers of *Broadway Melody* (1929), the first successful "all-talking, all-singing, all-dancing" screen musical, and the winner of the Academy Award for Best Picture (1929), they created a score so loaded with hits—"You Were Meant for Me," "Wedding of the Painted Doll," and the title tune—they were signed to do four other film musicals in rapid succession. They did three film musicals in 1930, one in 1932, and three in 1937. There were hits in a stage show, *Take a Chance* (1932) (words and music by B. G. De Sylva, Richard Whiting, and Nacio Herb Brown), including "Eadie Was a Lady," "Turn Out the Light," and "You're an Old Smoothie." But their giant hit came in 1933 with the film *Going Hollywood*. Bing Crosby introduced "Temptation" with a beguine background, rising with it to become one of the Top Ten box-office talents. His best-selling record catapulted the song into the No. 1 spot where it remained for three weeks in 1934. That it was a standard became clear when Perry Como recorded it in the mid-forties to garner a million seller. The passionate character of its assertations of love—"I'm just a slave to you"—lent itself to parody, and Cinderella G. Stump (Jo Stafford) and Red Ingle and the Natural Seven did a takeoff, country style, in 1947, calling it "Tim-tay-shun." They scored a million-seller.

Into the early forties, Freed and Brown continued to turn out film musicals and an impressive number of hits that became standards. "All I Do Is Dream of You" was introduced by Gene Raymond in the film musical *Sadie McKee* (1934). Debbie Reynolds revived it in *Singin' in the Rain* (MGM, 1952). Played under the title of *The Affairs of Dobie Gillis* (MGM, 1953), it was sung in the film by Debbie Reynolds and Bobby Van. For five weeks early in 1936, Freed and Brown's song "Alone," sung by Kitty Carlisle and Allan Jones in the Marx Brothers film *A Night at the Opera*, was at the top of *Your Hit Parade*. In 1935, Frances Langford introduced "Broadway Rhythm" in the movie musical *Broadway Melody of 1936*, which also featured Eleanor Powell, the distaff Fred Astaire. Langford also introduced "You Are My Lucky Star" in the same film musical, helping the song to reach the No. 1 spot on *Your Hit Parade* for a three-week run. After a time, Arthur Freed turned his talents to producing films and became the producer of the brilliant series of musicals MGM introduced in the forties and fifties. The most famous was *Singin' in the Rain* (1952), which used two other Freed and Brown songs, "You Were Meant for Me and "All I Do Is Dream of You," along with "You Are My Lucky Star."

Paul Francis Webster (1907–1984) was one of the most accomplished lyric writers creating material for the screen. Of the few songwriters who have won multiple Oscars, he captured three Academy Awards. In 1953, he and Sammy Fain shared the Oscar for "Secret Love" from *Calamity Jane*. Two years later he walked off with the Oscar for "Love Is a Many-Splendored Thing," again with Sammy Fain as the composer. And in 1965 he and composer Johnny Mandel won the Oscar for "The Shadow of Your Smile" from the film *The Sandpiper*.

Webster's first consequential song was "My Moonlight Madonna," a hit in 1933. The music was adapted from Zdenko Fibich's "Poème" by William Scotti, and Webster added lyrics. Introduced by Rudy Vallee, it was recorded by baritone Conrad Thibault, tenor Jack Fulton with the Paul Whiteman

Orchestra, and Arthur Tracy, radio's Street Singer. Two additional recordings helped popularize the poetic ballad: one by composer Victor Young, another by Freddy Martin operating under the pseudonym Albert Taylor.

"Two Cigarettes in the Dark" (music by Lew Pollack; words by Paul Francis Webster) was one of Bing Crosby's earliest recordings on the newly established Decca label. Webster used the various phases of smoking—striking a match, the glow of the cigarette, and smoke rings—as images of love. Cigarette smoking was not then linked to cancer and frequently served on screen as a symbol of sophistication and intimacy.

In 1941, Webster worked with Duke Ellington on a West Coast theatrical production, *Jump for Joy*. Its main performer was Herb Jeffries, who recorded the production with the Duke and his orchestra on RCA. The major song that came out of the work was "I Got It Bad and That Ain't Good" (music by Duke Ellington; words by Paul Francis Webster), which was introduced and recorded by Ivie Anderson on the production disk. Ella Fitzgerald also recorded the bluesy torch ballad for Decca.

While Webster fulfilled movie assignments all through the forties, fifties, and sixties, his high points were, of course, the songs that garnered Academy Awards. Several other songs are also memorable. The title song from the film *Friendly Persuasion* (1956), music by Dimitri Tiomkin, also known as "Thee I Love" (the film dealt with Quakers), was nominated for an Academy Award. A best-selling record was cut by Pat Boone on Dot. Also nominated for an Academy Award was the title song "April Love," music by Sammy Fain, which again was recorded sensitively by the star of the film, baritone Pat Boone, in 1957. In 1960, Tiomkin wrote the music for "The Green Leaves of Summer," introduced in the motion picture *The Alamo*, starring John Wayne and Laurence Harvey, where it was sung on the soundtrack by a chorus. With composer John Green, Webster wrote "Never Till Now," which was used instrumentally in the motion picture *Raintree County* (1957), starring Elizabeth Taylor.

The year 1933 sparkled with a remarkable number of gem-like songs with poetic imagery, unforgettable melodies, and rich harmonies. Jerome Kern and Otto Harbach created the evergreen "Smoke Gets in Your Eyes" and the beautiful "Yesterdays" (not to be confused with the Beatles' "Yesterday"), both in *Roberta*. Irving Berlin produced one of his many holiday perennials in "Easter Parade." Duke Ellington gave us one of his uniquely masterful instrumentals in the modernistic blue-toned "Sophisticated Lady," later lovingly lyricized by Mitchell Parish. And the little-known Frank Perkins wrote the melodious "Stars Fell on Alabama," also lyricized by Parish. Harold Arlen and Ted Koehler caught the spirit of the times in a song that has remained an oft-performed standard, "Stormy Weather."

The impact of the Depression was seen in the transformation of the ten-year-old Times Square Theatre—its last stage show was a revue, *Hot Rhythm*, in 1930—into a movie grind house. Only fourteen new musicals opened during the year, less than half the number three years earlier. Even the gangster Waxey Gordon could not beat the economic downdraft when he invested in a show by hit writer Ray Henderson, *Strike Me Pink*. And on February 27, the night that the Gershwins' *Pardon My English* closed, the Reichstag in Germany was burned down, leading to a violent attack on Communists—who were not responsible—by the Hitler regime. By then it seemed clear that the Big Bad Wolf was the fanatical Hitler, not the Depression. Among the "dangerous foreigners" against whom Der Führer campaigned in 1933 was Mickey Mouse!

Medley 1933

At 32 ½ minutes past three, Mountain Time, on December 5, 1933, Utah put the Repeal Amendment over, incidentally launching 52nd Street—a beehive of speakeasies in the twenties—as the premier street of world jazz clubs.

When he was eight years old in 1933, Sammy Davis, Jr., appeared in a motion picture short, *Rufus Jones for President*, wearing a mini tux and top hat.

Of the fourteen new musicals that opened in 1933, three were topical in subject matter—*The Threepenny Opera* by Kurt Weill and Bertolt Brecht, Irving Berlin and Moss Hart's *As Thousands Cheer*, and the Gershwins and George Kaufman/Morrie Ryskind's *Let 'Em Eat Cake*. Except for Jerome Kern's *Roberta*, these were curiously the only memorable musicals of the year.

The "torch" ballad "Why Was I Born?" by Oscar Hammerstein II and Jerome Kern was a favorite of many female vocalists who sang it on and off the screen. But it remained the property and signature of sad-faced Helen Morgan, who introduced it in *Sweet Adeline*, surpassing the performances she gave in *Show Boat* of other Hammerstein-Kern ballads.

He was known as the Singing Brakeman since he worked as a railroad man from his boyhood, but earned the cognomen of the Father of Country Music. Jimmie Rodgers, born in Meridian, Mississippi, on September 8, 1897, became a legend, recording over one hundred sides for RCA Victor between 1927 and 1933. From black railmen who were amateur musicians he acquired a love for the sound of the blues. He developed a unique style that he called Blue Yodels and which sold millions throughout the South. He suffered from tuberculosis from 1924 on, dying in the Hotel Taft in New York City during a recording session. He was so weak that he recorded sitting in a wheelchair.

"Undecided," a jazz instrumental by trumpeter Charlie Shavers, was one of the more popular numbers performed by the John Kirby Quintet at the Onyx on 52nd Street. An in-demand number, it was so little known that the knowledgeable Nat Shapiro associates it with Chick Webb, who introduced a vocal version as sung by Ella Fitzgerald in 1939. It did not become a pop hit until 1951, when it was recorded by the Ames Brothers with the Les Brown Band.

In February 1933, Bessie Smith, Empress of the Blues, made her only appearance on Jazz Street. Dressed in a cheap fur coat, which she did not remove, she sang six numbers accompanied by Bunny Berigan's backup combo: "Baby, Won't You Please Come Home?," "Mama's Got the Blues," "I'm Wild About That Thing," "The Gin House Blues," "Dirty No-Gooder's Blues," and the number that was the epitome of her art, "Nobody Knows You When You're Down and Out." Reports have it that Ella Fitzgerald and Mildred Bailey were both present and refused to take the floor after Bessie. Later in the year, in November, she did a session with Frankie Newton's combo, arranged by John Hammond, for whom she had recorded one hundred and sixty Columbia sides. It proved her last record date, for she never made the session scheduled for Mississippi in 1936, destroyed in a highly publicized midnight auto accident. "Bessie combines exceptional feeling for the blues with a remarkable sense of timing which gives her singing a swing comparable to that of the best jazzmen" (*The Jazz Record Book*, Charles Edward Smith).

In June 1933, Kraft Music Hall introduced a new product, Miracle Whip salad dressing, and turned to Paul Whiteman and Al Jolson to attract buyers. Auditioning for Whiteman, Jane Froman, who came from Chicago to appear in the *Ziegfeld Follies*, broke her ankle, and, despite a bad stutter, became the No. 1 female vocalist.

He was a genius at designing guitars, some still on the market today. Many believe he created the best electric guitar ever made—and with his virtuosity as a performer, he was the innovator of overdubbing, now a commonplace. Born in Waukesha, Wisconsin, June 9, 1916, he was playing Bluegrass on Chicago radio in 1933 as Rhubarb Red during the day and performing jazz at night as Les Paul. Later, working with his wife Mary Ford, he made a multi-overdubbing of voices and guitars on "How High the Moon" that yielded a million seller in 1951, the first of a series of hits that included "The World Is Waiting for the Sunrise" and "Vaya Con Dios."

Billie Holiday made her debut recording, singing the undistinguished "Your Mother's Son-in-Law" with the Benny Goodman Band, a date arranged by talent scout and record producer John Hammond, who first heard Billie in a run-down Harlem café.

John Popkin opened the Hickory House on 52nd Street, importing the logs from out-of-state for grilling customers' steaks; the business remained a landmark of jazz that outlasted all the other clubs on Jazz Street.

The influence of columnist Walter Winchell found expression in a song "Orchids to You" by Mack Gordon and Harry Revel, but no orchids to entertainer Al Jolson, who floored the columnist for a remark he printed about Jolson's wife.

Night-club entertainer and impresario Texas Guinan, whose byword was a reference to her patrons as "suckers," died November 5, 1933.

The owners of the illustrious 21 Club lent money to their patrons during the Bank Holiday to help them pay their bills.

Virtuoso pianist Art Tatum, who came from Toledo to astound both the jazz and classical worlds with his prodigious improvisations, cut his first sides in 1933, recording "Sophisticated Lady" and "Tiger Rag."

In 1933, Kurt Weill, the German operatic composer, was driven from his native land by the rise of the Nazis. Although his first venture in New York was an operatic pageant of Jewish history, composed as a collaboration with Max Reinhardt, it was finally presented in a much revised form at the Manhattan Opera House in 1937 under the title *The Eternal Road*. Weill made his mark as a Broadway composer of *Knickerbocker Holiday*, *Lady in the Dark*, *One Touch of Venus*, and *Threepenny Opera*, the English-language version of his *Dreigroschenoper*, Weill and Bertolt Brecht's great Berlin musical (1928). Although there are differences of opinion about his transition to Broadway, some deriding it as an apostasy, others see Weill as the innovator of a movement dedicated to revitalizing opera by infusions of energy from the popular musical theatre.

The financial and spiritual horizons of 1933 revealed signs of a turn to a better time, but the noises emanating from abroad were ominous.

❧ 11 ❧

What a Difference a Song Made
(1934)

It was not until 1934 that the theme song received recognition for its creative impact in a film, whether musical or nonmusical. That year the Motion Picture Academy presented its first Oscar for Best Song. In the running were Vincent Youmans's "Carioca" (words by Gus Kahn and Edward Eliscu), Ralph Rainger's "Love in Bloom" (words by Leo Robin), and Cole Porter's "Night and Day" (from the film *The Gay Divorcée*). The award went to "The Continental" (music by Con Conrad; words by Herb Magidson), which was one of several songs written especially for *The Gay Divorcée*, the film title of the Broadway hit *Gay Divorce*. To the movie moguls, it was less unusual to refer to a divorcée as gay than to a gay divorce. (The current meaning of "gay" would put a totally different connotation to the play or film.) In fact, only "Night and Day" was retained from Cole Porter's original theatrical score. How inept can film producers be?

To say that the award to Con Conrad (1891–1938) came as a surprise is an understatement, considering the composers with whom he was competing. Conrad K. Dober, as he was christened on his birth in New York, was a theatre pianist who performed in vaudeville both in Europe and the United States. Before he went to Hollywood in 1929 to write movie musicals, he had scored three pop hits: "Margie" in 1920, "Barney Google" in 1923, and "Lonesome and Sorry" in 1926. Before he won the Oscar, he collaborated on "You Call It Madness But I Call It Love," whose co-writers included Gladys Du Bois, Paul Gregory, and Russ Columbo. Tragically short-lived baritone Columbo, generally regarded as the first of the crooners, introduced the ballad and used it as his theme in the few years before his death in 1934. Conrad and Magidson produced only one other song of consequence after "The Continental." "Midnight in Paris" was introduced by Nino Martini in the film *Here's to Romance* in 1935.

At that year's Academy Awards, a Special Award was presented to Shirley Temple in grateful recognition of her outstanding contribution to screen entertainment during the year 1934. Shirley was five years old when she was discovered by Jay Gorney, the composer of "Brother Can You Spare a Dime?," in the lobby of a Los Angeles movie house during the Christmas holidays. Gorney persuaded Lew Brown, who was writing songs and producing films for Fox, to give her a screen test. She was so cute and displayed such charming savvy as a singer and dancer that she was immediately put under contract. Making her film debut in *Stand Up and Cheer*, she elicited such cheers from the audience that within the year she appeared in *Little Miss Marker*, stealing the film from stars Adolphe Menjou and Charles Bickford. Shirley's next triumphs were in *Baby Take a Bow*; *Now and Forever*, sharing billing with Gary Cooper and Carole Lombard; and *Bright Eyes*. She was then six years old.

Herb Magidson (1906–1986), the lyric writer of "The Continental," was educated at the University of Pittsburgh and worked for a New York publisher before he entrained for Hollywood in the 1929 California Gold Rush. Apart from the songs he wrote with Con Conrad, his biggest hit was "Music, Maestro, Please!," which made No. 1 on *Your Hit Parade* for four weeks in 1938 and became the No. 2 sheet music best-seller. His only other consequential song was "Enjoy Yourself (It's Later Than You Think)," a rhythm ballad with music by Carl Sigman. Although it was published in 1948, it did not become a hit until two years later when Guy Lombardo and His Royal Canadians made a best-selling disk on Decca.

Cole Porter may not have won the Oscar for his great standard "Night and Day," but in 1934 he had the biggest musical show of the year—*Anything Goes*. "It was more than just the runaway smash of the year," Gerald Bordman has observed. "More than merely a well-wrought, hilarious musical filled with unforgettable melodies and sophisticated lyrics, it was the quintessential musical comedy of the thirties." Out of its brilliant score came such timeless hits as the title tune, "Blow, Gabriel, Blow," "All Through the Night," "I Get a Kick Out of You," and a plethora of tricky and contemporary images in "You're the Top."

The public's taste for upscale sophistication was more than balanced or countered by a feeling for songs of a western character. One of the year's big hits was "Tumbling Tumbleweeds," written by Bob Nolan, a Canadian who became fascinated with the West after he settled in Arizona. Nolan was part of a group organized in 1934, known as the Sons of the Pioneers. It was led by Roy (Cincinnati-born) Rogers, and included Tim Spencer, who grew up in Oklahoma, Texas, and New Mexico. In 1935, the group acquired fiddler Hugh Farr and began performing on Station KFWB in Los Angeles, attaining enough popularity to make appearances with Will Rogers and at the Texas Centennial.

The initial recording of "Tumbling Tumbleweeds" was by the Sons of the Pioneers, but the best-selling version was produced by Bing Crosby in 1940. Gene Autry (b. 1907, Tioga Springs, Texas) introduced it in his first full-length film, *Tumbling Tumbleweeds* (Republic, 1935), and revived it in *Don't Fence Me In* (1945). Rogers sang it in *Silver Spurs* (Republic, 1943), as did the Sons of the Pioneers in *Hollywood Canteen* (Warner Bros., 1945).

In 1934, ASCAP made an award of $2,000 for the best popular song of the year. The prize went to "Solitude" by Duke Ellington, words by Eddie De Lange and Irving Mills. This was Ellington's first hit song and was popularized by him and his orchestra on an RCA Victor recording made in 1933. Ellington was a master at using the blues idiom in a unique way for the expression of different moods—in this instance, loneliness.

The lure and romance of the sea produced a number of hits in 1934. "Isle of Capri" was an English import, a tango with music by Will Grosz and words by Jimmy Kennedy, the British lyricist for whom it initiated a series of hits. It was introduced in the United States by Guy Lombardo and His Royal Canadians, but the first American recording was by Xavier Cugat and His Orchestra. Extensive performances and other recordings resulted in a sale of a million copies of sheet music. In 1935, jazz trumpeter Wingy Manone—the nickname referred to the loss of his right arm in a New Orleans streetcar accident when he was a youngster—cut a scattin'-jazzy disk that became a request number for him and a standard in the jazz field. Also in 1935, "Isle of Capri" was included in the *Provincetown Follies* stage show. The *Follies* also featured another Kennedy maritime opus, "Red Sails in the Sunset." The composer was also Will Grosz, using the pseudonym Hugh Williams. It was introduced in the United States by Ray Noble and His Orchestra, reportedly aggregating a sale of over a million song sheets. "Harbor Lights" by the same team was a torch song—she was on the ship and he was on the shore—that became a best-selling record for Rudy Vallee in 1937. The song did not attain its majority until a dozen years later, when it was revived by Sammy Kaye and His Orchestra and by Dinah Washington. Then in 1950 it went to the top of the charts, appeared twenty-nine times on *Your Hit Parade*, and sold over a million copies of sheet music. The universal quality of the song received special emphasis when a famous group, the Platters, recorded it and made a best-selling disk in 1960.

There is no indication that Jimmy Kennedy and his collaborator Michael Carr spent time in Mexico. But when Gene Autry toured England, he sang their song "South of the Border (Down Mexico Way)" and then went on to make a motion picture with that title (Republic, 1939). Autry's disk sold three million copies in two years. But Shep Fields and His Rippling Rhythm also had a successful version of the Latin ballad. Toward the end of 1939 the song made No. 1 on *Your Hit Parade*, holding the slot for five weeks, and finished the year as the top ranking sheet music seller.

Jimmy Kennedy continued to produce hits into the Fifties: "My Prayer" in 1939, "April in Portugal" and "Istanbul" in 1953. "My Prayer," adapted by Kennedy from a classical French composition, "Avant de Mourir" by Georges Boulanger, was on *Your Hit Parade* for fourteen weeks, climbing to the No. 2 spot. Sammy Kaye and His Orchestra had the recording that increased the song's popularity. Once again, the Platters made a recording during the early rock era that sold over a million in 1956. It was still a Platters hit tune forty years later, notably in Las Vegas, of all places.

Originating in 1947 as a Portuguese song, "Coimbra" by Paul Ferrao, "April in Portugal" acquired its English title when Chappell Music retained Kennedy to adapt it. Before it acquired its popular form it was known as "The Whispering Serenade" and was introduced by Georgia Carr on a Capitol recording. It became a hit in 1953 as "April in Portugal" on an instrumental recording.

"Istanbul" was a novelty song whose subtitle was "Not Constantinople." The music was by Nat Simon and the hit recording was by a robust-voiced group known as the Four Lads. The year was 1953, and it was Kennedy's last hit.

In an almost twenty-five-year collaboration, Richard Rodgers and Lorenz Hart wrote only one song that became a hit without being part of a stage or film production. "Blue Moon" began by being called "My Prayer." Dropped from the Jean Harlow production for which it was intended, it was recast as "The Bad in Every Man" and sung by Shirley Ross in the nonmusical film *Manhattan Melodrama*. It was then briefly known as "Act One" and finally became known as "Blue Moon." As such, it was published by Robbins Music as an independent number, achieving the largest sheet music sale of any Rodgers and Hart song until then. Between 1948 and 1963, it was tracked in six motion pictures: *Words and Music* (MGM, 1948), *Malaya* (MGM, 1949), *East Side, West Side* (MGM, 1950), *With a Song in My Heart* (20th Century-Fox, 1952), *Rogue Cop* (MGM, 1954), and Federico Fellini's *8 ½*

(1963). Except for the Fellini opus, every production was by the film company that owned Robbins Music. (20th Century-Fox was an adjunct of the combine that owned what was then known as the Big Three: Robbins, Feist, and Miller.) Curiously, the only recording of "Blue Moon" that reportedly passed the million mark was one made, inconceivable as it may appear, in the rock era by Elvis Presley.

Stanley Adams's role as President of ASCAP overshadowed his efforts as a songwriter. However, in 1934 he translated into English the Spanish song "Cuando Vuelva a Tu Lado" by Maria Grever. He titled it "What a Diff'rence a Day Made." It was widely performed and became a favorite of many female vocalists. But not until almost a quarter of a century later did it become a hit. Simply to say that it was then recorded by the salty-sweet voice of Dinah Washington and garnered enough disk jockey play to skyrocket the charts does not tell the real story.

Dinah Washington was a masterful singer who could handle any type of song from rhythm and blues to sophisticated white ballads. The Mercury label used her to cover for black record-buyers songs that broke as hits in other areas: country, pop, show music, jazz, and so on. When Mercury appointed Clyde Otis as its A&R chieftain—the first black in such an administrative post—I approached him about recording "What a Diff'rence a Day Made" with Dinah. Edward B. Marks Music Corporation, of which I was then General Professional Manager, owned the song's copyright. Dinah made a great recording, requiring only two takes. I was so convinced that her record could cross over that, even though I employed people to contact disc jockeys in key cities, I decided to personally promote the disk. I had no difficulty in persuading deejays at the major white stations to spin her record. But then I discovered that the Mercury promotion department was not backing my efforts—they were concentrating their promotion efforts on a number of major white artists, knowing that Dinah would sell 25,000 or more among black buyers. So it became a competitive battle, with Mercury contacting disk jockeys I had seen and reminding them that the Dinah Washington was not one of their plug platters. But Dinah's disk, once it was heard, had such tremendous appeal it overwhelmed the platter spinners and garnered repeat plays. And so the record broke for a hit as I was completing an itinerary that took me cross-country from New York to San Francisco, down the California coast, across the Gulf states, and ended in Miami, where Mercury announced at a disc jockey convention that Dinah had a pop hit—and, of course, made no reference to its efforts to sabotage my promotional activity.

"What a Diff'rence a Day Makes"—the tense was changed on Dinah's disk—received a Grammy as the best rhythm and blues record of the year. That was a slight misnomer, since it was a pop, not an R&B, disk. Dinah followed her Grammy winner with a version of "Unforgettable"—and pop publishers were suddenly lining up in the hope of securing a Dinah Washington disk. The color line had been crossed.

In 1934, two new powerful media of song exploitation entered the music scene. The first, as we have already noted, was adding an award for Best Song to the Oscars given annually by the Academy of Motion Picture Arts and Sciences. This enhanced the importance of popular songs, prompting songwriters to extend themselves and film producers to search for memorable theme songs as potential hits. Being nominated augmented the value of a song, and winning the Oscar extended the life and increased the earnings of a song and film.

The second new medium of song exploitation was the legit dinner or jazz club, which sprang up in impressive numbers, especially on West 52nd Street in mid-Manhattan. Creating a venue for small groups and soloists—largely because of their limited size—the 52nd Street clubs were more important in the development of jazz as an art form than the big bands through which many of the jazz artists earned their livelihood. The small club and group was for *listening*, not for dancing, and moved artists to extend themselves. On 52nd Street, jazz was largely a solo art form.

Stanley Adams (1917–1989)

Born August 14, 1917, in New York City, Stanley Adams attended New York University and earned an L.L.B. degree at its law school. His first professional songwriting assignment was producing lyrics for a revue at the Connie's Inn night club in the early thirties. He wrote songs for films and Broadway musicals. After serving on ASCAP's Board of Directors as a writer-member he was elected president in 1953 and served until 1956, was re-elected in 1959 and served until 1980. The recipient of many awards, he received a Presidential Citation in 1963.

Interview with Stanley Adams

1954 was a good year for me. I did the English lyrics for two Latin songs. "My Shawl" was originally known as "Ombo" in Spanish. It had music by Xavier Cugat, who made "My Shawl" his theme. "What a Diff'rence a Day Made" came from Mexico, where it was known as "Cuando Vuelva a Tu Lado," with Spanish words and music by Maria Grever, who wrote a number of hits that made it in the USA, including "Ti-Pi-Tin." You know what a hit "Diff'rence" became when it was revived in 1959 since you secured the recording by Dinah Washington when you were Professional Manager at E. B.

Marks. It had a second revival in 1976 when Esther Philips's record became No. 1.

Talking about revivals, let me tell you about a recent revival—one that came out of left field, as music men used to say. In 1938, I wrote a song with Hoagy Carmichael for a Paramount picture that had Louis Armstrong and Mae West, who was wonderful to work with—just marvelous. The picture was called *Every Day's a Holiday*, and the song, titled "Jubilee," was introduced by Armstrong. Very cute picture. Nothing happened to another song I wrote that year called "Wacky Dust." But its revival is worth a story.

Hoagy Carmichael, with whom I wrote "Jubilee," remained on the coast. I came back to New York at the behest of the Shuberts to do a *Ziegfeld Follies*. They had bought the title and asked me whether I would be interested in working on it with Dana Suesse. We had just started to work when it was called off. At this point Henry Spitzer, who was Max Dreyfus's Professional Manager at Harms, called me and asked me to do some songs with Oscar Levant. Oscar was a fantastic musician, and he knew Bunny Berigan, the jazz trumpeter, very well. Bunny asked us to write a theme song. The result was "Wacky Dust," meaning music for a hot cornet—the music was so crazy. For example, "It brings a dancing jag, and when it starts, only a sap'll refuse the Big Apple and Shag." The Big Apple and Shag were big dances of the day. Bunny recorded it, but did not use it as his theme. Ella Fitzgerald also cut it. And that's where the song ended.

About four years ago I got a call from Robbins Music, telling me that the group the Manhattan Transfer had recorded the song in London and that it had broken for a tremendous hit in Europe. It was in an album. But they took it out and released it as a single. When the album was released in this country, they did not use "Wacky Dust" as a single.

I started getting letters about the song's relation to the drug culture. The song was interpreted—misinterpreted—because of the word "dust." Naturally I resented this implication. Not too long ago, I was listening to Steve Allen, and he picked the title up to show that "angel dust" was in the air way back in the thirties. When I wrote him a letter, he corrected the impression he had given on the air. In any event, it's another proof of the fact that no one knows when a copyright is going to be picked up and revived.

I did try to find out how the Manhattan Transfer latched onto the song, and I was told that they were going over some old albums—probably Ella Fitzgerald—and were attracted by it. They did a marvelous vocal. Oh, when I wrote Steve, I pointed out that "Wacky Dust" had no more to do with drugs than did "Star Dust."

"Yesterthoughts" was an old Victor Herbert tune. Herman Starr of Warner Bros. Music gave me that tune to write up. We were in the middle of the ASCAP-BMI situation, when ASCAP songs were off the air. There was no contract between ASCAP and the networks, and all ASCAP songs were "boy-cotted." "Shadows on the Sand" endured the same fate. The music was by Will Grosz, who was very hot for a short time.

I did have a big hit in '42, which is somewhat outside the scope of your narrative. But it has an interesting story. George Meyer and I made an appointment to do some writing at the offices of Rocco Vocco. During the afternoon, George came up with that marvelous front phrase of the song that became known as "There Are Such Things." It was one of the few times that I wrote the lyric first and the music was put to it. While we were going over it, rehearsing it, Rocco came rushing in. After we played it for him, he said, "You wait right here." He called upstairs to the penthouse of the Brill Building, where Tommy Dorsey had his offices. Bregman, Rocco, and Conn were on the eight or ninth floor—and he arranged for Dorsey to hear the song the following day.

When we played the song for Tommy, he flipped. "It's everything you said it was," he said to Rocco, "but I'm going to publish it, not you." Instead of resisting, Rocco readily agreed, for he had a wonderful insurance policy for the future. After that, Tommy would have to play whatever Rocco brought him. That's how Dorsey happened to get the song. It was published by him. I believe that this was a Tuesday—and the musicians were going on strike the following week. So Tommy had to get it arranged and recorded before then. And he did, using the Pied Pipers and Frank Sinatra on the vocal. It was an enormous record, and the song was a smash. But Rocco had no way of refusing to let it go to Dorsey.

I just thought of another song of mine that developed unexpectedly into a hit. In a revue called *The Show Is On*, with a score by Vernon Duke and Ted Fetter, Hoagy Carmichael and I had one song. It was called "Little Old Lady," and, during the out-of-town run, the producer decided to dispense with it. But Yip Harburg liked the song so much that he wrote a special sketch for it in which a little old lady sold flowers at a stage door to the chorus girls. It was not supposed to be one of the show's major songs, but it had great charm. Guy Lombardo liked it as much as Yip Harburg, and he played it on his Sunday night, coast-to-coast show. It was like magic. Within a few days, calls came in from all over the country. In those days, song hits sold sheet music, and, before long, this little old song had amassed a sale of three-quarters of a million.

In the thirties—by comparison with the music business of today—there was a warmth, a camaraderie, an intimacy that have completely disappeared. The publishers and writers were very close; they mixed socially as well as being business acquaintances. We used to meet after hours at Lindy's, and the band leaders would drop in. It all had a feeling of family. Guys would often throw lines to other writers. It was a wonderful, wonderful feeling. In those days, most of the publishers owned their own business—Saul Bornstein, Jack Bregman, Max Dreyfus, and the others.

Today, the companies are in the hands of business interests who bought out the original owners. An entirely different psychology has developed. A songwriter has to offer something more than just a song to interest a publisher. And then the groups came in. The ordinary songwriter is out because the groups write their own songs, record them, plug, perform, and publish them.

There's no market for songwriters like myself today. But for that matter, there aren't too many songwriters of the thirties still around. Johnny Mercer is gone, Hoagy Carmichael, Eddie Heyman, Jerry Livingston, Walter Donaldson, Gus Kahn, DeSylva, Brown, and Henderson, Harold Arlen, Arthur Schwartz, and so many more. And a number who are still alive have been incapacitated by illness. But their songs and the memories that go with them live on.

Medley 1934

In January 1934, the No. 1 comedy-variety show in radio was Eddie Cantor and Rubinoff's Orchestra, followed by the Maxwell House Show, with Lanny Ross, and Don Voorhees's Orchestra, with Rudy Vallee and his Fleischmann Hour in the No. 3 spot.

First use of the word "jitterbug" occurred in a song with that title by Irving Mills and Cab Calloway, whose band introduced the song.

Lawrence Welk (1903–1992), born in Sharsburg, N.D., burst on the music scene with "Beer Barrel Polka," initiating a long-lived career on radio and TV.

Muzak, now sixty years old and sent by satellite to more than 110,000 businesses and syndicated to seventeen countries, began its service in 1934 in Cleveland, piping music into homes through telephone lines.

Described as the most glamorous, luxurious, and, at more than $20 million, the most expensive restaurant ever built in the United States, the Rainbow Room, sixty-five stories above Sixth Avenue, first opened its doors on October 3, 1934. Noël Coward and Cole Porter were part of the sophisticated café society that clinked glasses at the opening, a glittering realization of a project launched by John D. Rockefeller, Jr., in 1932 to express his confidence in the American economy.

A search for antecedents turns up this early use of the phrase "Rock and Roll" in an issue of *Song Hit Folio* for December 26, 1934. It is the title of a song by Sidney Clare and Richard A. Whiting, publishing by Irving Berlin, Inc., for the film *Transatlantic Merry-Go-Round*. The reference in the title and song is to the "rock and roll of the sea" and the romance in the motion.

Paul Whiteman recorded nine sessions at Victor, cutting over forty sides to surpass the output of all other bands, including Rudy Vallee, who was at the height of his popularity. Among the more impressive disks were "Deep Purple," augmented by Dana Suesse, whose popularity promoted the addition of a lyric by Mitchell Parish; "Smoke Gets in Your Eyes" and "Wagon Wheels," which hit best-seller charts during a viciously cold New York spell with temperatures dropping to 18 degrees below zero; and a 12-inch version of songs from Cole Porter's *Anything Goes*—a kind of cast album.

The Paul Whiteman scholarship competition was awarded on June 13, 1934, to David Diamond, a nineteen-year-old poverty-stricken student of modernist Roger Sessions, for his *Sinfonietta*, a 20-minute work inspired by Carl Sandburg's epic poem "Good Morning America." The monetary scholarship came to Diamond at a time when he was mopping floors at the Dalcroze Institute, which he attended eight hours a day, and working at a drugstore at 96th and Broadway from 10:30 P.M. to 3:00 A.M. every night. *Sinfonietta* was premiered at Philadelphia's Robin Hood Dell in June 1935.

"One Night of Love," a semi-operatic theme song by Gus Kahn and Victor Schertzinger, was sung by the Metropolitan Opera Company's Grace Moore in the film of the same name. The audience reaction was so strong that the door was opened for the film appearances of other operatic stars.

When the Hudson-De Lange Orchestra was playing at the Greystone Ballroom in Detroit, it was decided that the band needed a theme. Will Hudson composed an instrumental theme he called "Moonglow." Arriving in New York, he settled at Mills Music as a writer and arranger. Eddie De Lange, who had been a Phi Beta Kappa student at the University of Pennsylvania, added a lyric—and the ubiquitous Irving Mills became the third collaborator. When the Hudson-De Lange Orchestra played it at the Roadside Restaurant on Long Island, the piece became known as the "Sophisticated Swing" theme. It did not become a hit until 1956, when a counter-melody was written to it by George W. Duning (lyric by Steve Allen), which was recorded by Morris Stoloff's Orchestra on Decca and was used as the theme of the nonmusical film *Picnic*.

Decca Records entered the recording scene in 1934, financed by British coin, developing into a major label with "The Music Goes 'Round and 'Round," a 52nd Street audience-rouser, as its first best-seller and Bing Crosby as the company's star attraction.

In 1934, novelist Dashiell Hammett was at the peak of his success, having completed *The Thin Man*, his fifth novel. He was also working in Hollywood, a recognized celebrity at MGM, the author of *The Maltese Falcon*. He lived twenty-six years longer, but his drinking lost him jobs and friends, his health deteriorated, and he gambled away his money or gave it to anyone who begged—dying in debt.

The Quintette of the Hot Club de France, with jazz fiddler Stephane Grappelli and gypsy guitarist Django Reinhardt, made its first recording in 1934.

✤ 12 ✤

"The Music Goes 'Round and 'Round"
(1935)

By the mid-thirties, music had to swing in bands, combos, and extravagantly by soloists of all instruments. The meteoric rise of Benny Goodman was psychological as well as musical. After four years of frustration, economic shortages, and gloom, the American people were ready to seize on something that would give them a lift. Swing *did*.

"For the next ten years," Marshall Stearns has noted, "swing music made big money and bandleaders became as popular—and as unpredictable—as movie stars. . . . Bob Crosby's 'Dixieland Shuffle' was recorded in 1936, Tommy Dorsey's 'Marie' in 1937, Artie Shaw's 'Begin the Beguine' in 1938, and Glenn Miller's 'In the Mood' in 1939."

The year 1935 saw the birth of the crowning achievement of George Gershwin's career and the masterpiece of the season, *Porgy and Bess*, frankly described as "An American Folk Opera," even though it played the same venue as *Girl Crazy* and included several hit songs. These were "I Got Plenty o' Nuttin'," "It Ain't Necessarily So," the beautiful and rangy ballad "Bess, You Is My Woman Now," and the lovely "Summertime," which was adopted by Bob Crosby as the theme for his orchestra. Both the drama and music critics of New York's newspapers attended the opening on October 10, with the drama critics reacting more enthusiastically then the music reviewers. The opera, later recognized as one of America's major operas, ran for just 124 performances and failed to retrieve its $50,000 investment. Some attributed this limited initial acceptance to the unwillingness of people to listen to the tragedies of others in the atmosphere of the Depression. (In 1959, jazz pianist Nina Simone made a million-selling vocal record of "I Loves You, Porgy," on a small offbeat label, Bethlehem.)

For a number of Broadway's top songwriters, 1935 was a notable year. Rodgers and Hart delivered three outstanding songs in their score for *Jumbo*, a Billy Rose musical extravaganza that combined a circus with a musical comedy. "The Most Beautiful Girl in the World" was one of Rodgers's most ingratiating waltzes, which ran far beyond the standard 32 bars for 72 measures. It was introduced by Donald Novis and Gloria Grafton. The same duo warbled the love song "My Romance," but Gloria Grafton soloed in the heart-rending torch song, "Little Girl Blue," later a great favorite of the cabaret stylist Mabel Mercer.

Cole Porter also produced two classics. "Begin the Beguine," inspired by an Indonesian war dance he witnessed in the Dutch East Indies on a world cruise, was introduced by June Knight in the musical *Jubilee*. It apparently caused no great excitement. That happened the following year when Artie Shaw, contracted by RCA to record a swing version of Rudolf Friml's "Indian Love Call," insisted on recording the then little-known "Begin the Beguine" over the opposition of his record producer. Reports have it that the disk sold two million copies to become one of the biggest instrumental recordings by an American band.

Also from the score of *Jubilee* came "Just One of Those Things," introduced by June Knight and Charles Walters. Collaborator Moss Hart claims that Porter wrote the debonair song overnight while the show was in its pre-Broadway tryouts in Chicago.

From Jerome Kern's pen in 1935 came "I Won't Dance," written for the film version of his 1933 musical *Roberta* in response to Fred Astaire's request for a high-voltage dance number. Kern took the rhythm directly from a step that Astaire demonstrated for him. Dorothy Fields and Jimmy McHugh wrote the lyrics, and the song made *Your Hit Parade* in the No. 4 spot on its first broadcast and remained on the program for seven weeks, moving to the No. 2 spot during one of those weeks.

The other hit that came from *Roberta* was "Lovely to Look At," also with words by Dorothy Fields and Jimmy McHugh. Once again a composer encountered producer resistance, this time because the refrain was only sixteen measures and the last four bars were unusually complex. But Kern was adamant and would not make any changes. "Lovely to Look At" was No. 3 on the premiere presentation of *Your Hit Parade* and jumped to No. 1 the following week, remaining in various slots for a seven-week run.

Dorothy Fields and Jimmy McHugh achieved two other hits in 1935, both for the musical film *Every Night at Eight*. "I Feel a Song Coming On," an uptempo, rollicking tune made to order as an opening-night club number, was introduced by Frances Langford, who also sang "I'm in the Mood for Love." That song made ten appearances on *Your Hit Parade*, touching No. 1 for one week.

Among film contract songwriters, Nacio Herb Brown and Arthur Freed scored with "Alone," introduced by Kitty Carlisle and Allan Jones in the Marx Brothers film *A Night at the Opera*. The song held the top spot on *Your Hit Parade* for five weeks in 1936. They also had a hit in "Broadway Rhythm," introduced in the musical *Broadway Melody of 1936* and interpreted by dancer Eleanor Powell, who was described in the *New York Times* as possessing "the most eloquent feet in show business."

Although her name was Hildegarde Loretta Sell (b. 1906, Adell, Wis.), she was known simply as Hildegarde. Billie Holiday had her gardenia; Harry Richman had his cane and straw hat; and Hildegarde had her crumpled handkerchief. In 1935, she scored with the song "Darling, Je Vous Aime Beaucoup," written by her manager, Anna Sosenko. Sung by Simone Simon in the film *Love and Kisses* (1937), it was revived in 1955 by Nat Cole, who sold a million records.

Hildegarde's career as a singer and pianist lasted more than a half century. Facing her ninetieth birthday, February 1, 1996, she admitted that she was finally retiring during an interview by Chicago's ace showbiz interrogator, Sig Sakowicz, for his mammoth WMPA-radio interview collection. Remembered are her effective presentations, each with an overtone of sadness, of Kern's "The Last Time I Saw Paris" and Noël Coward's "I'll See You Again."

" 'I'm Gonna Sit Right Down and Write Myself a Letter" (music by Fred E. Ahlert; words by Joe Young) was a Tin Pan Alley hit in 1935 for clowning jazz pianist Fats Waller, but became a two-million disk seller in 1956 when it was recorded by Billy Williams.

The variety of songs that found a public in the opening year of the Swing Era is suggested by the popularity of "When I Grow Too Old to Dream," a European-sounding waltz by Sigmund Romberg to a lyric by Oscar Hammerstein II. It was introduced in the film musical *The Night Is Young* by Evelyn Laye and Ramon Novarro.

When Judy Garland auditioned at MGM, one of the songs she used to charm her judges was "Zing Went the Strings of My Heart" by James F. Hanley. It was sung and danced by Hal Le Roy and Eunice Healy in the revue *Thumbs Up* (later the title of a 1943 film). *Thumbs Up*, a twenty-week disappointment gorgeously mounted by John Murray Anderson, also offered "Autumn in New York," a haunting classic by Vernon Duke, sung by J. Harold Murray before a background of moving screens displaying shots of Manhattan.

Edward Eliscu (1902–   )

Born in 1902 in New York City, lyricist-actor-playwright-director-producer, Eliscu was active on Broadway and in Hollywood, and is mainly remembered for songs he wrote with Vincent Youmans: "Great Day," "More Than You Know," and "Without a Song" in 1929 and "Flying Down to Rio," "Carioca," and "Orchids in the Moonlight" in 1933. Long concerned with the problems of the songwriter, he served as President of the Songwriters Guild of America for five years. In November 1987, he received the ASCAP/Richard Rodgers award for outstanding contributions to the American Musical Theatre.

Interview with Edward Eliscu

In my family, my oldest brother, though self-taught, played the violin, mandolin, and ocarina. We had a piano, and I took piano lessons probably for a couple of months. But I never learned to read music, although I was interested in music at an early age. I was also interested in writing. I began as a writer and displayed a bent for light verse and parodies. I was also attracted to popular music quite early in my life. I can remember my mother singing "On a Bicycle Built for Two" and "Meet Me in St. Louis." I never played any instrument. I did perform as a child, but I did more reciting than singing.

My first "professional" engagement occurred when I was eight years old and recited Lincoln's *Gettysburg Address* at an open-air movie. In those years, during the summer, movies were frequently shown in vacant lots. You sat on uncomfortable benches, watching Lillian Gish, Bronco Billy, and other stars of the silent era. I was a special feature on July 4 and received $2 and a box of candy for my recitation.

In school, I functioned on a double track, reciting and writing. I combined reciting Patrick Henry's famous speech, *Give Me Liberty or Give Me Death*, as well as the Gettysburg Address—which may have sown the seeds of my later efforts to combine politics with entertainment. Although I was in several plays, I did not do anything musical. Then my interest in vaudeville was such that I began to perform songs that I had heard. I was the youngest in a family of four boys and three girls, and my mother sparked my interest in music by taking me to matinees at the Alhambra Theatre in Harlem while my sisters took me to the opera and to concerts.

At City College I was editor of the college newspaper and director of the Senior Class play, *Bye Bye Beowulf*, presented at the Morosco Theatre on Broadway. By the late twenties, I was acting on Broadway in *Quarantine* with Helen Hayes and in *The Racket* with Edward G. Robinson.

I was the first of the Social Directors at summer adult camps that later fostered Moss Hart, Danny Kaye, Max Liebman, and other creative people. I started that not long after I got out of CCNY. I wrote, produced, and performed in plays at Camp Copake. That gave me my start in writing original material and working under the pressure of doing an original revue each week. I had a highbrow streak, and while I did musical revues and clowning, I also was producing and acting in plays by O'Neill, Shaw, Shalom Aleichem, and Chekhov.

For my first Broadway show, *Quarantine*, with Helen Hayes and Sidney Blackmer, I was the assistant stage manager as well as an actor. Offstage, I played the guitar and sang in Spanish, which I had studied at De Witt Clinton High School.

In my spare time as an actor—and I had plenty of it between engagements—I wrote vaudeville and night club material for producers and performers like Leonard Sillman, Imogene Coca, Clayton Jackson, and Durante. Two roads led me to Vincent Youmans. One path was through Harms Music, which gave me my first show assignment as lyricist of *Lady Fingers*, a show with music by Joe Meyer and a book by Eddie Buzzell, the star. It was presented at the Vanderbilt Theatre by producer Lyle Andrews and ran for a little over one hundred performances.

I then wrote the lyrics for an operetta based on the life of Lucretia Borgia. It went the round of producers. Although it was like most operettas of the day, it did bring me to the attention of Vincent Youmans, who was producing and composing a show in 1929 called *Louisiana Lou*, later known as *Great Day*. After I auditioned some of my songs, he took me on, and I co-wrote the lyrics with Billy Rose. Although the show was a flop, it boasted a number of Youmans's great melodies, including "More Than You Know" and "Without a Song."

There was one idea song in *Great Day* that Billy Rose and I developed and were sorry to have it dropped from the show. It was a song about futility, and we titled it "Bismarck Is a Herring and Napoleon Is a Cake." Years and years later, I learned from a friend that there was a song in *Jamaica*, written by E. Y. Harburg and Harold Arlen (who was the rehearsal pianist for *Great Day*), with the title "Napoleon's a Pastry."* I guess a good idea never dies.

Youmans was not content to be just the fine composer he was. He wanted to be completely involved in every phase of a work for which he was writing melodies. He was an indefatigable worker with an intense feeling for the

---

*"A number of critics preferred the comic songs Lena Horne sang," Gerald Bordman wrote of *Jamaica* in *American Musical Theatre*, "a song like 'Napoleon' (in which she sang of how the great names of the past were exploited by commercial products). No critic recalled Arlen and Harburg had first used 'Napoleon's a Pastry' in *Hooray for What* (12-1-37)." *Jamaica* opened 10-31-57 and *Great Day* on 10-17-29.

songwriter's craft. He was an excellent pianist, but, unlike most composers, he never sang his songs when he was demonstrating them: he whistled the melody as he accompanied himself with chords. I can't read music, but I am told by those who can that he set down his compositions in a kind of short-hand in which the notes appeared without their rhythmic values. Perfectionist that he was when it came to his music, he was undisciplined about his body and neglected his health. He suffered from tuberculosis from his late thirties on. But even when he was in Denver for a cure, he would rest all day but go out and carouse through the night. He died when he was just forty-seven years old.

After I went out to the coast in February 1930, they put me to work with Nacio Herb Brown, who had already scored with "Wedding of the Painted Doll" and "Singin' in the Rain." We wrote the score for an operetta called *One Heavenly Night*. Evelyn Laye, who had just starred in the Noël Coward operetta *Bitter-Sweet*, appeared in it with John Boles. Following that, Nacio Herb Brown and I contributed "I'll Still Belong to You" to *Whoopee*, a United Artists picture starring Eddie Cantor, which had a score by Gus Kahn and Walter Donaldson, who had written the music for the Broadway musical of the same name.

On my return to New York in September 1930, I resumed writing for the theatre, most notably *The Third Little Show* and the *Second Garrick Gaieties*. I was doing sketches and songs, and I also edited *The Third Little Show*. Ned Lehac and I wrote "You Forgot Your Gloves," a song that should have gone further than it did. The title came out of a real situation involving my wife when we were in Atlantic City for the tryout of a show. It was rather cold, and we were driving back when she suddenly discovered that she did not have her gloves. When I said, "You forgot your gloves," somebody in the car said, "That's a song title." I thought so, too, and two years later I used it in *The Third Little Show*.

There was a lull in musicals. As a fledgling director, I coached young contract players, directed dialogue, and supervised tests. I also wrote occasional lyrics for RKO films, supplied with music by Max Steiner and Harry Akst. When the studio decided to do a big musical to be called *Flying Down to Rio*, producer Joe Brock sent for Vincent Youmans and engaged "a skinny dancer from Broadway," as Fred Astaire was then known around Hollywood. I was assigned to do the lyrics together with Gus Kahn.

The basic idea or concept of the film was Lou Brock's, who was head of the studio and who had lived in Brazil. "Orchids in the Moonlight," one of the major songs, was his idea. Other hits were the title song and "Carioca." Dolores Del Rio was the star, but Ginger Rogers and Fred Astaire, who were making their debut as a team and were second leads, stole the film. It was the beginning of a legendary partnership for them.

In 1937, I worked on a revival of operetta composer Franz Lehar's *Frederika*, doing the adaptation and lyrics for the story of a doomed love affair between the poet Goethe and the lovely Frederika. It's a good score. But the music was tied up at the time. By the time the Shuberts straightened out the legal situation, operetta was on the decline. Although no song emerged as a hit, the show continues to play around the world.

I spent little time in Tin Pan Alley, since most of my work was in the theatre or in films. But I occasionally visited Harms Music, then located at 62 West 45th Street.

The building had a tiny elevator, so small that it could hardly accommodate four songwriters. But Harms, headed by the brilliant Max Dreyfus, had at the time not only some of the greatest show writers of the day—Kern, Gershwin, Porter, Rodgers and Hart—but some of the most accomplished orchestrators: men like Hans Spialek, Max Steiner, Robert Russell Bennett, and others.

The man who later founded Miller Music—one of the Big Three after a time (Robbins, Feist, and Miller)—was professional manager of Harms. He got the Secretary of the Treasury, William Woodin, to finance him. Woodin wanted, like millions of Americans, to be a successful songwriter. He did become a member of ASCAP, and its *Biographical Dictionaries* lists half a dozen songs and instrumentals he wrote.

Of the people I remember there was Harry Akst, a fine pianist and accomplished songwriter—he wrote "Dinah" and "Am I Blue?"—who was an amusing and witty man with a mischievous sense of humor. Max Steiner was a tiny man and very capable; RKO was lucky to have him as part of its small music department. The Goldwyn organization and other independents had no music department like MGM and Warner Bros. That's why Feist sent me out in 1930, hoping that I would break into a small studio with no publishing tie-up. I had a drawing account and was permitted to earn additional fees for services to any studio.

Most of the fellows were under contract, which meant that the studio owned what they wrote "for hire." This arrangement had sad consequences for a lot of people, which I was able to avoid as an independent contractor. When the renewal came up for the songs in *Flying Down to Rio*, Harms was under the impression that I had written them for hire and that they therefore owned my share of the copyrights. On some technicality or other, the case went right up to the Supreme Court. We won it and established a precedent. On the Hollywood scene, I believe that I was helpful to songwriters in my position as an editor and screenwriter. I always tried to see that the fellows who wrote the songs got a good cue and a reprise.

Medley 1935

In 1935, the Village Vanguard, opened the year before by Max Gordon in a basement on Charles Street (with one exit, one ballroom, and no entertainment license), moved to its still-current address at 178 Seventh Avenue. First featuring local poets, then comedians (including Lenny Bruce), then folk singers (including Woody Guthrie), Gordon settled on a jazz policy in 1955. His interest was in new performers, and his alumni included Charlie Parker, Miles Davis, John Coltrane, and Bill Evans, among others.

Under Arthur Fiedler, the Boston Pops produced the first classical disk to sell a million copies, a 78 r.p.m. recording of "Jalousie." It was, of course, a crossover.

A number of lesser bands imitated Glenn Miller's unison clarinet-tenor sax sound. Bob Chester exploded the sound in "Maybe," a song that attracted recordings by the Ink Spots, the young Dinah Shore, and Sammy Kaye.

On April 19, 1935, Billie Holiday made her debut at the Apollo Theatre after Ralph Cooper spotted her at the Hot Cha Bar and Grill on 13th Street and Seventh Avenue.

"1935 was a swinging summer at the Onyx," publicist Jack Egan recalls. "The cats would drop around after they'd finished their regular chores and sit in with the McKenzie–Riley–Farley combo."

Cleo Brown, who had a sweet, sexy voice and the most solid left hand before Art Tatum, came up in the mid-thirties through the new power of radio, making her first hit in March 1935 with a trio version of "Lookie, Lookie, Here Comes Cookie" that included Gene Krupa on drums. Later she recorded a walloping version of "Pinetop's Boogie," her biggest hit, several years before the boogie-woogie craze.

Cleo Brown worked with Texas Guinan at the Chicago World's Fair in 1933 and Chicago's Three Deuces in 1934. She apparently retired from music in the fifties and went through a religious conversion. Bobby Short, who last saw and heard her in 1949 when she was working in Los Angeles, has said, "Cleo Brown was a great star for all of us when we were growing up."

Amateur Night at the Apollo Theatre in Harlem, which passed its fiftieth anniversary years ago, was inaugurated in 1935. By 1936, it gained wide exposure through broadcasts over Station WMCA, which carried the show live every Wednesday night at 11:00 P.M. for more than two decades. In the early years, winning first place led to a week's booking at the theatre. Not living up to audience expectations, as evidenced by boos and hissing, brought a tall man on stage with a shepherd's crook, the curve of which was placed around the unfortunate performer, who was yanked off stage.

In the thirties and forties, attendance at Amateur Night at the Apollo was a "must" for people in the music business. In the audience one could find talent agents, publishers, songwriters, managers—all hoping to spot a new talent. And through the years, among the performers who got their start at the Apollo Amateur Nights, were Sarah Vaughan, Ella Fitzgerald, Leslie Uggams, Gladys Knight, and James Brown.

Leroy Carr was a short-lived, alcoholic bluesman who died in 1935 at the age of thirty. He recorded extensively with jazz guitarist Scrapper Blackwell in a blues-pop-inflected style, exerting a marked influence on urban bluesmen of the thirties. He is remembered for his recording of "How Long, How Long Blues," and especially "In the Evening (When the Sun Goes Down)," which he wrote. Big Bill Broonzy has told the story of how a group of Chicago bluesmen drove through one long night from Chicago to Indianapolis where Carr lived just to hear him do "In the Evening."

Joe Williams adopted "In the Evening" as a single blockbuster after leaving Count Basie and gave the tune its best ride for years on his concert tours lasting into the nineties.

⤜ 13 ⤛

"Stompin' at the Savoy"
(1936)

(The writer of this journey through pop music time and space was a staunch devotee of Swing Street. My journeys, often browsing the joints with John Hammond, also brought art assignments such as the jazz personality portraits at the Downbeat Club. Further down the line, the craft was deployed at a chicken shack on 46th Street with sports figures the objects of brush and oil, defining my commercial art as graduation exercises after a working scholarship at the Art Students League. "And now," as I would schtickly proclaim to Top Banana Hank Henry two decades later in burlesque on another famous street, the Las Vegas Strip, "back to the script."–Ed.)

As dusk settled over Manhattan early in 1936, a steady stream of clubgoers entered the Onyx Club on 52nd Street. When the Onyx reopened (with guitarist Carl Cress as the silent moneyman), Joe Helbock booked a five-piece combo led by Red McKenzie. Included were two clowning cats—trombonist Mike Riley and trumpeter Ed Farley—who came up with a novelty song titled "The Music Goes 'Round and 'Round." They performed it with a comedy routine, describing with wide gestures the passage of sound through the curves and bends of a trombone or French horn. The phrase, "Oh, ho, ho, Oh, ho, ho—and it comes out here," caught on. The audience ate it up—and the club became SRO. Jazz fiddler Stuff Smith, who followed Riley-Farley, also drew crowds to the Onyx. "When Stuff got the feeling," Hoagy Carmichael has said, "he would change the fiddle bow to an inverted position so

143

that he could saw all four strings at once. Then he'd start pumping four beats to the measure while Jonah [Jones] and others did their work. One chorus would lead to another. It was a welling thing that led to pandemonium and a breaking point at about the 15th chorus!"

Stuff also wrote material that added to his popularity. In the month of his Onyx debut, he recorded his novelty "I'se a Muggin' " on Vocalion. Soon another novelty number Stuff had written took off on the same label: "You'se a Viper" ("viper" was a marijuana smoker, but in the atmosphere of the time, it had a humorous connotation). Stuff had a sense of the comic—he appeared in a battered black stovepipe resting rakishly on the back of his head—but he was also a jealous man. Despite his tremendous acceptance— he packed the club from February into October—he got Billie Holiday fired when as a secondary act she began to get rave notices in the papers.

While Stuff was still on the Onyx bandstand, the club sponsored "New York's first Swing Music Concert." It occurred on Sunday evening, May 24, 1936, and the Imperial Theatre audience remained for two-and-a-half hours after the curtain had descended on all the neighboring Broadway theatres. Fiddler Joe Venuti opened with a fourteen-piece band, while the Casa Loma Band closed the concert. In between, fourteen different combos appeared, most of them playing freewheeling, two-beat Dixie. The surprise smash of the evening was Artie Shaw and His String Swing Ensemble. The audience was so responsive that the group was compelled to play an encore—and it could only repeat "Interlude in B Flat," composed by Shaw for the concert. It was the only composition that the ad hoc group knew. By the time the concert was over, agents were waving contracts at Shaw, who was soon fronting the first of his big bands in Manhattan's Hotel Lexington. Although the Cotton Club was not on 52nd Street, it continued to be a big draw several blocks down Broadway, having moved in September of 1936 into the site of the Palais Royale. Out of its twenty-seventh *Hit Parade*, if not exactly a salute to the move, came "Alabama Barbecue" (words and music by Benny Davis and J. Fred Coots), as well as the very popular "Doin' the Suzy-Q" by the same team, and "Frisco Flo," introduced by Cab Calloway. "No Regrets" was a torch ballad by Roy Ingraham and Harry Tobias, unveiled by the Casa Loma Orchestra. It remained on *Your Hit Parade* for ten weeks, usually in the lower reaches, but it managed at one point to climb to No. 4.

Paul Douglas, announcer of CBS's pioneer jazz radio program, *Saturday Night Swing Club*, was one of the announcers with Ben Grauer of NBC and Budd Hulick, Colonel Stoopnagle's partner. Douglas later wrote in an article titled "Oh, Say Can You Swing": "If they had let one more person into the Imperial that Sunday night, he would have found himself in my lap."

The biggest hit of 1936 came from the film musical *Swing Time*, featuring the terpsichorean magic of Fred Astaire and Ginger Rogers. In one scene,

Ginger was shampooing her hair and Fred was kidding her about her appearance. Asked to write a song for the scene, lyricist Dorothy Fields came up with the title "The Way You Look Tonight." It was intended as a comical number, and Fred sang it tongue-in-cheek. But Jerome Kern created a melody that gave the lyric romantic overtones. Detached from the scene, it became a love song, capturing the Oscar as Best Song of the Year. It remained No. 1 on *Your Hit Parade* for more weeks (six) than any other song save one.

"Did I Remember?" (music by Walter Donaldson; words by Harold Adamson) was the other song. And who remembers it? It was an Academy Award nominee, featured in *Suzy*, starring Jean Harlow and Cary Grant. Since Harlow could not sing, Virginia Verrill dubbed her singing. Although Cary Grant had no singing voice to speak of, he managed a kind of half-spoken delivery, having the charm of the type of singing for which Rex Harrison became famous.

Swing Time also contained "A Fine Romance," which was frankly subtitled "A Sarcastic Love Song" and in which Ginger needled Fred during a snowstorm for his lack of affectionate warmth. "A Fine Romance" entered the *Hit Parade* before "The Way You Look Tonight" and remained on the charts for eight weeks, but it never rose above the No. 4 slot.

The song that hit No. 1 five times, just behind the two leaders, was "Is It True What They Say About Dixie?" (music by Gerald Marks; words by Sammy Lerner and Irving Caesar). It was not in any show, or in a film. Obviously the songwriters were seasoned Tin Pan Alley writers who knew how to plug their wares. Both Rudy Vallee and Al Jolson were persuaded to give airtime to the song, so much airtime that its popularity was confirmed by the *Hit Parade*.

Extensive plugging undoubtedly also accounted for the popularity of "Lost" (words and music by Phil Ohman, Johnny Mercer, and Mary O. Teetor), another Tin Pan Alley song without a show or film showcase. It made No. 1 for four weeks, as did "Goody Goody" (words and music by Johnny Mercer and Matt Malneck). But "Goody Goody" was recorded and performed on national radio by Benny Goodman and His Orchestra.

The Goodman band also scored with "Sing, Sing, Sing," a swinging number written and introduced by Louis Prima, but became a best-selling record for Goodman. Drummer Gene Krupa was featured in the first extended drum solo on a disk. A classic of the Swing Era and a favorite of the Goodman band was "Stompin' at the Savoy," a rhythmic song celebrating the famous and the biggest of the Harlem ballrooms. The credits read: "words: Andy Razaf; music: Benny Goodman, Chick Webb, and Edgar Sampson." Those who were close to the Chick Webb band, which recorded the number in 1934 before publication, believe that the composer was really Edgar Sampson (1907–1973), a versatile musician who played the saxes and violin. He was an accomplished arranger-composer and joined the Chick Webb band in 1934. Webb's disk made little impression. But when the number was recorded by Goodman in 1936, his disk became a best-seller, and "Stompin' at the Savoy" was transformed into a swing classic.

It is somewhat of an exaggeration, but, generally speaking, the swinging songs introduced by the big bands did not make *Your Hit Parade*, whose choices seemed to cater to ballads from films, Broadway shows, and Tin Pan Alley. Nevertheless, "In the Chapel in the Moonlight," by Billy Hill, recorded by Shep Fields and His Orchestra, made No. 1 on *The Parade* for three weeks.

The year 1936 was a good one for Bing Crosby, Al Jolson, Fats Waller, and especially Shirley Temple. Appearing in two film musicals, *Pennies from Heaven* and *Rhythm on the Range*, Bing made an Academy Award nominee of the title song of the former and recorded and popularized Johnny Mercer's tongue-in-cheek cowboy song "I'm an Old Cowhand (from the Rio Grande)" in the latter. "Pennies from Heaven" went to No. 1 for a four-week stay at the end of 1936 and the early weeks of 1937. Its acceptance led to its being interpolated in the 1953 film *Cruisin' Down the River*. (In 1980, the title was used by a British television series describing the adventures of a sheet-music salesman of the 1930s; the series also featured a number of popular songs from the period. The next year, comic Steve Martin made a film version of the same story.)

Child prodigy Shirley Temple was just eight years old but appeared in four films, *Poor Little Rich Girl, Captain January, Stowaway*, and *Dimples*, dancing and singing a dozen songs. Numbers by Gordon and Revel like "You Gotta Eat Your Spinach, Baby" and "You Gotta S-M-I-L-E To Be H-A-Double P-Y" were obviously written to give play to her cuteness and youthful charm. But the ballad "When I'm with You" by Gordon and Revel made No. 1 on *Your Hit Parade* for two weeks. And "Goodnight, My Love," introduced by Shirley and reprised by Alice Faye in *Stowaway*, made the *Parade* in 1937. Top box-office attractions, these films led to Shirley Temple's making more than twenty movies in the thirties and to being the top Hollywood box-office star in several of these years.

Of the songs in *Sing Baby Sing*, "You Turned the Tables on Me" (music by Louis Alter; words by Sidney D. Mitchell), introduced by Alice Faye, was given a special award for creativity by ASCAP and became a favorite with jazz ensembles, specifically those of Benny Goodman and Louis Armstrong.

One ballad of the year that passed into the jazz repertoire—Vernon Duke's (and Ira Gershwin's) "I Can't Get Started with You," introduced in the *Ziegfeld Follies of 1936* by Bob Hope and Eve Arden—has one other distinction. In *Have Tux Will Travel*, Bob Hope claims that his singing of the song in *Ziegfeld Follies* "put me into pictures. Mitchell Liesen and Harlan Thompson, who were preparing a script for *The Big Broadcast of 1936* for Paramount, saw me in the number with Eve Arden and hired me." The jazz trumpet great, Bunny Berigan, made the song a hit in a recording by his own band, featuring him as vocalist.

Drawing crowds to the Yacht Club on 52nd Street, Fats Waller, his derby sitting at a rakish angle on his head, introduced a number of comical numbers: "The Panic Is On" by George Clarke, Bert Clarke, and Winston Tharp; "You Stayed Away Too Long" (music by J. C. Johnson; words by George Whiting and Nat Schwartz); and "Your Feet's Too Big" by Ada Benson and Fred Fisher.

By contrast, there was the Hungarian import with English words by Sam M. Lewis. "Gloomy Sunday" was advertised and promoted as "the suicide song" in its native habitat. It was introduced in the United States by Paul Robeson, leading in 1941 to a best-selling record by Billie Holiday. "Gloomy Sunday" is said to have prompted twenty-one suicides in Hungary. Its composer, Rezso Seress, also committed suicide.

The year 1936 was one of cataclysmic events: FDR's landslide re-election to the presidency; Hitler's invasion of the Rhineland and Mussolini's of Addis Ababa; the outbreak of the civil war in Spain. But no event quite stunned the public (at least in Great Britain and the United States) as the abdication of the British throne by Edward VIII. No words spoken in 1936 had the excitement, thrill, or romance of what millions heard over the radio on December 2, 1936, when he indicated that he planned to give up the throne and marry Mrs. Wallis Simpson, an American divorcée, "the woman I love." There is doubtless little or no connection that in that year Cole Porter wrote "I've Got You Under My Skin," Isham Jones composed "There Is No Greater Love," and Rodgers and Hart wrote the intimate "There's a Small Hotel."

The continuing market for Latin rhythms and sounds evidenced itself in an adaptation of a melody by Cuban composer Ernesto Lecuona of "Malagueña" fame. The original Spanish lyric of "Say 'Si, Si' " was by Francia Lubin, based on the Cuban lyric "Para Vigo Me Voy." Al Stillman wrote the English lyrics when the song was introduced by Xavier Cugat with Lina Romay delivering the vocal. (Four years later, the Andrews Sisters produced a best-selling disk, and Gene Autry sang it in the film *Carolina Moon*.)

While *Rose Marie* was a Broadway smash in 1924, the famous duet of Jeanette MacDonald and Nelson Eddy in "Indian Love Call" became a million-selling record with the release of the film version of the Rudolf Friml operetta in 1936. Reportedly theirs was the first musical show tune to mount the million mark.

For the popular dance team of Fred Astaire and Ginger Rogers, Irving Berlin produced "Let's Face the Music and Dance" in the movie musical *Follow the Fleet*. This was another dance scene in which a costume made problems. Ginger wore a dress that had very heavy sleeves. With every turn, Astaire feared being walloped by a flying sleeve. What he feared did occur at one point when he was struck in the mouth and eye and temporarily stunned. The scene was saved in that the camera happened to be focused on Ginger.

Cole Porter was well represented by "Easy to Love" in *Born to Dance* and by "It's De-Lovely" in *Red, Hot and Blue*. "Easy to Love" was staged so that Reginald Gardiner was seen in Central Park conducting an invisible orchestra in Ponchielli's "Dance of the Hours," which magically turned into "Easy to Love," sung by actor Jimmy Stewart. It was also performed by Frances Langford. "It's De-Lovely," introduced by Ethel Merman and Bob Hope, made *Your Hit Parade* for ten weeks, starting in November 1936 and finally making No. 1 on January 16, 1937.

The year also brought a film biography of the great Ziegfeld, who had died in 1932. In a long review in the *New York Times*, Frank S. Nugent wrote: "The picture has the opulence, the lavishness, the expansiveness, and the color of the old Follies; it has the general indifference to humor which was one of Ziegfeld's characteristics, and it has the reverential approach with which we suspect Mr. Ziegfeld might have handled his own life story." Although the special music and lyrics were by Walter Donaldson and Harold Adamson, with a Harriet Hoctor ballet (music by Con Conrad and lyrics by Herb Magidson), reviewer Nugent singled out Berlin's "A Pretty Girl Is Like a Melody," "with overtones of *Rhapsody in Blue* [as] never having been equalled on the musical comedy stage or screen."

Lionel Hampton (1908–   )

Vibraharpist extraordinaire, virtuoso drummer, and two-fingered piano player in the Earl Hines groove, he was born in Louisville, Kentucky, in April 1908. He was raised by his mother in Birmingham and then, from 1916 on, in Chicago. Here, along with Sid Catlett, he studied drums and absorbed influences from Zutty Singleton. In 1927, he migrated to California and worked with Paul Howard's Quality Serenaders, and made his record debut in 1929. He is noted for his extravagant exuberance as a performer and for high-spirited antics like throwing his sticks in the air and dancing on his drums. "Flying Home," which he wrote and which was his showpiece with the Benny Goodman Band, became a hit record for him in 1942 when he recorded it with his own band. He continues to pursue an active if not exhausting schedule of one-nighters and recording.

Interview with Lionel Hampton

In 1930, I was playing with Les Hite's Orchestra at Sebastian's Cotton Club on the outskirts of Los Angeles. It was a place where movie stars and the jet set came to hear black music and enjoy black entertainers. Louis Armstrong appeared as a headliner. He left his own band in New York City, so we backed him up. He liked us so well that he invited us to do a recording session with him.

When we got to the recording studio, there was a vibraharp standing in a corner. Louis asked me what it was, and I told him it was a new instrument being brought into the percussion family—a modernized xylophone with tubular metal resonators and motor-driven propellers to produce a vibrato. I had played a xylophone when I lived in Chicago and was in Major Clark Smith's *Chicago Defender*'s newspaper boys band. I played snare drums in the marching band and xylophone in the concert orchestra.

I used to fool around with the vibes and play jazz. I was really into jazz even at that time. When Louis asked whether I could play the vibraharp, I said, "Yes." I knew that it had the same keyboard as the xylophone. To show him, I played a solo from one of his records. So we recorded Eubie Blake's "Memories of You," and Louis liked it so much I played several other solos on the vibraharp. That was the start of the vibes, and I played with Louis for nine months. But I didn't really make the vibes my main instrument until I got a set of my own when I had my own band. It was my late wife Gladys who urged me to stick with the vibes, and so I did.

When I had my own orchestra, I got a job at the Paradise Club, which was at 6th and Main in Los Angeles. It was right across the street and opposite the Red Car Pacific Electric Depot, which brought sailors from ships at San Pedro and Long Beach. The place had sawdust on the floor. You could get a pitcher of beer for twenty-five cents and it was a sailors' hangout.

In August 1936, on the 19th or 20th, Benny Goodman was in California, playing an engagement at the Palomar Ballroom. His brother-in-law, John Hammond, had been in the Paradise and heard us play. He brought Benny down, and Benny brought his clarinet, Teddy Wilson, and Gene Krupa. The next I knew, all three of them were up on the stage, and we jammed for almost two hours. Benny liked what he heard so well he phoned me the next day. I didn't believe he'd call me, and I didn't take the call. But he did reach me and invited me to play a record date, which I did. We recorded "Moonglow" and "Dinah." They were put out under the name of the Benny Goodman Quartet. When Benny invited me to come and join him, I did, in November 1936.

Funny thing about the Paradise Club was that, after that jam session, they took the sawdust off the floor, put tablecloths on the tables, and began charging people $1.50 just to get in. For the three months that I remained there, we'd jam around the clock. It was pretty hard pulling me away from there because we were doing fantastic business. I had a good band: Tyree Glenn on trombone, Don Byas and Herschel Evans on sax, and other star players.

It was on November 11, 1936, that I walked out onto the stage of the Manhattan Room of the Hotel Pennsylvania to play my first date with the Benny Goodman Band. It was one of the first times that black and white musicians played together. It was instant integration and important socially as well as financially. We were getting the top money of any musicians in the country. There was no displeasure manifested by the audience. The music was so outstanding that people were listening instead of looking.

When the band played the South, prejudice sometimes took an ugly form, as Benny Goodman reported about a fair in the Southwest in the summer of 1937. "We noticed about the second day," Goodman said, "that a couple of city police on duty around the place didn't like the attention that Lionel and Teddy were getting. They didn't say anything, but every time that one of the kids came up and asked either of them for an autograph (naturally calling them *Mr. Hampton* or *Mr. Wilson*), they'd act nasty. . . . On the third night, after we had finished a session with the quartet, one of the guests ordered some champagne for Lionel. As the waiter got to the stage door, one of the officers stopped him and said, 'Where you goin' with that?' The waiter answered, 'It's for Mr. Hampton.' 'The hell with that stuff,' this guy yelled, and flung out his arm, knocking the tray, glasses, ice and champagne out of the waiter's hand."

I stayed with Benny until mid-July 1940, when I stepped out to form my own band. I organized it in Los Angeles. There was this young man who showed up with a clarinet wrapped in a newspaper. When I asked him where his horn was, he said he didn't have one. So I had him play something on the clarinet, which I accompanied on the piano. I heard something in his style, and I got him a tenor sax—and that's how Illinois Jaquet was born.

My band was a breeding ground for other top names: Cat Anderson on trumpet, whom I got out of a band in South Carolina; Quincy Jones, who came from Seattle, Washington, to play trumpet and arrange; Fats Navarro, who was another giant trumpet player; Kenny Dorham, a trumpet player from Texas; Art Farmer, a trumpet player out of Phoenix; and Charlie Mingus, bass player and composer out of Nogales and California.

Then there was Dinah Washington—she started as a gospel singer—a girl who worked in the washroom of Joe Glaser's club and doubled at the Garrick Bar in Chicago. When I heard her at the Garrick on Glaser's urging, I invited her to the Regal Theatre on the South Side where my band was playing. After she sang "Evil Gal Blues," I was ready to hire her, but I didn't like her name. She was born Ruth Jones in Tuscaloosa and was singing under that name. I asked he if she minded changing her name. "I don't care what you call me," she said, "so long as you give me a job." And so, on the impulse of the moment, I named her Dinah Washington—I don't know why.

When I introduced her at the Regal Theatre in a backstage interview, a guy standing next to her said, "There goes my chance of being in the band." We did medleys in the show, and I guess I surprised him when I had him sing the second medley that night. I liked him and hired him—and that was Joe Williams, who later made it big with the Count.

Clifford Brown, another fine trumpet player, came out of the band. We had Earl Bostic, who played alto and arranged, and came from Tulsa; Dexter Gordon, a tenor player out of California; Benny Golson, another tenorman and composer out of Philadelphia.

Shortly after I came into New York to join Goodman in '36, Victor approached me about making records with a small band. Starting in 1937, I made a series on the Bluebird label for about four years, cutting some in New York, some in Chicago, and some in Los Angeles. I have been told that Victor intended these to compete with the small band recordings that Teddy Wilson was making with Billie Holiday for Brunswick. I used top players from the bands of Benny Goodman, Cab Calloway, Duke Ellington, Earl Hines, and others. We did top tunes as well as originals, like Benny Carter's arrangement of "I'm in the Mood for Swing." Sometimes when I play jazz, it's not only an emotional experience but a spiritual one. I've reached heights with the big band when I and my men were just about carried away. Once when we were playing "Flying Home" on a barge on the Potomac River and we were reaching a climax in the last chorus when everyone goes "rum-ba-da, dum-ba-da, RUM—POW," I yelled, "Hit it!," and the bass player was so high, he leaped right into the water.

The thirties were good years in retrospect. I had the opportunity of playing with two of the great giants of music, Louis Armstrong and Benny Goodman, and I picked up a world of experience from those two guys.

Milt Hinton (1910–)

Born in Vicksburg, Mississippi, in June 1910, he first studied violin but switched to bass while in high school in Chicago. His major associations during the thirties were with Eddie South, known as the Dark Angel of the Violin, and with the Hi-De-Ho Man, Cab Calloway. After leaving Cab in 1951, he went on to play with Count Basie, Louis Armstrong, and Benny Goodman, among other bands. Respected for his superior musicianship, he has frequently been quoted as saying: "A musician has to have lived to play great jazz or else he'll just be a copy." He has continued an active career into the 1990s. On January 12, 1988, he was flown to Munich, Germany, to play a tune for the reopening of the Munich Opera House, and in the summer of

1988 he taught Master Classes at the Summer Jazz Institute at Skidmore College.

Interview with Milt Hinton

When I came to Chicago from Mississippi in the early twenties, the city was in the Depression and the times were not too good for jazz or the musicians. Al Capone ran the Cotton Club, and Ralph Capone had the only other hot spot, with a band led by Boyd Atkins. My first professional job playing with a big band was with Atkins, a saxist/violinist who wrote "Heebie Jeebies," first recorded by Louis Armstrong. In 1930, I went to work for Tiny Parham, a pianist/organist.

My first big job was at the Show Boat Cabaret, where Louis Armstrong had been playing. To take Louis's place, they sent for Jabbo Smith, a rapid-fire trumpeter like Dizzy Gillespie who could play anything with a cup mouthpiece. The band had Cassio Simpson on piano, Floyd Campbell on drums, and a lineup of three saxes and two brass. We played jazz and original blues. The place was owned by gangsters and operated as a bookie joint during the daytime, taking bets over the telephone on horseraces. At night, it became a cabaret. They didn't like us around during the daytime to rehearse, practice, or write. When Jabbo goofed a number of times, showing up late, they put Cassio in charge. Cassio had a fetish for writing tunes about food, like "Chittlins and Greens," "Stringbeans and Rice." It was a solid band, and we played the Regal Theatre on the South Side of Chicago.

The people who had the Show Boat were also tied up with the Three Deuces. I worked there with Zutty Singleton, who was the kingpin of the New Orleans "clan." Lee Collins, who replaced Louis in King Oliver's band, was on trumpet, a brother of Cozy Cole's was on piano, and Everett Barksdale played guitar. Art Tatum was the relief pianist, playing solo during intermissions. It was my job when Art was playing his last tune to return to the stage and join him. It was quite a challenge to keep up with his magnificent harmonic changes and shifts in tempo. This was around 1935. Fletcher Henderson was at the Grand Terrace at that time with Roy Eldridge, Chu Berry, John Kirby, and others. They would close at 1:00 A.M. We played until 4:00 A.M. So they would come over to the Three Deuces and jam with us.

I started with Eddie South, the fantastic jazz fiddler, in 1931–32 when he returned from a sensational four-year tour of the Continent. A guy named Sam Skolnick wanted to put him in a downtown Chicago hotel with four or five violins—like Emery Deutsch with a continental flavor. This would be a small group within a big band. We used to rehearse in a Chinese restaurant called Chu Chin Chow. After all the rehearsing and activity, they decided that the time was not right to put a black band with a continental flavor in a downtown hotel. Skolnick had signed up a group of us for forty weeks at $75 a week. They could not find a hotel to place a big band. So they bought back the contracts, paying each musician $300 for a release. They didn't give me my money but they gave me a job at a West Side club, The Rubaiyat. It was small and plush, and we had a five-piece combo with Eddie South as the featured artist. We played for a time with a drummer.

In 1932, when the Democratic Convention was held in Chicago and FDR was nominated as the presidential candidate, the headquarters was at the Congress Hotel. They decided to put Eddie South in the lobby. It had a beautiful fountain with a small island in it, and that was our bandstand. All the top politicians of the day came by to hear us. We stayed there for quite a while and then went on to California. Here we played at a club on Hollywood Boulevard called the Ballyhoo—just three pieces, no piano, myself on bass, Everett Barksdale on guitar, and Eddie South. All the big stars of the screen came to hear Eddie, who was certainly the finest violinist to play jazz and a man who could have made it in the concert field in a less prejudiced time.

In the Ballyhoo, they had a dance act, Latin style. Carmen Miranda danced with two men, one of whom was Cesar Romero. They went on to big careers. For them, we had to play "La Comparsita" and other Latin numbers. We were out there for twenty-six weeks, a very lucrative engagement. We made our first commercials for some product. In those days, there was no tape and no splicing. If you made a mistake, you had to go back and do the whole thing over, right from the beginning. Lionel Hampton showed up at one point. We knew him from Chicago, and we had not seen him since our school days. Lionel came down to the railroad station—there were no planes or airports then—and he brought his band to greet us.

Returning to Chicago, I worked with Eddie South in 1934. We made some recordings: "Old Man Harlem," on which I did a vocal, and "My Oh My," on which Eddie did the vocal. In '35 I worked with Zutty Singleton at the Three Deuces. Cab Calloway was then doing a picture, *The Singing Kid*, with Al Jolson. His regular bass player, Al Morgan, left him on the Coast to form his own band, and Cab came East needing a bass player. Keg Johnson, one of his trombonists, who knew me from Chicago, urged Cab to visit the Deuces and hear me.

When you entered the Three Deuces, you came right off the street. There was a bar and tables. The night club was downstairs. Cab came down while Art Tatum was playing. When Art was finished, we played and Cab invited us to his table. He turned to Zutty and asked, "Can I have him?" Zutty nodded: "Sure, you can have him." Nobody asked me, and Zutty just gave me away. People who overheard the conversation started to applaud. Cab came to the bandstand with Zutty, and they took a bow. It was about 2:30

in the morning then, but I called my mom to tell her that Cab Calloway, who was a big name, had asked me to join him—she had me packed so that by 4:00 I was down at the railroad station on my way.

On the train, I took a lot of ribbing from the men in the band. But Cab's friendliness helped me face them down. He told me that they were going to do a lot of one-nighters and that he would get a good bassist when he got to New York. I agreed, and I stayed with Cab for fifteen years—from February 1936 until 1951.

The one-night stops in the South were pretty terrible. With Cab, we always traveled first class in a Pullman and sleeping was no problem. But eating was. No white restaurant would serve us or even give us food to take out. In Longview, Texas, the prejudice was so awful that a guy would say: "I'll pay a $100 fine just to smash one of those boys." In Fort Lauderdale, Florida, we wouldn't get off the bandstand at intermission time just to get a drink of water without a police escort. When we met white musicians we knew, we'd sometimes have a jam session in the Negro section after hours. But in some southern cities, it was impossible because the white cats would get into trouble if the police found them in the Negro section. We got along with southern musicians. They would come in to listen and talk, but they wouldn't fraternize with us. Cab had so much work that he eventually stopped touring the South.

He was a wonderful man to work for. He was a strict disciplinarian but easy to get along with when you did your job. He paid well, better than many other leaders. And we traveled first class. If we had to take a bus, we would go with Greyhound. At Christmas time, there would be a $100 bonus for each man. He would also give us train fare to go home for the holidays and return fare. They were good years, the fifteen that I played with him.

Medley 1936

With 1936 came the closing of the Harlem Opera House, built for opera in 1889 by Oscar Hammerstein and segregated until after World War I. During the Harlem Renaissance it became a premier showcase for black talent, along with the Apollo Theatre, Lafayette Theatre, and Cotton Club. Eubie Blake and Noble Sissle of *Shuffle Along* fame played the House, and Ella Fitzgerald made her debut there.

Buddy Rich (1918–1987), the virtuoso drummer, left the family vaudeville act—he sang, danced, and drummed—to join Joe Marsala's band in 1936. Two years later he was heard in his first recorded drum solo—a 17-second explosion—on Marsala's disk of "Jim Jam Stomp."

After three years as vocalist, Mildred Bailey, the Rockin' Chair Lady, left the Paul Whiteman band to join forces with her husband, jazz vibraharpist

Red Norvo. For three years, 1936–39, they performed on the radio as Mr. and Mrs. Swing, and Mildred made some of her best recordings—"Please Be Kind," "Blame It on My Last Affair," "Georgia on My Mind," and "Rockin' Chair."

Interest in the college scene, avidly cultivated in the songs and shows of the twenties, carried over into the thirties. Rudy Vallee, who featured collegiate material, adapted "The Whiffenpoof Song" and showcased it on his program after he heard it performed in 1936 by the Whiffenpoof Society, a branch of the Yale Glee Club. He had originally heard the number as an undergraduate at Yale. The word *whiffenpoof* comes from an imaginary character in a Victor Herbert operetta, with other words of the song adapted from Rudyard Kipling's poem, "Gentlemen Rankers." In 1947, both Robert Merrill and Bing Crosby recorded it, with Crosby's rendition, backed by Fred Waring's Glee Club, selling over a million copies.

Making his Apollo Theatre debut in 1936, Andy Kirk and His Clouds of Joy performed "a piece of folk origin" known as "The Slave Song." Jack Kapp of Decca assigned the song for a rewrite to Sammy Cahn and Saul Chaplin, who titled it "(It Will Have to Do) Until the Real Thing Comes Along." It was then discovered that an earlier rewrite of the song, the work of Mann Holiner and Alberta Nichols, had been introduced in 1931 in Lew Leslie's *Rhapsody in Black*. A lawsuit or threat of one led to the credits in the song being listed as Sammy Cahn, Saul Chaplin, Mann Holiner, Alberta Nichols, and L. E. Freeman. A best-selling record by Andy Kirk featured a vocal by Pha Terrell.

✴ 14 ✴

"Sing Me a Song of Social Significance"
(1937)

George Jean Nathan, the eminent critic, described it as a "miscegenation" of a Union Square soap box with a talented juke box," and Virgil Thomson characterized it as "the most appealing socialism since *Louise*." They were referring to *The Cradle Will Rock* by Marc Blitzstein, which had the most bizarre and dramatic premiere of any Broadway show.

A WPA Theatre production, with John Houseman as producer and Orson Welles as director, it was in its dress rehearsal stage when suddenly an order came from federal theatre officials in Washington canceling the production. Their objection was to its left-wing, anti-capitalist outlook. Apparently, notification of the cancellation reached Houseman, as I heard him tell it at a revival in 1981, just before the first night audience began entering the Maxine Elliott Theater. While he and members of the cast sought to entertain an audience that grew increasingly restive, other cast members scurried about the theatre district in search of an empty theater or auditorium—one that could be used without government finances. The nearby Venice Theatre was finally found and rented, whereupon Houseman and Welles led a march of the entire audience twenty blocks north to the new venue.

Since the costumes and the scenery belonged to the federal theatre, they had to be left behind. Forbidden by an order of the Actors Guild to perform, cast members bought tickets and sat with the audience, performing from their seats. Because the musicians were also enjoined by their union from participation, the score was performed on an upright piano on stage by the composer himself, who also served as an impromptu commentator.

The inverse result of this makeshift presentation was that the musical gained not only unusual media attention but dramatic impact. "Much that was specious and contrived," David Ewen notes, "was eliminated by Blitzstein's rambling and charming commentary." Even the music itself seemed to benefit from the piano rendition and the informal proceedings The *New York Times*'s Brooks Atkinson called it "the most versatile triumph of the politically insurgent theater."

The work was repeated nineteen times at the Venice Theatre, financed by a private investor. Still performed without scenery, orchestra, or costumes— now by design rather than necessity—*The Cradle Will Rock* moved to the Windsor Theatre in the Bronx, where it stayed for 108 performances, proving a mildly profitable venture.

The *Post* called it "a Puckish proletarian romp." Although epithets like discordant and strident were used to describe the plot and score, no one denied the talent behind the acerbic condemnation of life in a company town. "Whether or not one agreed with its [anti-capitalist] politics," David Ewen wrote, "Blitzstein emerges as one of the most provocative and exciting new writers for the musical theater in several years."

But so did Harold J. Rome, whose *Pins and Needles* had its premiere just a few weeks before *The Cradle* on November 27, 1937. It was presented at what had once been the Princess Theatre—the venue of the Kern-Wodehouse mini-musicals of the 1910s—but now bore the more challenging name of the Labor Stage. With the unconventional sponsorship of the International Ladies Garment Workers Union, the cast consisted entirely of rank-and-file members of the union—tailors, cutters, weavers, machinists—and only weekend performances were scheduled so as not to interfere with their work schedules. It was an integrated show, and its songs were all an expression of the show's pro-labor, anti-fascist outlook. Romance was given a sociopolitical treatment in "One Big Union for Two," "It's Better with a Union Man," and "Sing Me a Song of Social Significance." "Doing the Reactionary" satirized capitalism, while "Three Little Angels of Peace" ridiculed fascism. The most sentimental song was a ballad, "Sunday in the Park," celebrating the frugal pleasures of working people.

No advertisements were placed for the premiere performance, and no major music critic was in attendance. Nevertheless, its low budget and, perhaps, its fresh, unconventional point of view kept the revue on the boards for a staggering 1,108 performances, first at the 299-seat Labor Stage, later at the 849-seat Windsor Theatre in the Bronx. Even recognizing that the run might have been shorter in a larger house, there is no questioning the show's phenomenal popularity. In number of performances, it was the decade's second longest-running musical.

"Listening to dance bands the other night," composer/arranger Gordon Jenkins wrote in September 1937, "I heard 458 chromatic runs on accordions, 911 'telegraph ticker' brass figures, 78 sliding trombones, 4 sliding violas, 45 burps into a straw, 91 bands that played the same arrangement on every tune, and 1,100 imitations of Benny Goodman."

At the time, 18,000 musicians were reported on the road, with dance music grossing $80 million, and 400,000 musicians working. Unquestionably, swing was at a peak in the summer of 1937.

But the Depression was not over. In fact, it suddenly took a turn for the worse. The number of shows produced on Broadway fell to the lowest figure in thirty years; 13,130 theatres became nationwide Depression casualties, and Broadway's Criterion Theatre, opposite the famed Astor Hotel, was transformed into a Woolworth's.

The sober tenor of the American citizenry was revealed in a series of Broadway musicals that turned from typical fare of the musical to more challenging subjects. *Swing It*, a short-lived black July musical, was concerned with economic problems. *I'd Rather Be Right*, with a book by George S. Kaufman and Moss Hart and a weak score by Rodgers and Hart, was a friendly mockery of the Roosevelt administration. Figures from the administration were identifiable, and FDR was played by George M. Cohan, who hated Roosevelt and had to be prevented from inserting sarcastic lines of his own.

But the strongest show was traditional in type—not of subject matter—but of cast and song. Out of *Babes in Arms* came Alfred Drake, Mitzie Green, Ray Heatherton, and Dan Dailey, among others. And Rodgers and Hart delivered one of their finest and most memorable scores, with "The Lady Is a Tramp," "Where or When," "Johnny One Note," "I Wish I Were in Love Again," and the wistful "My Funny Valentine." Produced for a mere $55,000, the show racked up 289 performances.

They were hardly front-runners, but Bud Green and Michael Edwards produced what was apparently the biggest hit of the year. "Once in a While" was introduced as an instrumental by Tommy Dorsey and His Orchestra under the title "Dancing with You." Coming at the end of the year, it made No. 1 for more weeks (seven) on *Your Hit Parade* than any other song that year.

In terms of *Your Hit Parade*, the "runner-up" two hits were "Boo Hoo" and "It Looks Like Rain in Cherry Blossom Lane," each of which maintained the No. 1 spot for six weeks. "Boo Hoo," introduced by Guy Lombardo and His Royal Canadians, was adapted from an earlier Carmen Lombardo song called "Let's Drink." The hit version was created by Carmen Lombardo and John Jacob Loeb and Edward Heyman, and it was interpolated in the non-musical film *Dead End*, starring Humphrey Bogart and Joel McCrea (Samuel Goldwyn, 1937). Guy Lombardo also introduced "It Looks Like Rain in Cherry Blossom Lane" (words and music by Edgar Leslie and Joe Burke).

Two of the songs that made the *Parade* for four weeks each were also Academy Award nominees. "That Old Feeling" (words and music by Sammy Fain and Lew Brown), introduced in *Walter Wanger's Vogues of 1938* by Virginia Verrill, became a favorite of Jane Froman, whose voice was heard on the soundtrack of her film biography *With a Song in My Heart* (1952). "Whispers in the Dark" (music by Frederick Hollander; words by Leo Robin) was introduced by Connie Boswell with André Kostalanetz and His Orchestra in *Artists and Models* (Paramount, 1937).

Larry Clinton (1909–1985), a talented arranger, swing composer, and band leader, established a reputation for adapting classics into pop tunes or swing numbers. But in 1937, he scored a hit with a nonsense novelty, "The Dipsy Doodle," which was introduced by Tommy Dorsey and His Orchestra, vocal by Edythe Wright, and which became Clinton's theme when he launched his own band that year. One of his earliest jobs was as a sideman-arranger with Ferde Grofé. As the thirties progressed, he arranged for Isham Jones, Glen Gray, Bunny Berigan, and the Dorsey brothers.

"The Dipsy Doodle," which was also recorded by Tommy Dorsey, became the accompaniment of a dance at a time when several other composers tried to create songs for dances. For the finale of the film *New Faces of 1937*, bandleaders Harry James and Ben Pollack devised a song called "Peckin'," which became a popular dance. A third dance-song was "The Shag," written by the Tin Pan Alley songwriters Jerry Livingston and Milton Ager.

The sound of Hawaiian music seemed to have a special appeal for American listeners. "The One Rose That's Left in My Heart" (words and music by Del Lyon and Lani McIntyre) originated in the land of the leis and made *Your Hit Parade* for six weeks but never rose above the No. 6 slot. However, "Sweet Leilani" (words and music by Harry Owens, leader of his Royal Hawaiian Orchestra), introduced in the movie musical *Waikiki Wedding* by Bing Crosby, won the Academy Award for the best song from a film. It reportedly became the first of twenty-two records to sell over a million for Bing, who sold more than forty million disks during a recording career that embraced 2,600 titles.

Working in Hollywood, George Gershwin produced four of his most beguiling melodies. They were heard in two film musicals, *A Damsel in Distress* and *Shall We Dance*, both starring Fred Astaire. "A Foggy Day" was steeped in the atmosphere of London mist and achieved a burst of feeling in the final lines, when he saw her there, "And in foggy London town the sun was shining ev'rywhere." Sinatra, for whom this song was a perennial favorite, enhanced the ending by repeating "shining" numerous times. In the same film, the Gershwins contributed "Nice Work If You Can Get It," introduced by a trio of girls, abetted by Astaire, who later reprised the song solo, pounding at the same time on various percussive instruments.

Shall We Dance, starring Ginger Rogers as well as Astaire, offered "Let's Call the Whole Thing Off" and "They Can't Take That Away from Me." The former was typical of the fight-and-make-up scenes of many Astaire-Rogers films, its pettiness emphasized by a lyric in which they quarreled about pronunciation—"tomayto" vs. "tomahto," and so on. Fred sang "They Can't Take That Away from Me" to Ginger, riding on a ferry boat from Hoboken, creating the only Gershwin song to have been nominated for an Academy Award. It lost, as we know, to "Sweet Leilani." No comment.

For Cole Porter, another of the great Broadway show tune writers, *Rosalie* was his second Hollywood assignment—the first had been *Born to Dance* in 1936. Apparently, Louis B. Mayer rejected one melody after another that Porter offered for the title tune. "I wrote six tunes under that title," Porter later recalled. "I handed in the sixth to Louis B. Mayer, who told me to forget Nelson Eddy (who was to sing it) and go home and write a honky-tonk song. It was a hit. I didn't like it. The one he threw out was better." Those who hear in the hit version some of the clichés and conventions of Tin Pan Alley believe that Porter consciously used them tongue-in-cheek—and then was amazed to find that the song went to No. 1. It was sung by Nelson Eddy and a chorus to a dance by Eleanor Powell. And it was one of those mammoth numbers with which Busby Berkeley challenged his competitors to equal or surpass.

By contrast, "In the Still of the Night," also in *Rosalie*, was a sophisticated, minor-keyed, modulating melody that expressively gloved the dreamy lyric. It was also introduced by Nelson Eddy, becoming a song that was later a hit for Della Reese (her first) and, in 1956, a million seller for the R&B group the Five Satins.

On the Avenue was a cliché backstage musical whose major redeeming feature was a sensational ballad by Irving Berlin. "I've Got My Love to Keep Me Warm" was introduced by Dick Powell and Alice Faye. In 1958, Les Brown and His Orchestra made it a best-selling record.

"So Rare" (music by Harry Herst; words by Jack Sharpe) was really a rare instance of a hit song. Jimmy Dorsey recorded it in 1937, and it went to No. 1 on *Your Hit Parade*—but just for one week. Twenty years later, the owner of a small Cincinnati label, Fraternity, hired Lou Douglas to make a new arrangement and persuaded Jimmy Dorsey to cut a new record. The new version, in the song's twentieth year, remained on the charts for thirty-eight weeks and became one of the Top Ten hits of 1957, the rock 'n' roll year.

Dorsey died of cancer shortly after he was awarded a Gold Record and less than a year after brother Tommy had choked to death in his sleep.

This survey of 1937's hits would be incomplete without a reference to "Caravan" (music by Duke Ellington and Juan Tizol; words by Irving Mills), later a Gold Record for Billy Eckstine in 1949 and a million-selling record for Ralph Marterie in 1953; "I Can Dream, Can't I?" (music by Sammy Fain; words by Irving Kahal), introduced by Tamara in the musical *Right This Way* and a million seller for Patty Andrews in 1949; and "I'll Take Romance" (music by Ben Oakland; words by Oscar Hammerstein II), the title song introduced by Grace Moore in the film musical.

"Thanks for the Memory," introduced by Bob Hope in *The Big Broadcast of 1938*, released in 1937, became his theme. It is not a romantic song as the title suggests, for all the memories are of the type to be treated tongue-in-cheek. A recording by Hope and Shirley Ross helped the song mount *Your Hit Parade* for three weeks, after which it went on to win the Academy Award as the Best Film Song of 1938.

Bessie Smith, Empress of the Blues, did not play the Apollo Theatre until 1937 (March 19). By that time, Bessie had long lost her following. Many regard 1929, the year she recorded the coruscating "Nobody Knows You When You're Down and Out," as marking the terminus of her popularity. Toward the end of the thirties, she took tentative steps to try to regain her standing, and the Apollo booking was one such move.

In the dark early hours of September 26, 1937, Bessie Smith was traveling in a Packard on Route 61 in Mississippi to make her night's booking. About ten miles north of Clarksdale, the car in which she was a passenger rammed into the back of a stationary truck. The impact sliced off the roof of the Packard and threw it over onto its right side.

"Her arm was almost torn out of its socket," clarinetist Mez Mezzrow stated. "They brought her to the hospital but it seemed like there wasn't any room for her just there—the people around there didn't care for the color of her skin. The car turned around and drove away, with Bessie's blood dripping on the floor mat. She was finally admitted to another hospital where the officials must have been color-blind, but by that time she had lost so much blood that they couldn't operate on her, and a little later she died. 'See that lonesome road, Lawd, it got to end,' she used to sing. That was how this lonesome road ended up for the greatest folk singer this country ever heard—with Jim Crow directing the traffic."

Mezzrow's version of her death—inaccurate in many details—seemingly originated with members of the Chick Webb Band, which played Memphis shortly after the tragedy. But the claim that she was the victim of southern racism gained its greatest currency as the result of an article printed by *Down Beat* a month after the accident. Written by John Hammond, it appeared

under the provocative heading, "Did Bessie Smith Bleed to Death While Waiting for Medical Aid?" In the course of the article, which mentioned the Chick
Webb Band as a source, Hammond wrote: "When finally Bessie did arrive at
the hospital she was refused treatment because of her color and bled to death
while waiting for attention." Hammond did include a paragraph in which he
added: "If the story is true, it is but another example of disgraceful conditions
in a certain section of our country." Despite his questioning approach, the
impression it left—and given wide circulation for years—was that Bessie's
death was the result of southern discrimination, an impression that later led
Edward Albee, the Pulitzer Prize–winning playwright, to write *The Death of
Bessie Smith*.

Chris Albertson, who wrote *Bessie*, a well-received biography of the Empress of the Blues, believed that we will never know the whole story. But John
Chilton, a highly regarded historian of jazz, prints what is now widely regarded as the authentic version of the tragic accident.

Shortly after the Packard struck the parked truck, "the driver of the rel-
atively undamaged truck," Chilton writes, "drove from the scene of the accident to call for an ambulance. Dr. Hugh Smith, a noted surgeon from
Memphis, who was driving to do some night fishing, came upon the scene of
the accident. He found Bessie Smith lying in the road in a critical condition,
having suffered severe injuries to her chest, abdomen, and right arm. Having
rendered first aid to Bessie, Dr. Smith and his companion began clearing the
back of his car to make room for the injured woman. Shortly afterwards they
were forced to jump clear just before the back of his Chevrolet was rammed
by another car—two passengers in the oncoming vehicle were both injured
in the collision. Two ambulances arrived. The one drove Bessie to the Afro-
American Hospital in Clarksdale. After being operated on for the amputation
of her right arm she died at 11:30 A.M. from a combination of shock and
severe injuries."

Medley 1937

When George Gershwin died on a Hollywood operating table, following sur-
gery for a brain tumor, novelist John O'Hara said, "George Gershwin died
on July 11, 1937, but I don't have to believe it if I don't want to."

"I had to live for this," Gershwin complained to a friend a week before
his death, "that Sam Goldwyn should say to me, 'Why don't you write hits
like Irving Berlin?' "

O'Hara's comment leads me to recall precisely where I was when I first
heard the news of Gershwin's death. I didn't believe it. But there it was in
the *New York Times*. It was early morning. I had just driven my wife to the
railroad station in Croton, New York, where we were living for the summer.

I bought the *Times*, as I usually did, and was driving back to the summer house when my eye caught the name "Gershwin" on the paper lying beside me. I stopped the car and parked immediately on what was the main road in Croton. Sitting there, I read with disbelieving eyes that Gershwin was gone. I read the story a second time, a third time—and still could not get myself to believe it.

It did not make sense. "The young composer," as Edward Jablonski writes, "typified eternal youth in a vibrant, strident America wakening to its potential and power in the arts, business, industry, finance, sports, in a world only recently shocked into the twentieth century."

On New Year's Eve 1937, Paul Whiteman inaugurated a new CBS series, *Chesterfield Presents*, in which the emphasis was on big-band swing and the appeal to the young dancing crowd. (Camel was sponsoring Benny Goodman every Tuesday, and Raleigh's was presenting Tommy Dorsey on Friday.) Initial problems were solved when the band began to be picked up on location, instead of broadcasting from Hollywood, and Paul Douglas, a swing enthusiast, was hired as announcer. The vocals were handled by Joan Edwards and the Modernaires, a close-harmony quartet with a feeling for swing numbers. Apart from adding some of the best-known swinging musicians, Whiteman developed a group known as the Swingin' Strings.

She was of German-Norwegian origins, but her Russian name, Vera Zorina, came from her dancing in the mid-thirties in the Ballets Russes de Monte Carlo. In 1937, she made the transition from ballet to musical comedy, appearing in the London production of Rodgers and Hart's *On Your Toes*, the innovative show that introduced ballet into the American musical. It led to her starring the following year in *Goldwyn's Follies* on the screen and Rodgers and Hart's *I Married an Angel* on Broadway. That year, she married George Balanchine, the choreographer of all these shows. Both Balanchine, who brought ballet to Hollywood, and Zorina signed seven-year contracts with Goldwyn, and their marriage broke apart during that period; he married ballerina Maria Tallchief and she wed Columbia Records executive Goddard Lieberson.

A newcomer of a different stripe was Canada's Deanna Durbin (b. 1921), who had an operatic soprano voice. Appearances on the Eddie Cantor Show and a short with Judy Garland led to her first starring role in *Three Smart Girls* (1937).

There are many songs that do not make the *Hit Parade* but somehow eventually turn into classics. One is an adaptation of a Scottish folk ballad, recorded by Maxine Sullivan, originally a native of Pittsburgh named Maxine Williams. Slender and pert, she was drawing crowds at the Onyx singing offbeat numbers like Joyce Kilmer's "Trees" in a soft, rhythmic, melodic style. "The characteristics which I consider important in singing," she told an interviewer, "are the way in which I hit notes—softly and without effort, a relaxed feeling at all times and a feeling for what I am singing." Claude Thornhill, pianist-arranger with a flair for fresh tonal sounds and novel instrumental combinations, generated the idea of her doing swing versions of two Scottish ballads: "Annie Laurie" and "Loch Lomond." Thornhill arranged, played, and produced the Vocalion record. It caught on and sold steadily, making listener demands for live presentations so constant that Maxine became known as the Loch Lomond girl. (Incidentally, the Sullivan surname became hers as a result of the credits on the Vocalion record, whose executive probably thought an Irish-sounding name more appropriate for a Scottish ballad.)

Although the record never made the Top Ten, it apparently sold so well that it became the center of a controversy in April 1938. In a front-page *Down Beat* story, singer Ella Logan charged that she was the first to swing old songs, not Maxine Sullivan. Months later Maxine simply denied that she had ever claimed to originate the concept. "Swinging the Classics" became widely controversial during 1938.

The death of Pulitzer Prize–winning novelist Edith Wharton was overshadowed by the death of Gershwin. On May 28, President Roosevelt pressed a telegraph button in Washington, D.C., that opened the long-awaited Golden Gate Bridge to automobile traffic. The first Pedestrian Day began twenty-four hours earlier when 200,000 people walked, strolled, or danced across the bridge.

In February, Ben Bernie, playing at the Cocoanut Grove in Los Angeles, took umbrage at a remark made by a reveler, and took a swing at the gent. In July Amelia Earhart and her plane were reported lost in the Pacific—and never located.

Count Basie offered a job to blues singer Helen Humes, who turned him down, but surrendered at the urging of John Hammond and sang with Basie for four years from 1937 on.

Hollywood made a film, *Fifty-Second Street*, with a nondescript score.

Mayor La Guardia outlawed burlesque in New York City.

Just as Fred Astaire and Ginger Rogers were Hollywood's dancing couple of the years, so William Powell and Myrna Loy were the quintessential romantic comedy couple.

On 52nd Street, Leon and Eddie was the top-grossing night club.

✦ 15 ✦

"One O'Clock Jump"
(1938)

"An evening of American Negro music shook the stage," Howard Taubman wrote in the *New York Times* on December 24, 1938, "the rafters and the audience at Carnegie Hall last night. It had a little of everything—and a lot of swing . . . There were Spirituals, Holy Roller hymns, harmonica playing, blues, boogie-woogie piano playing, early New Orleans jazz, soft swing and—finally without adjectives—swing."

The title of the program was *From Spirituals to Swing*, characterized in *The Black Perspective in Music* as a "landmark in the history of American music." Presented by the *New Masses*, it was conceived, produced, and hosted by John Hammond. It was dedicated to Bessie Smith, who was described in the notes by James Dugan and John Hammond as personalizing "the grandeur and warmth of Negro music."

The note-writers proceeded to mention the "automobile accident in Virginia [*sic*]" and added: "Taken to a hospital, she was denied admission because she was a Negro," a claim that was repeated later in the program notes: "They could play their last inhuman joke on her by turning her away from the white folks' operating table." These statements, later proven false, added fodder to the controversy, discussed in the previous chapter.

Divided into seven sections, the concert opened with recordings of African tribal music. The seven sections were named:

165

I. *Spirituals and Holy Roller Hymns*
   It included Sister Rosetta Tharpe, courtesy of the Cotton Club.

II. *Soft Swing*
   An ad hoc group that included Lester Young (tenor saxophone and clarinet—the latter given to him by Benny Goodman).

III. *Harmonica Playing*
   Sanford Terry of Durham, North Carolina, who was blind.

IV. *Blues*
   Included Joe Turner, James Rushing, and Helen Humes.

V. *Boogie-Woogie Piano Playing*
   Albert Ammons, Meade "Lux" Lewis, Pete Johnson (Hammond had been looking for Lewis, who recorded his own "Honky-Tonk Train Blues" in the early twenties, for over five years—and finally found him washing cars in a Chicago South Side garage).

VI. *Early New Orleans Jazz*
   Sidney Bechet and His New Orleans Feet Warmers.

VII. *Swing*
   Count Basie and His Orchestra, Basie's Blue Five, and the Kansas City Six.

"A good time was had by all," Taubman observed, "except, perhaps, by the manager of Carnegie Hall, who might have been wondering whether the walls could come tumbling down."

In 1938 the black influence in popular music manifested itself in a number of ways. "Boogie Woogie," composed by Clarence ("Pinetop") Smith and first recorded by him in 1928 as "Pinetop's Boogie Woogie," was recorded by Tommy Dorsey and His Orchestra and sold a million copies. "Yancey's Special" (music by Meade Lux Lewis; words by Andy Razaf), introduced by pianist Lewis and dedicated to Jimmy Yancey, was featured by Bob Crosby and His Orchestra, with Bob Zurke on piano.

The boogie numbers performed by Dorsey, Lewis, and Crosby anticipated a boogie-woogie craze that swept popular music in 1939 and the early forties. The craze, involving the Andrews Sisters, Will Bradley's Orchestra, and pianists Freddie Slack and Bob Zurke, was stimulated in part by the Boogie Woogie Trio who appeared at the "Spirituals to Swing" concert and later made recordings and went on a cross-country tour.

The big bands featured a flock of bluesy numbers: "Gin Mill Blues," introduced by jazz pianist Joe Sullivan in 1933 and showcased by Bob Crosby and His Orchestra; "Good Morning Blues" (words and music by Count Basie, Ed Durham, and James Rushing), introduced by Count Basie and His Orchestra; "Jeep's Blues" (music by Edward Kennedy Ellington and Johnny Hodges), introduced by the Duke and recorded by Johnny Hodges and His

Orchestra in a best-selling Vocalion record; "Ol' Man Mose" (words and music by Louis Armstrong and Zilner Randolph), introduced by Armstrong with a best-selling record by Eddy Duchin with his orchestra, vocal by Patricia Norman; and "Steppin' into Swing Society" (music by Edward Kennedy Ellington; words by Irving Mills and Henry Nemo), introduced by the Duke.

The most important of the black songs was "One O'Clock Jump," music by William "Count" Basie, the theme of his orchestra, a favorite of the Goodman band, and later a million-selling record for Harry James and His Orchestra.

In the genre of black jive, Slim and Slam (Bulee "Slim" Gaillard, guitar, and Leroy "Slam" Stewart, bass) produced three novelties that became popular. "Tutti-Frutti" was written by Doris Fisher and Slim Gaillard, and a song with the weird title "Vol Vist Du Gaily Star" was the work of Gaillard and Bud Green. The most successful of the three was "The Flat Foot Floogie (With the Floy Floy)," a riff with words whose meaning was quite elusive, but whose sound made it a jazz standard and a pop hit. It was written by Gaillard, Stewart, and Green, and made them 52nd Street favorites at Kelly's Stable and the Hickory House. With the sponsorship of Martin Block, then the kingpin of *Make Believe Ballroom*, they began recording for Vocalion, cutting "Flat Foot Floogie" on February 17, 1938. (Much later, in 1946, Gaillard created "Cement Mixer (Put-ti, Put-ti)," a song that was improvised when they lacked a fourth side for a date at the time he heard a cement mixer doing its put-put-put outside the studio.)

Gaillard was a gangling giant of a man with a droll sense of humor on stage and off. A natural musician as well as a natural clown, he played the piano with the back of his hands and the vibraphone with swizzle sticks. He could play "Jingle Bells" on a snare drum, producing the pitches by sliding the fingers of one hand along the drumhead as he beat out the rhythm with the other. He and Slam were one of the hottest vocal-instrumental duos of the thirties and forties until World War II broke them up. A comic genius of jazz like Fats, Slim, whose favorite song was "Any Time, Any Place, Anywhere," has said: "I love to—I live to—improvise the impromptu." Slam's hot jazz ingredient was humming obligato to bass strums and slap.

Of the new artists who made their debut in 1938, few stirred as much excitement as the Andrews Sisters. The Supremes of the thirties and forties, they were of Greek extraction and came from Minneapolis: Patti (b. 1920), Maxene (1918–1995), and La Verne (1915–1967). In the early thirties, they toured in vaudeville with the Larry Rich Band. But after playing clubs, theatres, and radio, their careers were given a tremendous lift when their management was undertaken by music publisher Lou Levy, the recipient of a Songwriter Guild award. Their rise into the big time came with their 1938 recording of "Bei Mir Bist Du Schoen," a 1932 Yiddish popular song with music by Sholom Secundo and an English lyric by Saul Chaplin and Sammy Cahn—it was Cahn's first song. In 1938, Priscilla Lane sang the ballad in the Warner Bros. film *Love, Honor and Behave*. Two weeks at No. 1 on *Your Hit Parade*, "Bei Mir Bist Du Schoen" was the No. 3 sheet-music seller of the year and sold a million copies of the Andrew Sisters' disk.

The sisters are remembered for a large number of resounding hits. The raucous "Boogie Woogie Bugle Boy" (music by Don Raye; words by Hughie Prince) was introduced by them in an Abbott and Costello film, *Buck Privates*, and became an Academy Award nominee. Other hits include "Rum and Coca-Cola," "I Can Dream, Can't I?," "Pistol Packin' Mama," "Don't Fence Me In," with Bing Crosby, and "Christmas Island," with Guy Lombardo. The Andrews Sisters had verve and a jazzy, shrill kind of sound, leaning toward numbers that swung, but they also achieved appealing harmonies in the ballads.

The biggest song of the year, based on eight appearances in the No. 1 spot on *Your Hit Parade*, was "My Reverie." The words were by Larry Clinton, an arranger-composer who had evinced a talent for making pop versions of the classics. "My Reverie," adapted from a Claude Debussy theme, was one of the grand sheet-music sellers of the year.

The two songs that approached "My Reverie" in popularity were "Ti-Pi-Tin" and "A-Tisket, A-Tasket"—each occupying the No. 1 slot for six weeks. Introduced by Horace Heidt and His Brigadiers, Maria Grever's "Ti-Pi-Tin" was the No. 1 sheet music seller of the year and No. 2 in radio plays. The English lyrics, regarded as several notches below the quality of the music, were by Raymond Leveen.

"A-Tisket, A-Tasket" was adapted from a nursery rhyme by Ella Fitzgerald and Al Feldman, who wrote arrangements for the Webb Band. Recorded by the Chick Webb Band, which Fitzgerald led after the hunchback drummer's death in 1939, "A-Tisket, A-Tasket" helped popularize the band and enlarge Ella's audience, adding pop appeal to her jazz following. The song's acceptance was so great that it finished as the year's top radio tune. (In his Norton Lectures at Harvard in 1977, Leonard Bernstein stated that the same melodic motif ["A-Tisket, A-Tasket"] was used by children all over the world to tease each other. Research does not reveal very many instances of such musical universality cutting across cultures.) Ella Fitzgerald's great vocal charm was stilled by her death at age seventy-seven in 1996.

Frank Loesser (1910–1969) wrote songs for college shows. He attended CCNY, was a newspaper reporter, performed in vaudeville as a pianist-singer-caricaturist, and wrote special material for vaudeville acts before he became a professional songwriter and then one of the outstanding composer-lyricists of the Broadway musical theatre. In 1938, he collaborated with Hoagy Carmichael and Burton Lane to produce a number of outstanding songs. There were three songs with Hoagy: "Small Fry" was popularized in recordings by Johnny Mercer and Bing Crosby—the latter sang the cute song to thirteen-year-old Donald O'Connor, making his screen debut in *Sing You Sinners*. "Heart and Soul" was written as an independent number, yet it was interpolated in a 1938 movie short, *A Song Is Born*, by Larry Clinton and His Orchestra, and the following year Gene Krupa and His Orchestra played it in the film *Some Like It Hot*. "Two Sleepy People," perhaps the best-known of the three, was sung in *The Big Broadcast of 1938* by Bob Hope and Shirley Ross.

The biggest song Loesser was associated with in 1938 was "Says My Heart," with music by Burton Lane. It was introduced by Harriet Hilliard of Ozzie and Harriet in the film musical *Cocoanut Grove*. The song made No. 1 on *Your Hit Parade*, remaining in the top slot for four weeks, and was ranked No. 3 in radio performances for the year and No. 4 in sheet-music sales.

After a time, Loesser began writing his own music, becoming, like Irving Berlin, Harold Rome, and Cole Porter, among the few who were adept in creating melodies as well as lyrics. Like Berlin, he was also his own publisher, and produced a series of smash hits in the forties—"Baby, It's Cold Outside" was one—and several enormous Broadway musicals, including the great *Guys and Dolls* (1950) and an operatic-type show, *The Most Happy Fella* (1956). Chain smoking and martinis ended a brilliant career at an all-too-early age.

The show composers did their bit to enrich popular music during the year. Rodgers and Hart contributed "Falling in Love with Love," a lilting waltz, to a musical adapted from Shakespeare's *Comedy of Errors* and titled *The Boys from Syracuse*. Cole Porter's sole adventure into a serious subject, a musical satire on communism and American diplomacy, unexpectedly introduced the scintillating Mary Martin to Broadway audiences. Although she had a minor role in *Leave It to Me!*, she stopped the show with "My Heart Belongs to Daddy," sung in a baby-like voice (typical of flapper theatrics in the twenties) while she simulated a striptease.

The last film George Gershwin worked on before the operation for a brain tumor that cost him his life was *The Goldwyn Follies of 1938*. Two memorable hits emerged from the score. "Love Walked In" and "Love Is Here to Stay" were both introduced by Kenny Baker. "Love Walked In" was on *Your Hit Parade* for fourteen weeks and zoomed to No. 1, where it remained for four. "Love Is Here to Stay" was reportedly incomplete at Gershwin's death, and its twenty bars were developed (sans credit) into the finished song by his good friend Vernon Duke.

One of the most beautiful ballads of 1938 was "September Song," composed by Kurt Weill to a poetic lyric by playwright Maxwell Anderson for the musical *Knickerbocker Holiday*. It was one of the first Broadway shows that used a historical setting to comment on contemporary issues. Set during the reign of Governor Peter Stuyvesant in New Amsterdam in the mid-seventeenth century, it concerned itself with the problem of democracy versus totalitarianism. The dictatorial Stuyvesant was played by Walter Huston, father of director/writer John Huston, with such charm that audiences found themselves drawn to his untenable ideas. Huston had a nasal, husky voice and was not a singer, but he half-recited, half-sang "September Song"—voicing his fears of growing old as he thought of the young girl he was about to marry—with such depth of feeling that he stopped the show each evening. (When Weill learned that Huston was to play Stuyvesant, he telegraphed him in Hollywood, inquiring the range of his voice. To which Huston replied: "No range—no voice.") Huston's recording of "September Song" remains a masterpiece, although Bing Crosby had a best-seller of the song on Decca, as did Stan Kenton. In the motion picture adaptation of *Knickerbocker Holiday*, the eloquent ballad was sung by Nelson Eddy. But when they needed a recurrent theme for the non-musical film *September Affair*, starring Joan Fontaine and Joseph Cotten (Paramount, 1951), they used Walter Huston's rendition on the soundtrack.

Among the songs that Bing Crosby introduced in 1938 was "I've Got a Pocketful of Dreams" (music by James V. Monaco; words by Johnny Burke) in the film *Sing You Sinners*. With Crosby's recording drawing extensive plays, it went to No. 1 on *Your Hit Parade* for four weeks and was reportedly the No. 1 sheet-music seller of the year. Crosby also popularized a song that had been written fifteen years earlier in 1923, titled "Mexicali Rose" (music by Jack Tenney; words by Helen Stone). Plugged on the radio in 1926 by the Cliquot Club Eskimos, it became a stereotype of songs about Mexico and its women because of its frequent use in westerns. After Crosby revived it as a popular song, Gene Autry made a film titled *Mexicali Rose* (1934), while Roy Rogers used it in *Song of Texas* (1943). In 1931, Autry starred in a Republic film titled *(There's a) Gold Mine in the Sky*, based on a song of the same name by those purveyors of saccharine sentiment couched in cliché street language—newspaper columnists Charles and Nick Kenny.

One rather unusual song from 1938 was "You Go to My Head" (music by J. Fred Coots; words by Haven Gillespie). It was introduced by the Casa Loma Band, with Kenny Sargent—later Lombardo's vocalist—singing. A song of unusual length, it was also characterized by a melody that made large leaps and spanned more than the usual octave and three or four notes. Frank Sinatra made it a favorite, while Perry Como's conductor, Mitch Ayer, used it as the theme for his orchestra.

The other unusual hit of 1938 was "Jalousie," a number that was written twelve years earlier by a Danish composer, Jacob Gade, who called his selection "Tango Tzigane." Arthur Fiedler and the Boston Pops took a shine to it, and it became the first million-selling disk of a light orchestral piece. It is said that more than two hundred recordings have been made of it throughout the world.

The summer of 1938 was a historic time in popular music and jazz, not unlike the time of Benny Goodman's appearance at the Palomar in Los Angeles. It was the period that saw the launching of the Big Band Era on 52nd Street.

The "stages" of the clubs on Swing Street were really not made for aggregations of twelve to fifteen musicians. Originally functioning as basement servant quarters—several steps down—of townhouses of the wealthy, they were narrow and so small that sixty people at postage-stamp tables jammed the place. Add the heat and humidity of New York summer to cigarette and cigar smoke and the situation was nearly intolerable.

But as Willard Alexander, manager of the Count Basie Band, has told it, "By the summer of 1938 there seemed no place for Basie to go." Unable to book him into any of the big Eastern rooms, for reasons they could not understand—color was not the explanation since they did book Ellington, Cab Calloway, Louis Armstrong—they were unable to transform a working band into a name band.

"Then I got the idea of putting him on 52nd Street," Alexander said. "It was crazy. The clubs couldn't accommodate a big band on those stands, and they were so small fourteen men would blow the walls out."

Desperate, Alexander approached the two owners—who were doing no business in the summer heat—with the proposition that he would install air-conditioning if they booked Basie. The Famous Door owners bought it, and Basie hit pay dirt.

"And how he did hit! He was a resounding smash," Alexander recalled, "from the moment he struck the first opening notes on the piano—splink, splank! The lines began forming and it was SRO the entire time. All his men were star soloists. But there was no band that played with the coordination and presence of Basie's. Those guys didn't play together. They used to breathe together. That's what gave the band its fantastic punch, no matter how softly they played . . . in that small space, fourteen men played as one! You could feel the pulsations inside you. We had a CBS wire, and soon people all over the country were sitting in on the birth of a great band!"

Jazz historian Charles Edward Smith was among those who cannot forget "Count Basie's fourteen men playing 'King Porter Stomp' with such steam that the leader's hands dropped off the piano and he sat listening to them with a slight, incredulous smile."

In 1938, Benny Goodman gave a precedent-shattering concert at Carnegie Hall, after which Gene Krupa left the band to form his own. Goodman also played Mozart with the Budapest String Quartet. But Artie Shaw's band was voted No. 1 over Goodman's in *Down Beat's* annual poll. Shaw's rise was powered not only by a sensational engagement in Boston but by his two-sided hot version of Cole Porter's exotic "Begin the Beguine." Billie Holiday became the first black vocalist featured with a white band when Shaw hired her after she left the Count Basie Band, a move that made headaches for both in 1938's prejudiced world. Billie later complained that she was too white for the Count Basie Band and too black for Shaw's. When the latter played the Hotel Edison in Manhattan, Billie was not allowed to enter through the main lobby; she had to use the delivery entrance in the rear. "I'll never sing with a dance band again," she said later, bad-mouthing both Basie and Shaw. A Carnival of Swing at Randall's Island in New York drew 24,000 fans who stayed for 5 ¾ hours and almost committed "destruction by admiration."

On October 30, Orson Welles presented a radio drama titled *War of the Worlds* over CBS. The script dealt with an imagined invasion of the earth by inhabitants of Mars. As the story unfolded and described an attack on the Pulaski Skyway in New Jersey, panic developed among listeners. Frantic phone calls came into the station and police were called out to cope with a crowd that besieged the CBS building. The actors and Welles were totally unaware of the uproar they were creating until the broadcast was over. It became one of the spectacular news stories of 1938, the jitteriness under-standable, perhaps, because of what was happening in Europe. Hitler cap-tured Vienna, a major intellectual center of the time. Mussolini aped Hitler and put a ban on music by Jews. Thomas Mann fled Germany and settled in the United States. In May, the House Un-American Activities Committee be-gan its scandalous witch-hunt under Texas Democrat Martin Dies.

"Cherokee" was never a hit in the traditional sense, yet it was quite pop-ular and developed into a standard. That was true of many tunes, particularly instrumental melodies in the Swing Era, and a natural consequence of the hundreds of bands making records and broadcasting.

"Cherokee" was the work of British bandleader Ray Noble, who intended to write a suite, with each section dedicated to a different Indian tribe. Though Noble had a sweet or dance band rather than a swing band, the first to record "Cherokee" was Count Basie, who made a two-sided, swingy ver-sion. Basie's disk so enchanted Charlie Barnet's young fiery arranger that Billy May knocked out the swingiest arrangement he could create. Because it featured a walloping tenor sax, Barnet's instrument, "Cherokee" soon be-came the band's theme. At the same time, Charlie Parker, an alto saxist with Jay McShann's band, began working with the harmonics to the tune. His version of it, "Ko Ko," in his Savoy recording, would be one of the great bebop classics of the forties.

"Undecided" was another instrumental that was never a hit but has out-lasted No. 1 songs on *Your Hit Parade.* "Undecided" was written by Charlie

Shavers, trumpeter-arranger with the slick John Kirby Sextet, a favorite of the 52nd Street scene. Once the Kirby group recorded the arrangement in 1938, it became a favorite with numerous instrumentalists, such as Red Norvo, and swing bands including Benny Goodman, who made a septet recording.

To name all the rhythm tunes that were part of this syndrome would require almost an entire book.

Van Alexander (1915–   )

Composer, author, and arranger Van Alexander was born May 2, 1915, in New York City. He was an arranger for Chick Webb, Paul Whiteman, Benny Goodman, Les Brown, and many others and formed his own orchestra in 1938, recording for Bluebird, Victor, and Varsity labels. He went on to score twenty-two motion pictures and numerous television segments.

Interview with Van Alexander

It was in the latter part of the thirties that I became involved with swing. In the early thirties, I was in high school, George Washington High in Manhattan. I studied harmony and other phases of music with Otto Cesana, who had a studio on 57th Street on the top of Aeolian Hall. In Los Angeles, I studied with Mario Castelnuovo-Tedesco. By 1936, I was doing arrangements for a number of bands, including Paul Whiteman, Les Brown, and Benny Goodman.

I got my start with Chick Webb through Moe Gale, who handled the band and was part owner of the Savoy Ballroom. Nothing really happened with the Webb band until "A-Tisket, A-Tasket" broke for a hit. In 1938, they were playing up in Boston at a place called Laveggio's Restaurant. I would travel up each week on the train, bringing three arrangements with me. Most of them were of popular tunes of the day. Very likely, the publishers were footing the bills for the arrangements, although I can't be sure of that. I had a deal with Moe Gale for $75 a week, which was a lot of money in those days to a young kid in his early twenties.

Ella Fitzgerald, who was also in her early twenties and was singing with the band, approached me with the idea of trying to do something with the old nursery rhyme, "A-Tisket, A-Tasket." I thought it was a good idea, but I was just too busy. Each week when I'd come up to Boston, she would be disappointed because I hadn't done anything with her idea. Finally, I told Chick about it and promised to bring an arrangement when I came up the following week.

In retrospect, I must admit that I had no idea that it would turn out as it did. It was strictly a novelty thing and I added extra lyrics for the guys in the band to shout out—"Was it red? Was it blue? Was it green?" A Robbins Music song-plugger, Leo Talent, was at the rehearsal when the band played it down. He phoned Abe Olman, who was the general manager, and suggested that he might want to get an air-check of a new number the band was doing called "A-Tisket, A-Tasket." I didn't know what we had. But everybody went crazy the minute they heard the thing. The first thing we knew, it made *Your Hit Parade* and other people began recording it. It went to No. 1 on the *Parade*, where it remained for seventeen weeks. It really established Ella and me and, of course, the Chick Webb Band.

As I talk to you, I'm looking up at the wall in my music room. It's now fifty years later [1988], and Chick's record was nominated for the Grammy Hall of Fame. They also gave me a plaque as the co-writer and arranger. It's satisfying to know that it has a lasting quality. It's still being played all over the world, as I can tell from performances listed on my ASCAP statements. I'm truly grateful to both Ella and Chick. I was a green kid just out of high school who used to go to the Savoy Ballroom to dance. In those days, it was known as the Home of Happy Feet.

I came to California in 1945, and in 1965 I did an album for Capitol Records in which I recreated the themes of the bands that played at the Savoy. It was called *The Home of Happy Feet*. Unfortunately, that name was not known to the majority of people around the country, so they re-issued it as *The Savoy Stomp*. It included "Let's Get Together," Chick's theme; Don Redman's "Chant of the Weed"; Teddy Hill's "Uptown Rhapsody"; Lucky Millinder's "Ride, Red, Ride"; and, of course, an instrumental version of "A-Tisket, A-Tasket." I had arranged for all of these bands as an offshoot of my work for Chick.

I really don't know how my tie-up with Webb happened. Being an *ofay* kid in Harlem was a little unusual. Chick had other arrangers, of course, like the marvelous Edgar Sampson and Charley Dixon. It was a wonderful opportunity for me. It's how I met Benny Goodman, for whom I did a number of charts. Chick would always say to other bandleaders, "Why don't you use the kid? He can write some great things." He was very unselfish.

He was a sweetheart to work with. The first arrangement I wrote for him was "Keeping Out of Mischief," a Fats Waller–Andy Razaf tune. The band would rehearse at the Savoy after they finished playing at 1:00 A.M. The guys would have something to eat and the rehearsal would start about 2:00. They had three or four arrangements before mine. This was my first chance and it got to be 4:30 or 5:00 A.M. Finally, they played my arrangement. In the meantime, my mother was phoning the police, worried that her young son was in Harlem at such an hour. I'll never forget that night. Chick offered me $5, asking if that was okay. I said, "Fine." I not only did the arrangement but copied the parts—which takes hours. I had done another tune and I was getting $5 for each. But I had to wait for Charley Buchanan, who was the manager of the Savoy, to give Chick the $10. It took another half hour to get hold of him. It was quite a night—and one that I will never forget.

Some of the great nights at The Track—as the Savoy was known to insiders—were the evenings when bands engaged in a battle of music. One of the most memorable was the battle between Benny Goodman and Chick Webb. It was May 11, 1937. Benny had Gene Krupa, Ziggy Elman, and all those top instrumentalists. Chick had his regular band. He would play three or four tunes, and then Benny would play an equal number. There were about five thousand people there that night. To get to the Savoy, you had to walk up a flight of stairs—it was on the second floor. People were crowding the bandstand and jumping up and down so that the floor was heaving. We thought that it would give way, and we'd all land in the basement. People were lined up for blocks, and the police were out in droves. The consensus was that Chick "cut" Benny that night. There was no voting. The decision was in the applause, but a lot of the critics agreed. It was a little incongruous to see the little hunchback drummer playing against Gene Krupa, who said himself that he didn't stand a chance against Webb.

After "A-Tisket, A-Tasket" happened, I was approached by Eli Oberstein of Victor Records. He was starting a little stable of songwriting bandleaders. Each of us was given $100 a week as a draw and then at the end of the year, they would split up whatever surplus was left. He managed to interest Larry Clinton and Les Brown, among others. But it was a wacky deal. However, $100 a week looked pretty good in 1938, and the idea that I could start my own band was attractive, not to mention recording for Bluebird/Victor. I took the deal and stayed with Victor for about a year, which was just about the time that Oberstein remained at Victor. He had to leave for some reason or other and then he started a Varsity label on which I made a number of sides.

For a while, the band did pretty well, almost all on the East Coast. We played a number of the big spots like the Paramount, Loew's State, and the Capitol. We did all the one-night stands through New England for the Shribman brothers. I was young, and bandleading was exciting. Moreover, I had just gotten married and my wife traveled with me.

In this period, I also did a lot of what were known inside the business as stock arrangements. These were published by the music publishers for use by average bands. To this day, when I go to a record session, I invariably run into a musician who remembers playing my stock arrangements. Publishers paid $100 for a tune; after a time I got $125 and $150. That work petered out when I moved to California.

The other night I had dinner with Benny Carter at the home of a friend. Jokingly I said to Benny, "I wonder what the guys at Brittwood's Café are doing?" Brittwood's was a watering hole near the Savoy Ballroom. Benny wondered how I could remember those days. I was not drinking then, except a bit of a wine called Muscatel. A few days ago, I was playing golf with Ray Brown and mentioned Brittwood's. He exclaimed, "My God, how old are you?" They were great days for me.

Benny Carter is a remarkable man. He is over eighty years old, and he's as active as a young man, God bless him. I don't know how he does it. He travels all over the world. He told me he was going on a concert tour of Europe and he had five arrangements to finish before the week was out. I think it's great. I don't mind talking about the past, as apparently he told you he does. It's part of your life. Why not talk about it? But I live in the present. I'm not as busy as I'd like to be. I play golf and I'm watching my grandchildren grow up—and, hopefully, to see them through college.

Incidentally, in the thirties, I didn't write only for black bands. I did arrangements for Kay Kyser, Bunny Berigan, Abe Lyman, Freddy Martin, and others. But Chick Webb and the Savoy Ballroom were like home base. When he died on June 16, 1939, the funeral was in Baltimore, his hometown. My wife and I drove down for the services. It was a real hot day in June, in the hundreds. We couldn't get anywhere near the chapel. Traffic was stopped for blocks around. Trolley cars were stalled, with people standing on top of them. It was as if the president of the country was being buried. Finally, I got hold of an officer, identified myself, and he got us through the crowd into the chapel. Ella sang "My Buddy" over the coffin, and there wasn't a dry eye in the place. The crying was audible. Teddy McRae, who played tenor in the band, played a solo. It was a most touching occasion.

I am grateful for my career in the music business, but will never forget how it all started with Chick and Ella at the Savoy Ballroom.

Medley 1938

On January 16, a casual passerby might have been surprised by the billboard in front of Carnegie Hall. It read: "S. Hurok Presents the First Swing Concert in the History of Carnegie Hall: Benny Goodman and His Swing Orchestra!" It was the first purely jazz concert held in the Taj Mahal of classical music— there were pickets. But they were protesting Goodman's having performed on behalf of the Spanish Loyalists. For jazz fans, it was a major event, and the Hall was sold out. Goodman was apprehensive about having yielded to the urging of the agency that promoted *The Camel Caravan*, Goodman's radio show. (Harry James cracked: "Tonight I feel like a whore in church.")

The concert was a triumph, reaching a rousing climax during a 12-minute version of "Sing, Sing, Sing." George T. Simon wrote in *Metronome*: "BG and his veritable virile vipers had, in the opinion of a record gate, cut to the core John Barbarolli and the Philharmonic Cats [the house band]." Critics who regularly covered Carnegie were not impressed and wrote smart-alec reviews. "A jam session is only a long cadenza," wrote Deems Taylor, "and cadenzas bore me."

A fan—Albert Marx, who married Goodman's vocalist Helen Ward in 1938—insisted on recording the concert. He gave a copy to Goodman, who promptly filed it away in the back of the closet where it was discovered by a daughter in 1950. Recognized as a legendary find, it was released and immediately became a tremendous seller as the sound of *Benny Goodman at Carnegie Hall.* It became one of the earliest recordings voted into NARAS's Hall of Fame.

Larry Clinton in 1938, after he had begun recording with his own band on Victor, transformed Debussy's "Reverie" into the hit "My Reverie," which he recorded with Bea Wain on the vocal. The following year, he helped revive Peter De Rose's "Deep Purple." Among the classics that he converted into pop hits was a theme from Tchaikovsky's *Romeo and Juliet,* which went to No. 1 on *Your Hit Parade* in 1939 as "Our Love" (music by Clinton; words by Clinton, Buddy Bernier, and Bob Emmerich).

One of the most unusual tributes paid to a songwriter by his colleagues occurred in 1938. Other writers—Richard Rodgers, for one—produced a lush list of hits. But no writer displayed the versatility, innovative freshness, musical growth, and scope (from "Swanee" to *Porgy and Bess*) of George Gershwin, whose sudden death in 1937 stunned the world.

The tribute took the form of an elegant book, edited and designed by Merle Armitage, an operatic impresario and writer of biographies of classical composers. Armitage encountered no dificulty in eliciting encomiums from the leading composers, songwriters, conductors, and critics. Among popular music figures who contributed memorial statements were Jerome Kern, Harold Arlen, Irving Berlin, Oscar Hammerstein II, Paul Whiteman, and Rudy Vallee. Indicative of the impact of Gershwin's work were panegyrics from Walter Damrosh, Arnold Schoenberg, Serge Koussevitsky, and George Antheil. What emerged in this tribute were the exuberance of Gershwin and his music and the brilliant embodiment in that music of the rhythmic vitality of the American tempo and spirit.

✙ 16 ✙

"Over the Rainbow"
(1939)

They were living in a Jersey City third-floor walk-up; his wife Nancy was working as a secretary at $25 a week to augment his meager earnings as a singer at the Rustic Cabin on Route 9W, the Jersey Post Road. He was jubilant that night in June 1939 when he came home with the news that he had been signed by Harry James as male vocalist at $75 a week.

Frank Sinatra's first appearance with the James band was at the Hippodrome Theatre in Baltimore during the week of June 30. He sang two numbers, "Wishing" and "My Love for You," without attracting any particular notice. Except for a three-week stay at the Atlantic City Pier, the James band spent the summer of '39 playing at the Roseland Ballroom on Broadway. There he received his first critical notice. Writing in *Metronome*, George T. Simon approved the "very pleasing vocals of Frank Sinatra whose easy phrasing is especially commendable." Later, Simon revealed that he had written the comment as a result of being pressured by the manager of the James band on behalf, not of the band, but of Sinatra. Subsequent notices—in an October *Billboard* when the band was playing at the Hotel Sherman in Chicago and in *Variety* of a James band recording—were lukewarm.

But in this period the James band recorded "All or Nothing at All" (August 31, 1939). Sinatra participated in six recording sessions with the band, all in 1939. By January 1940, he was singing with the Tommy Dorsey Band, the realization of a dream, for in those days every singer wanted to work with either Dorsey or Glenn Miller.

Popular recognition was gradually arriving for Harry Haag James (1916–86) of Albany, Georgia. His middle name came from the Mighty Haag Circus with which his mother worked as a trapeze performer and his father a bandleader. Starting with the "hot" drums in his father's band at six, he mastered the trumpet by ten and was soon conducting the second band for the Christy Brothers Circus. He attended school in Beaumont, Texas, where the family settled, and at fifteen was traveling with Joe Gales's Orchestra. In 1935, while he was working with Ben Pollack, he composed "Peckin'," which became a dance craze among youngsters and led to an association with Benny Goodman, in whose band he played lead trumpet 1937–39.

Shortly after he formed his own band in 1939—partly with a loan of $42,000 from Goodman—James recorded, on February 20, "Ciribiribin," a song originally written in Italy in 1898 by A. Pestalozza. It revealed James's amazing ability to reach high notes. The record was an immediate success and catapulted James into the ranks of star jazzmen. A later recording that added stature was "You Made Me Love You" in 1941, by which time he was in the big time. A sensational engagement followed at New York's Paramount Theatre early in 1943.

In the succeeding year, James appeared in films made on almost every lot, with 20th Century Fox signing him to a long-term contract in 1946. In the early 1950s, he fell in love with actress Betty Grable, whom he married—it was his second marriage—and with whom he played an extensive vaudeville tour in 1953; they were divorced in October 1965. He returned to playing until the year of his death, frequently in the major rooms of the Las Vegas Strip. The band's style was on the sweet side, with Harry's high-flying trumpet supported by a mass of strings. His repertoire was varied, including blues, boogie, Viennese waltzes, instrumental trumpet specialties, even classical compositions.

The Tommy Dorsey Band was celebrated for the attention it paid to vocals, nurturing the well-known Pied Pipers as well as Sinatra, who told *Metronome* that he "enjoyed his work with Dorsey because he saw to it that a singer is always given a proper setting."

Although the Dorsey Band could swing as well as the best of the big bands, it was notable for its handling of ballads. Unquestionably, it was the velvet-smooth, romantically sensuous sound of Dorsey's own horn—the horn of the Sentimental Gentleman of Swing, as he was known—that set the mood, enraptured his singers, and appealed to his audiences. "With the possible exception of Claude Thornhill," Simon has observed, "no other band played ballads so prettily, so effectively and so musically." Dorsey's musicianship and instrumental virtuosity won plaudits from all his associates, including Sinatra, with whom he was at odds—because both had violent tempers and also because of what it cost Sinatra to buy out his contract. Nevertheless, Sinatra always said: "Tommy taught me everything I knew about singing. He was my real education." What Sinatra credited Dorsey with especially was his mastery of breathing: "In the middle of a phrase," Sinatra observed, "while the tone was being carried through the trombone, he would take a quick breath through a sneak pinhole in the corner of his mouth, and play another four bars with that breath." The mooing lyricism of Dorsey's solos imparted to Sinatra's singing a flowing quality that was a unique and over-powering characteristic of his style.

A rich array of instrumentalists passed through the Dorsey Band before his accidental death in 1956. Among these were drummer Buddy Rich, pi-anist Joe Bushkin, clarinetist Buddy De Franco, trumpeters Ziggy Elman and Charlie Shavers, and arrangers Paul Weston, Sy Oliver, and Nelson Riddle.

(Alton) Glenn Miller of Clarinda, Iowa (1904–1944), whose band has been characterized as the most popular dance band of all time, witnessed the explosive acceptance of his band in 1939. Before he formed it early in 1937, he enjoyed the most extensive experiences possible for a musician in every phase of popular music-making. Growing up in Nebraska, Oklahoma, and Colorado, he worked as a trombonist with Boyd Senter (1912–22), attended the University of Colorado, played with Ben Pollack's star-studded band (1926) in Chicago, gigged with Red Nichols, Benny Goodman, and the Dor-sey Brothers, played in Broadway pit bands, toured with Smith Ballew as band director and arranger (1932–34), performed in the Dorsey Brothers Band (1934), and in early 1935 organized and joined Ray Noble's first U.S. band. He made recordings for the first time under his name with some Noble instrumentalists in the spring of 1935. He spent 1936 arranging for Glen Gray, Ozzie Nelson, and others, working on the radio with Freddie Rich and playing briefly with Vincent Lopez.

The band he organized early in 1937 possessed good personnel, recorded for Decca and Brunswick, played a solid engagement at the Blue Room in New Orleans' Hotel Roosevelt, toured, and broke up at year end, a financial flop.

Virtually unknown in 1938, he began attracting notice in 1939, when he developed a unique sound by using a high-register clarinet doubling lead over the tenor sax. It was ear-arresting, intriguing, and had musicians arguing about how he got the sound.

On April 10, 1939, he recorded "Little Brown Jug," using a Bill Finnegan arrangement of the old song written in 1869 by R. A. Eastburn (pseudonym for J. E. Winner). It became the first of a series of million sellers. The second was "In the Mood" (music by Joe Garland; words by Andy Razaf), recorded on August 1, 1939, and again a million seller that remained at the top of the jukebox chart for 21 weeks. The third and fourth were "Sunrise Serenade" (music by Frankie Carle; words by Jack Lawrence) and "Moonlight Serenade" (Glenn Miller; words by Mitchell Parish), both recorded in April 1939. Popular on both sides, the record reached a sale of over two million by 1944. "Moonlight Serenade," which was Miller's signature theme, started as an exercise he wrote while he was studying with Joseph Schillinger, whose mathematical approach was of great interest to the big bandleaders.

Although "Wishing," written by Buddy De Sylva and introduced in the nonmusical film *Love Affair*, was not a million seller for Miller, it was the fourth best-selling record, their best sheet-music seller, and No. 1 on *Your Hit Parade* for four weeks. One always thinks of De Sylva as part of De Sylva, Brown, and Henderson, but this was a song for which he alone wrote both words and music. In December 1939, Miller began a radio show for Chesterfield that ran until September 1942.

If 1939 was a good year for Glenn Miller, so was 1940, with "Pennsylvania 6–5000," "Tuxedo Junction," "Blueberry Hill," and "Falling Leaves." And 1941, with "Chatanooga Choo Choo," "A String of Pearls," "and "Elmer's Tune." In 1942, he had "I've Got a Gal in Kalamazoo," "Serenade in Blue," "Don't Sit Under the Apple Tree," "American Patrol," "Juke Box Saturday Night," and "Moonlight Cocktail." His band starred in the films *Sun Valley Serenade* and *Orchestra Wives*. The Sun Valley opus had Sonja Heine for box-office draw, while *Orchestra Wives* spotted film stars in the band—Cesar Romero on piano (Chummy MacGregor provided the off-camera fingers), Jackie Gleason on bass (Doc Goldberg doing actual sounds), and George Montgomery on camera as trumpeter Johnnie Best did the soloing.

In September of 1942, what was regarded as the best of the big bands broke up. Miller had decided to enlist in the Army Air Force. A captain at first, he was soon promoted to major, and directed a large AAF band with strings that broadcast regularly in the United States and recorded on V-discs, scoring with "St. Louis Blues March." Later, in the dark of the night of December 15, 1944, Miller and an AAF Colonel took off from England in a plane bound for Paris. It was in anticipation of the band's coming over later. The plane was reported missing and never found. Miller was declared dead on December 18, 1944.

In 1939, Artie Shaw had his fourth million-record seller, "Traffic Jam." Written by himself and Teddy McRae, it was recorded in Hollywood in June. It followed such other million sellers as Cole Porter's "Begin the Beguine," "Nightmare," and "Back Bay Shuffle," written by Shaw and Teddy McRae and recorded in 1938. But in 1939, Arthur Arshawsky (b. 1910 in New York), at the peak of his career, said: "I hate the music business"—and walked out on his band and headed for Mexico, leaving Tony Pastor in charge.

In 1940, Shaw came back with a new band including strings and scored a major record hit with "Frenesi." About the same time, he made hit records of "Star Dust" and "Moonglow," winning plaudits for his "Concerto for Clarinet." He was given a medical discharge from the Navy in 1944, after which he revived his big band. In the 1950s, he revived the Gramercy Five, a combo that had an intriguing sound as a result of his using jazz pianist Johnny Guarnieri on harpsichord. The most literate and best-read of the big bandleaders, he wrote a well-received autobiography, *The Trouble with Cinderella* (1952), and later, in 1965, wrote the novella *I Love You, I Hate You, Drop Dead*. The composer of many large-scale jazz numbers, he also functioned as a New York theatrical and film producer. Not the least of his accomplishments was his marriage to six of the most beautiful women and actresses of the day. In November 1952, Victor presented him with eight gold records to commemorate his twenty-one years with the label and the sale of over a million of each of the disks.

Woodrow Wilson Herman (1913–1987), better known as Woody Herman, was born May 16, 1913, in Milwaukee, Wisconsin, and cut his first million seller in April 1939. "Woodchopper's Ball," a fast blues, was a joint work by him and blues songwriter Joe Bishop. Working in a vaudeville troupe at the age of eight, Herman was known as "The Boy Wonder of the Clarinet." He joined Tom Gerun's Orchestra in 1929, sharing vocals with Tony Martin and Ginny Simms, after studying at the Marquette School in Milwaukee and gigging with local bands. A short stint with Harry Sosnick led to his joining Isham Jones, whose orchestra he conducted on Jones's retirement and organized on a cooperative basis in 1938. In 1946, he premiered Stravinsky's *Ebony Concerto* at Carnegie Hall and placed first in polls in the major jazz magazines. With shifts in his personnel and reorganization, Herman's Herd, as it became known, was voted best band in 1949. "Laura," the theme by David Raksin from the film of the same name (Johnny Mercer later wrote a superb lyric), was a million seller in 1945.

In 1939, the Benny Goodman aggregation was responsible for the popularization of several numbers. "Darn That Dream" (music by James Van Heusen; words by Eddie De Lange) was a standard that emerged from a swing version of Shakespeare's *A Midsummer Night's Dream*. The show was a thirteen-performance fiasco, despite the intervention of a black cast that included Louis Armstrong as Bottom, Butterfly McQueen as Puck, and Jackie "Moms" Mabley as Quince—and the playing of the Benny Goodman Sextet.

As 1939 progressed, more and more big bands were responsible for creating hits. Jimmy Dorsey's recording of "Deep Purple," was the No. 1 radio tune for three weeks, the No. 2 sheet-music seller, and the No. 3 jukebox winner of the year. It was just behind "Over the Rainbow" in the number of weeks it occupied the No. 1 spot—six weeks against "Rainbow's" seven.

Brother Tommy Dorsey and His Orchestra converted "Heaven Can Wait" (music by Jimmy Van Heusen; words by Eddie De Lange) into a *Hit Parade* leader. The vocal was by Jack Leonard, whose entry into the armed forces opened a berth for Frank Sinatra. "Heaven Can Wait" held the No. 1 spot on the *Parade* for two short weeks

Guy Lombardo and His Royal Canadians introduced and popularized "Penny Serenade" (music by Melle Weersma; words by Hal Halifax), a song written in England in 1938, when it was first heard in the United States. It became the top-ranking jukebox hit for eleven weeks. Ray Noble, with a big band in the Lombardo genre, composed and lyricized the elegant romantic ballad "The Very Thought of You" in 1934 when it was one of the Top Ten songs for fifteen weeks. It was revived in 1939, leading to a film of that title starring Faye Emerson and Dennis Morgan in 1944.

Larry Clinton, who had demonstrated a penchant for swinging the classics, introduced and popularized two adaptations. One was "The Lamp Is Low," adapted by Peter De Rose from Maurice Ravel's impressionistic, whole-toned scaled "Pavane pour une Infante Défunte" and lyricized by Mitchell Parish. The other was "Our Love," adapted by Clinton himself from Tchaikovsky's *Romeo and Juliet*. A top radio tune, it made No. 1 on *Your Hit Parade* for two weeks.

Insofar as adaptations went, Sammy Kaye and His Orchestra were chiefly responsible for making popular the classical composition "Avant de Mourir" by Georges Boulanger, adapted by English songwriter Jimmy Kennedy, with a lyric he titled "My Prayer." Although it never made No. 1, it was on *Your Hit Parade* for fourteen weeks, eventually reaching the No. 2 spot.

André Kostelanetz and His Orchestra—hardly a big band—popularized "Moon Love," a theme from Tchaikovsky's Fifth Symphony, which Kostelanetz adapted. Lyrics were added by Mack Davis and Mack David to create a song that went to No. 1 on *Your Hit Parade* for four weeks in 1939.

Paul Whiteman made a *Hit Parade* song of "Stairway to the Stars," based on a theme from "Park Avenue Fantasy," an instrumental composition by Matt Malneck and Frank Signorelli published in 1935, to which Mitchell Parish added words in 1939. "Stairway to the Stars" occupied the No. 1 spot on the *Parade* for four weeks.

The Latin trend previously observed persisted in 1939. "Brazil," a samba composed by Ary Barroso in 1939, did not make it until four years later, when an English lyric was added by the talented lyric writer, Bob Russell. Then it popped up in five films, including Walt Disney's full-length animated cartoon *Saludos Amigos* (1942), and it was recorded by Eddy Duchin, Jimmy Dorsey, and, of course, Xavier Cugat.

Jimmy Kennedy was involved in the creation of "South of the Border (Down Mexico Way)," which he wrote with Michael Carr for Gene Autry, whose recording reportedly sold three million copies in two years. But it also provided the title and musical theme for an Autry film (Republic, 1939). The outstanding sheet-music seller and fifth best-selling record of the year, it made No. 1 on *Your Hit Parade* for five weeks. Shep Fields and His Rippling Rhythm cut an attractive recording using typical Mexican instruments and rhythms.

A curious hit emerged from a film, *Balalaika*, in which the Russian Art Choir and Ilona Massey introduced "At the Balalaika" (music by George Posford; words by Bob Wright and Gregory "Chet" Forrest). The selection originated in England and the original music by Posford was adapted by Herbert Stothart and the original lyrics superseded by those of Bob Wright and Chet Forrest. The song made *Your Hit Parade* for nine weeks without ever rising above No. 3.

Another import came from Czechoslovakia. Written by Jaromir Veivoda as "Skoda Lasky," meaning "Lost Love," it was anglicized as "Beer Barrel Polka" (!) by Lew Brown in 1934 and was made a million seller by Will Glahe and His Orchestra in 1938. With performances and recordings by Sammy Kaye and His Orchestra, and the exuberant Andrews Sisters, it became the No. 5 sheet-music seller and the No. 1 jukebox song, remaining a jukebox favorite for twenty weeks. Its popularity increased—as might be expected—during the tensions of World War II.

James Kern Kyser (Kay Kyser) (1906–1985) was born in Rocky Mount, North Carolina, on June 18, 1906. He had a band that could play jive and jump numbers as well as sweet. Kyser organized his first band at college in his home state, and emphasized comedy, both in his own style and that of the band. Attired in cap and gown, he hosted an extremely popular radio show called "Kollege of Musical Knowledge." His ace trumpet player, Merwin Bogue, was a stuntman who went by the name of Ish Kabibble. Kyser and his band appeared in as many as eight films in the forties, including *Swing Fever* (1943), debuting in 1939 in *That's Right You're Wrong*. Although it was introduced by Hal Kemp and His Orchestra, he had a million-selling Columbia record in a nonsense novelty, "Three Little Fishes," written by "Saxie" (Horace Kirby) Dowell. The number was so popular and so catchy that, according to reports, an inmate of the Kansas State Penitentiary killed another convict who would not stop singing it.

Another nonsense novelty popularized by Kyser in 1939 was "Scatterbrain" (words and music by Frankie Masters, Kahn Keene, Carl Dean, and Johnny Burke), performed by the band in their debut film. But this novelty was also frequently performed by Frankie Masters and His Orchestra, whose theme it became, and the bands of Benny Goodman and Freddy Martin. One of the top radio tunes of 1939, it also made No. 1 on the jukebox chart and *Your Hit Parade*, where it held the top spot for five weeks at the end of 1939 and the beginning of 1940. It was used as a big production number in the Judy Canova comedy film *Scatterbrain* (1940).

Kyser had the most catchy recording of "Friendship," a mock hillbilly number Cole Porter wrote for the musical *Du Barry Was a Lady* that was a show-stopper for Ethel Merman and comic Bert Lahr.

They were employed as porters at New York's Paramount Theatre when their big break came. Until then, they had been working up arrangements that were hot and jivey. They even played England with the Jack Rhythm Band in the mid-30s without making much of an impression. Then they changed to a slow ballad style in which high tenor Bill Kenny sang a chorus sweetly and was followed by bass-voiced Orville "Happy" Jones, slowly talking the words over soft background harmony by the group. The gimmick was a winner—and gave them their first hit when an agent heard them rehearsing in between their Paramount chores and arranged for them to make a Decca record, "If I Didn't Care," a Jack Lawrence ballad. They scored their first million seller in a duet with Ella Fitzgerald on "Into Each Life Some Rain Must Fall" (music by Doris Fisher; words by Allan Roberts) in 1944. On their own, they cut a gold disk in 1946 of "To Each His Own," a song discarded from the film of the same name. Together with the Mills Brothers, the Ink Spots were the first black artists to cross the color line and make it on radio.

On October 11, 1939, tenor saxist Coleman Hawkins—"Bean," to his friends, because of his love for every kind of bean—reluctantly entered the recording studios of RCA Victor to record a song that had become the talk of his appearance at Kelly's Stable on 52nd Street. It was the torch ballad introduced by Libby Holman in the movie *Three's a Crowd*. As he tells it, "At Kelly's Stable, sometimes at night, after a couple quarts of Scotch, very late, I'd sit down and kill time and play about ten choruses of 'Body and Soul.' And then the boys would come in and play harmony notes in the background until I finished up. That's all there was. But then Leonard Joy of Victor came in the club and asked me to record it. I said, 'Why?' I didn't even have an arrangement on it."

What Hawkins captured in his late-hour performances was the sense of broken love affairs, of loneliness and longing. To express that feeling of bittersweet emotion on a record without the club atmosphere and the Scotch was a challenge. Bean rose to it. The record became one of the first solo jazz disks that sold over a million and contributed to his recognition at the No. 1 tenor-sax soloist in polls in *Esquire*, *Down Beat*, and *Metronome*. It also gave stature to the song that led Big Nick Nicholas, an associate of Bobby Short, to say in 1986: "In the old days if you couldn't play 'Body and Soul,' you didn't work."

Until Lester Young (1909–1959) and his cool tenor succeeded Coleman Hawkins in the Fletcher Henderson Band around 1933, Hawkins's full-bodied brawny tenor was regarded as the acme of the instrument's sound. Before he made his debut with Mamie Smith's Jazz Hounds, Coleman Hawkins (1904–69) of St. Joseph, Missouri, played the piano at five, the cello at seven, the sax at nine, and studied music theory at Washburn College in Topeka, Kansas. After working with Wilbur Sweatman's band and in various Harlem night spots, he joined Henderson for a ten-year sojourn, 1923–33, playing the Club Alabam and Roseland Ballroom between 1923 and 1927. Forming his own combo in 1933 with Henry (Red) Allen on trumpet, Horace Henderson on piano, and J. C. Higginbotham on jazz, he toured Europe in a package with the noted bandleader Jack Hylton. After recording "Body and Soul," he soloed with small combos in New York and Los Angeles, and later with Jazz at the Philharmonic, reaching a peak of popularity by 1945. Unlike many members of his generation, he was not opposed to bop and worked with some of the top bopsters. He left a rich legacy of recordings on a variety of labels, including Apollo, Keynote, HMV, EMI, Savoy, Capitol, and Victor.

In popular music, 1939 was a year not only of legendary songs but legendary performances. The biggest hit by far was the rangy ballad that came out of the film *The Wizard of Oz*, "Over the Rainbow" (music by Harold Arlen; words by E. Y. Harburg). It helped establish the film as a classic, and its singer, Judy Garland, then only sixteen years old, as a star of the first magnitude. Her recording with the backing of Victor Young's Orchestra was a million seller. "Over the Rainbow" went on to win the Academy Award for Best Song. It was No. 1 on *Your Hit Parade* for more weeks—seven—than any other song that year.

The high point of E. Y. Harburg's creativity in the thirties came, of course, with *The Wizard of Oz*. Even apart from that great standard "Over the Rainbow," there is hardly a song from the film that does not sound in one's mind the moment its title is mentioned: "We're Off to See the Wizard," "Ding Dong, the Witch Is Dead," and so on. What Harburg emphasizes about the score is that Harold Arlen and he were writing "not just songs but scenes . . . not just thirty-two-bar songs but what would amount to the acting out of entire scenes, dialogue in verse and set to Harold's modern music. . . . Things like the three lullaby girls . . . and the Coroner, who came to avow that the Witch was dead. . . . All that was thought up by us, it wasn't in the book. Even a thing like 'Over the Rainbow'—there was no such thing as a rainbow mentioned in the book.

"When we brought in the song, all we were thinking about was a little girl who was in trouble with her folks, in conflict with them, at an age when she wanted to move away, and knowing that somewhere, someplace, there was a colorful land that wasn't this arid flat plain of Kansas. . . . That gave them the idea of doing the whole first part of the picture—when she's in Kansas—in sepia, black, and white, and then when she got to Munchkin Land, the fairyplace, it became colorful. The whole new country was rainbow country." (Harburg told an audience at New York's 92nd Street Y that Arlen used as the middle strain of the song a whistle with a distinctive trill that he generally employed in summoning his dog.)

The year 1939 had few show tunes that became popular, doubtless because of the limited number of musicals being produced. But Rodgers and Hart created a gem in "I Didn't Know What Time It Was" from *Too Many Girls*, a musical about football and the college scene. Richard Kollmar and Marcey Wescott introduced the burnished ballad that eschewed the A-A-B-A structure and instead pursued an A-A^1-B-A^2 setup.

In glancing back at the songs appearing in 1939—and for that matter through the thirties—"[They] Didn't Know What Time It Was" might be considered a cogent comment. Despite the show that dealt with sociological and political themes, and an occasional oblique reference in film and Tin Pan Alley songs, popular music displayed limited awareness of what was to come. Not even the appearance of Mussolini on the cover of *Life* seemed to fully arouse the creators of popular music to the bloody and violent era the world was edging into.

Mitchell Parish (1900–1993)

Born in Shreveport, Louisiana, on July 10, 1900, but raised in New York City, Parish turned from an early interest in medicine to songwriting when Irving Mills offered him a job as a staff writer at Mills Music. Reportedly the writer of more than a thousand lyrics, he achieved a dazzling number of standards, mostly on words he added to extant instrumental melodies. It was a pattern initiated by his fantastic success with the lyric he wrote to Hoagy Carmichael's hit melody, "Star Dust," in 1929. He also displayed a penchant for using nature imagery—stars, wind, rain, moonlight—as romantic settings.

After twenty-five years of being away from the academic world, he began attending New York University, was elected to Phi Beta Kappa in his junior year (1949), and was graduated summa cum laude (1950).

Interview with Mitchell Parish

Yes, I guess 1939 was a blockbuster year for me—with "Deep Purple," "The Lamp Is Low," "Lilacs in the Rain," "Moonlight Serenade," and "Stairway to the Stars." Peter De Rose and I each received the *Hit Parade* award for "Deep Purple" as the best popular song of 1939.

I did "Moonlight Serenade" to a melody of Glenn Miller's. Today, it's a very big standard. It's as big a standard as "Star Dust." Well, I don't know, let's put it this way: it's a standard. There's no question about that. Glenn wanted the lyricist of "Star Dust" to write the words to his melody, and he came to me and asked me to write the lyric.

As for "Deep Purple," Peter De Rose and I were both on the staff of Robbins Music. We wrote a few songs together, and I liked the melody. It was introduced on the radio as a concert piece some time in 1934 by Paul Whiteman. With my lyric, it became a best-seller for Larry Clinton and His Orchestra on Victor Records, with Bea Wain doing the vocal. "Deep Purple" was not only the biggest song of the year, it was also No. 1 for seven successive weeks on *Your Hit Parade* in 1939.

I know that many people did not find it easy to work with Jack Robbins, the head of Robbins Music. I got along with him very well because he respected me and I respected him. He did have his little tantrums. He had a habit of calling everybody "son-of-a-bitch," including his own sons. So nobody took him seriously in that respect. He couldn't stand incompetence or carelessness. He had no patience with such people, and he was not above telling them they were incompetent. That did not endear him to people. We got along because I wouldn't stand for his shenanigans. I refused to "yes" him. If I didn't agree with him, I would tell him so. What he couldn't stand was people who "yessed" him all the time—sycophantic people who wanted to curry his favor and avoid ruffling his feathers. They would agree with him on everything, and he didn't like that. Of course, it was not just a matter of disagreeing, but of having a reason for it. He could respect such disagreement. I got along with him because I wouldn't take any nonsense from him. Of course, I was in a position where I didn't have to take it. I was not working on a salary where he could fire me. I was in a position to think independently, and I spoke my mind.

On foreign songs, I would rather be able to work from the plain melody and not be tied to a foreign idea. As an example, "Take Me in Your Arms" (1932) was a big hit in Germany under the title 'Liebe War Es Nie,' which means, "It Never Was Love." When I got it, I discarded the German title and the whole idea. I regarded the tune as if it had just been written. I prefer to do that with all foreign songs, treat the melody as an independent thing.

I did the same thing with "Bolero," a tune from France—not Ravel's Bolero. I disregarded the title completely, and the idea. With me, it became "All My Love," and it made it with that title on the *Hit Parade* with a Patti Page record sometime in the fifties.

One of the first instrumentals for which I wrote a lyric was Ellington's "Mood Indigo." You're probably surprised because if you check the credits on the song, you'll find three names: Duke Ellington, Irving Mills, and Barney Bigard. My name is not on it. In fact, Ellington recorded it under the title "Dreamy Blues" before I was asked to write the lyric—which I did without getting credit. You see, it was during the Depression years (1931), and I didn't then have a good bargaining position. I was married and had two kids, and I depended on the publisher for the bread on our table. I want to make it clear that Duke Ellington had absolutely nothing to do with this. I also wrote the lyric to "Blues in My Heart" that year, and the credits on that song read: Words and music by Benny Carter and Irving Mills.

I resented the fact that I wasn't receiving credit for what I was writing. It was demeaning, but because of my circumstances, I had to agree not to have my name on the song. "Mood Indigo," as you know, had three names on it; the publishers claimed they didn't want a fourth. The result was that I decided that I had to emancipate myself from this kind of situation. So I went and took a Civil Service exam—I have a law background—for a position in the Criminal Courts of New York. I came out on top of the list, and I got a job as a Court Officer. Now I didn't have to accept terms I didn't like. The regular salary emancipated me. "Mood Indigo" served a purpose: I might not have taken the Civil Service exam otherwise. I kept the job for ten years before I resigned. It was an interesting job, and I got to know all the city's judges and many famous people like Tom Dewey, La Guardia, and others. They knew I was writing songs, and one of the judges once asked me to write a song about the courts. I told him: "You tell me what there is to sing about the court, and I'll write a song about it."

When it came to publishers, I didn't play the whole field. I was loyal to two sets of publishers: Jack Mills at Mills Music and Jack Robbins at the Big Three, the Metro-Goldwyn firm of Robbins, Miller, and Feist. I did place a few songs with others like Irving Berlin's company, Shapiro-Bernstein, Remick and Forster Music in Chicago. But they were isolated songs. The bulk of my catalogue was with Mills Music and Robbins. Even today when I look back at the music publishing business, I think of Jack Mills and Jack Robbins as the best publishers of the period. With all his foibles, Jack Robbins was a very good music man, very fine, colorful—and the same for Jack Mills. They were inspirational publishers.

Today's music publishing field is a cold business. But in those days, if you brought Mills or Robbins a song they liked, they'd enthuse about it. They'd call in their secretaries, their shipping clerks, and their staff, and they'd act excited. They'd comment on how great the song was, and they made you feel like writing your best. It was like a paternalistic thing. You wanted to please them and be praised by them. And they'd work on a song—get recordings, arrange performances, take ads, and love it.

Apart from "Star Dust," I guess "Deep Purple" and "Sleigh Ride" [with Leroy Anderson] are my favorite songs. But I once wrote a little song called "Hands Across the Table." It's only 24 bars altogether—an 8-bar verse, and a 16-bar chorus. It does not follow the standard construction: 32 bars, with four segments of eight bars each. If I remember, it was introduced by Lucienne Boyer in *Continental Varieties*, a revue in 1934. It was not a smash hit or even a big standard. I think it's a little gem.

I have a few songs that should be bigger than they are. One of them is "Emaline," which I wrote with Frank Perkins and is usually identified with Mildred Bailey. I wrote "Stars Fell on Alabama" with Perkins, too. It became a favorite of Jack Teagarden—you know, the singing trombonist.

Even though you're concerned with the thirties, I'm sure you will want to mention the show currently on Broadway that's based entirely on my lyrics [*Stardust*, 1987]. It's quite unusual to have a show oriented around a lyricist and not a composer.

You know, Willie Nelson has an album called *Star Dust*, which has been on *Billboard*'s album chart for ten years. I believe that's a record. He did a concert recently at the Westbury Music Fair. He brought me on stage and we both received a plaque. And Barry Manilow just recorded the ballad in his new album, *Swing Street*. Maybe the thirties are coming back, and, even if they aren't, many of the great songs of those years have never died.

Medley 1939

Film historians agree that Hollywood's creative energies peaked in 1939, an *annus mirabilis*—"twelve months of magic," in the words of *Time*—that produced *Gone With the Wind, Mr. Smith Goes to Washington, Ninotchka, Stagecoach, Goodbye Mr. Chips, Dark Victory, Wuthering Heights*, and, among others, the musical fantasy *The Wizard of Oz*.

Nat King Cole, later the superlative singer, launched his celebrated trip in which he played jazz piano in Los Angeles in 1939. A follower of Earl Hines, whom he heard and studied at the Grand Terrace in Chicago where he was raised, he played an arresting single-note melodic style. With his Trio, which functioned until he went solo in 1950, he made 115 sides, registering "Straighten Up and Fly Right" in 1942 as their first hit.

Having sung with Paul Whiteman, Willard Robison, and the Saturday Night Swing Session, Lee Wiley (1915–1975?) began making records with small jazz groups, mostly of the Dixieland persuasion. Her choice of repertoire largely favored show tunes, and with her sensitive reading of lyrics and throaty voice, she quickly became a favorite vocalist of show composers like Richard Rodgers, Cole Porter, George Gershwin, Harold Arlen, and others.

Among the numbers that originated with a band—usually written by a member—was "And the Angels Sing," No. 1 on *Your Hit Parade*, popularized by the Benny Goodman Band. In its origin, "And the Angels Sing" was a traditional melody played at Jewish functions for a happy, whirling dance known as the hora. The tune was brought to Goodman by Ziggy Elman, a high-flying trumpeter (born Harry Finkelstein), found by Goodman playing in a band on the Atlantic City Pier. Goodman interested Johnny Mercer in writing the lyrics. While Elman and his high-register notes made an instrumental *fralich* recording for Bluebird, Goodman made the best-selling swing version with Elman doing the solo.

In 1939, Billy Strayhorn joined Duke Ellington, becoming his collaborator and alter ego, and Chick Webb laid down his drumsticks for good.

The limited invasion of politics and sociology into the music scene found expression in 1939 in two events. "Franklin D. Roosevelt Jones," a song by Harold J. Rome in the musical revue *Sing Out the News*, won a special ASCAP award. The second was the Hollywood opening of a liberal or leftist revue, *Meet the People*. Edward Eliscu was responsible for the skits, Jay Gorney wrote the music, and both collaborated on songs like "Union Label," "The Same Old South," "Jitterbug," and "Chi Chi Castenango." It opened one year later at the Mansfield in New York, the same night as *Pal Joey*, and was only mildly successful.

On January 3, 1939, the jumping Jimmie Lunceford Band recorded " 'Tain't What You Do" for the first Vocalion session. The song was by trumpeter-arranger Sy Oliver and singing trombonist Trummy Young of the band. Sy told George T. Simon that the idea was Trummy's, given to him one day at five A.M. when he returned to their room after a night of jamming.

"I must say," Sy said, "that it was one of his better five A.M. ideas, and so I wrote down the title on a sheet of paper and later stuck it in my briefcase and forgot about it. One day when we were off, I was sitting on the front porch of a rooming house in Knoxville, Tennessee, and I began rummaging through my case. I came across the title, and it really hit me, so I called Trummy, and that very afternoon we sat down and worked it out, and then I wrote the arrangement and brought it to the band." It became one of the Lunceford Band's most famous numbers and biggest selling disks.

There have been only three Broadway theatres named after songwriters. Two are the Gershwin and the Richard Rodgers, both of whom certainly warranted being memorialized in an area to which they contributed so much priceless music. The other (for a short period at 359 West 30th Street) was the Jack Lawrence, named after the man who bought it and whose catalogue of hits was created either in Tin Pan Alley or Hollywood, not on Broadway. Lawrence was born in Brooklyn in 1912. He possessed a good baritone voice sometimes heard on the radio, and wrote mostly lyrics. His first hit was "Play, Fiddle, Play" (1932), written to a melody by Arthur Altman and violinist and orchestra leader Emery Deutsch, and introduced by Deutsch, who used it as his radio theme with the A&P Gypsies.

Lawrence's two biggest hits were "If I Didn't Care," popularized in 1939 by the Ink Spots on a best-selling Decca disk, and "All or Nothing At All," recorded in 1939 by Harry James with a vocal by Frank Sinatra. The James record was moderately successful, but the song became a million seller when it was revived under Sinatra's name in 1943, shortly after one of his explosive appearances at the Paramount Theatre. The switch in billing was indicative not only of Sinatra's popularity but of a major turn in popular music from the era of the big bands to that of the big baritones, from the Swing Era to the Sing Era. As for the Ink Spots' recording of "If I Didn't Care," for which Lawrence wrote both words and music, it was their first big hit following a period when they worked as porters at the New York Paramount.

Epilogue

There were bands in the twenties and earlier, before the Big Bands of Swing, and there were bands afterwards. But no set of bands elicited the kind of adulation and affection as the group that included Glenn Miller, Benny Goodman, Artie Shaw, Count Basie, Tommy Dorsey, Jimmie Lunceford, and a host of other swingers. The big bands made the country's ballrooms bounce to a steady four beat and became the medium through which new songs were introduced and plugged into hits. Even today, reissues of these big bands sell in huge quantities; people are forever buying new books about them, and occasional appearances of bands run by alumni of the tradition are well attended.

The year 1935 was the initial *annus mirabilis* for the big bands not only because the Goodman Band launched the Swing Era but also because *Your Hit Parade* made its initial appearance on coast-to-coast radio. Before 1935, popular music and the country at large operated in the dark shadows of the Depression. The Swing Era created a togetherness for a people working to overcome the ravages of economic upheaval.

In the thirties, 52nd Street, emerging from the period of Judas-hole speakeasies and Prohibition raids, blossomed as Swing Street, a cognomen recently added to the emblems on lampposts at the corners of Fifth and Sixth Avenues.

During the thirties and forties, in the dozen or more clubs on the block, you could hear every type of combo and artist. "On 52nd Street," says jazz pianist Marian McPartland, then a Hickory House performer, "in several hours, nursing a few drinks, you could travel musically from New Orleans up to Harlem and Bop." Hit songs and artists like Billie Holiday, Art Tatum, and the Count Basie Band zoomed to stardom on the Street—as it was known to cab drivers and jazz aficionados.

In the thirties, films were flooded with songs—not only musical movies but feature films and even Westerns. Early in the decade, Hollywood drew heavily on the hit songwriters of Tin Pan Alley and the Broadway stage. Although the studios quickly developed a coterie of contract songwriters, through the decade a strong interaction existed between Hollywood and New York.

Broadway musicals turned a 45-degree angle during the thirties, from lightweight girl-meets-boy entertainment to a view of topical problems. The satire was sugarcoated, but each of the members of the golden ensemble of show-composers essayed a show with a sociological and political story.

The twenties had a kind of unified outlook embodied in the mores and morals of the flapper and the gangster. The image that most closely typified the music of the next decade was that of the name bandleader. But the thirties were a kind of transition period, struggling to cope with the problems of economic stringency and international dictatorship. The fruit of its efforts ripened in the forties.

No. 1 Songs—Your Hit Parade

1935

"Soon," 4/20—W: Ira Gershwin; M: George Gershwin; New World Music Corp.

*"Lovely to Look At," 4/27—W: Dorothy Fields & Jimmy McHugh; M: Jerome Kern; T. B. Harms Co.

**"Lullaby of Broadway," 5/4, 5/11—W: Al Dubin; M: Harry Warren; M. Witmark & Sons

"What's the Reason," 5/18, 5/25—W: Coy Poe & Jimmie Greer; M: Truman "Pinky" Tomblin & Earl Hatch; Bourne Co.

"Life Is a Song," 6/1, 6/8—W: Joe Young; M: Fred Ahlert; Robbins Music Corp.

"In a Little Gypsy Tea Room"—W: Edgar Leslie; M: Joe Burke; Edwin H. Morris & Co., Inc.

"Chasing Shadows," 6/22, 6/29, 7/6, 7/20, 8/2—W: Benny Davis; M: Abner Silver; De Sylva, Brown & Henderson, Inc.

"In the Middle of a Kiss," 7/27—W and M: Sam Coslow; Famous Music Corp.

"Paris in the Spring," 8/10—W: Mack Gordon; M: Harry Revel; De Sylva, Brown & Henderson, Inc.

"And Then Some," 8/17—W: Tot Seymour; M: Vee Lawnhurst; World Music, Inc./ Famous Music Corp.

"East of the Sun," 8/24, 9/7—W and M: Brooks Bowman; Ann-Rachel Music Corp.

"You're All I Need," 8/31—W: Gus Kahn; M: Bronislaw Kaper & Walter Jermann; Robbins Music Corp.

"I'm in the Mood for Love," 9/21—W and M: Jimmy McHugh & Dorothy Fields; Robbins Music Corp.

*Nominated for Academy Award.

**Winner of Academy Award.

* "Cheek to Cheek," 9/28, 10/5, 10/12, 10/19, 10/26—W and M: Irving Berlin; Irving Berlin Music Corp.

"You Are My Lucky Star," 11/2, 11/9, 11/16—W and M: B. G. De Sylva, Lew Brown & Ray Henderson; Chappell & Co., Inc./Ann-Rachel Music Corp.

"Red Sails in the Sunset," 11/23, 11/30, 12/7, 12/14—W: Jimmy Kennedy; M: Hugh Williams (pseudonym, Will Grosz); The Peter Maurice Co., Ltd., London/Shapiro-Bernstein & Co., Inc.

"Treasure Island," 12/21—W and M: (No ref.); Publisher: (No ref.)

"A Little Bit Independent," 12/28—W: Edgar Leslie; M: Joe Burke; Bregman, Vocco & Conn, Inc.

Top Three No. 1s

1. "Chasing Rainbows" (tied with) "Cheek to Cheek"
2. "Red Sails in the Sunset"
3. "You Are My Lucky Star"

1936

"A Little Bit Independent," 1/4—W: Edgar Leslie; M: Joe Burke; Bregman, Vocco & Conn, Inc.

"The Music Goes 'Round and 'Round," 1/11, 1/18, 1/25—W: "Red" Hodgson; M: Ed Farley & Mike Riley; Ann-Rachel Music Corp.

"Moon over Miami," 2/1—W: Edgar Leslie; M: Joe Burke; Bourne Co.

"Alone," 2/8, 2/15, 2/22, 2/29, 3/14—W: Arthur Freed; M: Nacio Herb Brown; Robbins Music Corp.

"Lights Out," 3/7, 3/21—W and M: Billy Hill; Shapiro, Bernstein & Co., Inc.

"Goody Goody," 3/28, 4/4, 4/11, 4/18—W and M: Johnny Mercer and Matt Malneck; Commander Publications/Malneck Music

"Lost," 4/25, 5/2, 5/9, 5/30—W and M: Phil Ohman, Johnny Mercer & Mary O. Teetor; Robbins Music Corp.

* "A Melody from the Sky," 5/16—W: Sidney D. Mitchell; M: Louis Alter; Famous Music Corp.

"You," 5/23—W: Harold Adamson; M: Walter Donaldson; Leo Feist, Inc.

"Is It True What They Say About Dixie?," 6/6, 6/13, 6/29, 6/27, 7/11—W and M: Irving Caesar, Sammy Lerner & Gerald Marks; Irving Caesar/Marlong Music Corp./Samuel A. Lerner Publications

"The Glory of Love," 7/4—W and M: Billy Hill; Shapiro, Bernstein & Co., Inc.

"Take My Heart," 7/18, 7/25—W: Joe Young; M: Fred E. Ahlert; Warock Corp./Fred Ahlert Music Corp.

"These Foolish Things," 8/1, 8/8—W: Holt Marvell (pseudonym for Eric Maschwitz); M: Jack Stachey & Harry Link; Boosey & Co., Ltd., London/Bourne Co.

"When I'm with You," 8/15, 8/22—W: Mack Gordon; M: Marry Revel; Robbins Music Corp.

* "Did I Remember," 8/29, 9/5, 9/12, 9/19, 9/26, 10/3—W: Harold Adamson; M: Walter Donaldson; Leo Feist, Inc.

* "When Did You Leave Heaven," 10/10, 10/17—W: Walter Bullock; M. Richard A. Whiting; Robbins Music Corp.

** "The Way You Look Tonight," 10/24, 10/31, 11/7, 11/14, 11/21, 11/28—W: Dorothy Fields; M: Jerome Kern; T. B. Harms Co.

"I'll Sing You a Thousand Love Songs," 12/5—W: Al Dubin; M: Harry Warren; Remick Music Corp.

"In the Chapel in the Moonlight," 12/12, 12/26—W and M: Billy Hill; Shapiro, Bernstein & Co., Inc.

*"Pennies from Heaven," 12/19—W and M: Johnny Burke & Arthur Johnston; Ann-Rachel Music Corp.

Top Three No. 1s

1. "The Way You Look Tonight" (tied with) "Did I Remember"
2. "Is It True What They Say About Dixie?" (tied with) "Alone"
3. "Goody Goody" (tied with) "Lost"

1937

"In the Chapel in the Moonlight," 1/2—W and M: Billy Hill; Shapiro, Bernstein & Co., Inc.

"Pennies from Heaven," 1/9, 1/23, 1/30—W and M: Johnny Burke & Arthur Johnston; Ann-Rachel Music Corp.

"It's De-Lovely," 1/16—W and M: Cole Porter; Chappell & Co., Inc.

"Goodnight, My Love," 2/6, 2/13, 2/27, 3/6—W: Mack Gordon; M: Harry Revel; Robbins Music Corp.

"With Plenty of Money and You," 2/20—W: Al Dubin; M: Harry Warren; Harms, Inc.

"This Year's Kisses," 3/13, 3/20, 3/27—W and M: Irving Berlin; Irving Berlin Music Corp.

"Boo Hoo," 4/3, 4/10, 4/17, 4/24, 5/1, 5/8—W: Edward Heyman; M: Carmen Lombardo & John Jacob Loeb; Ahlert-Burke Corp./Flojan Music Publishing Co./ Frank Music Corp.

"September in the Rain," 5/15, 6/5, 6/12, 6/19, 6/26—W: Al Dubin; M: Harry Warren; Remick Music Corp.

"Carelessly," 5/22, 5/29—W and M: (No ref.); Publisher: (No ref.)

"It Looks Like Rain in Cherry Blossom Lane"—W and M: Edgar Leslie & Joe Burke; Edwin H. Morris & Co., Inc.

[Note—there were no new songs for June or July.]

"Sailboat in the Moonlight," 8/2, 8/21, 8/28—W and M: John Jacob Loeb & Carmen Lombardo; De Sylva, Brown and Henderson, Inc.

*"Whispers in the Dark," 9/4, 9/18, 9/25, 10/2—W: Leo Robin; M: Frederick Hollander; Famous Music Corp.

"So Rare," 9/11—W: Jack Sharpe; M: Jerry Herst; Robbins Music Corp.

"That Old Feeling," 10/9, 10/16, 10/23, 10/30—W and M: Lew Brown & Sammy Fain; Leo Feist, Inc.

"Remember Me," 11/6—W: Al Dubin; M: Harry Warren; M. Witmark & Sons

"You Can't Stop Me from Dreaming," 11/13—W and M: Cliff Friend & Dave Franklin; Remick Music Corp.

"Vieni, Vieni," 11/20—English W: Rudy Vallee; Italian-French W: George Keger & Henri Varna; M: Vincent Scott; Vincent B. Scott, Paris/M. Witmark & Sons

"Once in a While," 11/27, 12/4, 12/11, 12/18, 12/25, 1/1, 1/8—W: Bud Green; M: Michael Edwards; Miller Music Corp.

Top Three No. 1s
1. "Once in a While"
2. "Boo Hoo"
3. "September in the Rain"

1938

"Once in a While," 1/1, 1/8—W: Bud Green; M: Michael Edwards; Miller Music Corp.

"Rosalie," 1/15, 2/5—W and M: Cole Porter; Chappell & Co., Inc.

"Bei Mir Bist Du Schoen," 1/22, 2/12—English W: Sammy Cahn & Saul Chaplin; Yiddish W: Jacob Jacobs; M: Sholom Secunda; Harms, Inc.

"You're a Sweetheart," 1/29, 2/19—W: Harold Adamson; M: Jimmy McHugh; Robbins Music Corp.

"I Double Dare You," 2/26—W and M: Terry Shand and Jimmy Eaton; Shapiro, Bernstein & Co., Inc.

** "Thanks for the Memory," 3/5, 3/12, 3/19—W and M: Leo Robin & Ralph Rainger; Paramount Corp.

"Ti-Pi-Tin," 3/26, 4/2, 4/9, 4/16, 4/23, 4/30—English W: Raymond Leveen; Spanish W and M: Maria Grever; Leo Feist, Inc.

"Please Be Kind," 5/7—W and M: Sammy Cahn & Saul Chaplin; Harms, Inc.

"Love Walked In," 5/14, 5/21, 5/28, 6/4—W: Ira Gershwin; M: George Gershwin; Gershwin Publishing Corp/Chappell & Co., Inc.

"Cry Baby Cry," 6/11—W and M: Jimmy Eaton, Terry Shand, Remus Harris & Irving Melsher; Shapiro, Bernstein & Co., Inc.

"Says My Heart," 6/18, 6/25, 7/2, 7/9—W: Frank Loesser; M: Burton Lane; Famous Music Corp.

"Music, Maestro, Please," 7/16, 7/23, 8/6, 8/13—W: Herb Magidson; M: Allie Wrubel; Bourne Co.

"I Let a Song Go Out of My Heart," 7/30—W: Henry Nemo, John Redman & Irving Mills; M: Edward Kennedy "Duke" Ellington; Mills Music, Inc.

"A-Tisket, A-Tasket," 8/20, 8/27, 9/3, 9/10, 9/17, 9/26—W and M: Ella Fitzgerald & Al Feldman (aka Van Alexander); Robbins Music Corp.

"I've Got a Pocketful of Dreams," 10/1, 10/8, 10/22, 10/29—W: Johnny Burke; M: Jimmy Monaco; Ann-Rachel Music Corp.

* "Change Partners," 10/15, 11/5—W and M: Irving Berlin; Irving Berlin Music Corp.

"My Reverie," 11/12, 11/19, 11/26, 12/3, 12/10, 12/17, 12/24, 1/7—W and M (adaptation from Debussy): Larry Clinton; Robbins Music Corp.

"You Must Have Been a Beautiful Baby," 12/31—W: Johnny Mercer; M: Harry Warren; Remick Music Corp.

Top Three No. 1s
1. "My Reverie"
2. "Ti-Pi-Tin"
3. "A-Tisket, A-Tasket"

1939

"My Reverie," 1/7—W and M (adaptation from Debussy): Larry Clinton; Robbins Music Corp.

"You Must Have Been a Beautiful Baby," 1/14, 1/28—W: Johnny Mercer; M: Harry Warren; Remick Music Corp.

*"Jeepers Creepers," 1/21, 2/4, 2/11, 2/18, 2/25—W: Johnny Mercer; M: Harry Warren; M. Witmark & Sons

"Deep Purple," 3/4, 3/11, 3/18, 3/25, 4/1, 4/8, 4/15—W: Mitchell Parish; M: Peter De Rose; Robbins Music Corp.

"Heaven Can Wait," 4/22, 4/29—W: Eddie De Lange; M: Jimmy Van Heusen; Remick Music Corp.

"Our Love," 5/6, 5/13—W and M (adaptation from Tchaikovsky): Larry Clinton, Buddy Bernier & Bob Emmerich; Chappell & Co., Inc.

"And the Angels Sing," 5/20, 5/27, 6/3, 6/10—W: Johnny Mercer; M: Ziggy Elman; Bregman, Vocco & Conn, Inc.

*"Wishing," 6/17, 6/24, 7/1, 7/18—W and M: B. G. De Sylva; De Sylva, Brown & Henderson, Inc.

"Stairway to the Stars," 7/15, 7/22, 7/29, 8/5—W: Mitchell Parish; M: Matt Malneck & Frank Signorelli; Robbins Music Corp.

"Moon Love," 8/12, 8/19, 8/26, 9/2—W and M (adaptation from Tchaikovsky): Mack David, Mack Davis & André Kostelanetz; Famous Music Corp.

**"Over the Rainbow," 9/9, 9/16, 9/23, 9/30, 10/7, 10/14, 10/28—W: E. Y. Harburg; M: Harold Arlen; Leo Feist, Inc.

"Day In, Day Out," 10/21—W: Johnny Mercer; M: Rube Bloom; Bregman, Vocco & Conn, Inc.

"Blue Orchids," 11/4—W and M: Hoagy Carmichael; Famous Music Corp.

"South of the Border," 11/11, 11/18, 11/25, 12/9, 12/23—W and M: Jimmy Kennedy and Michael Carr; The Peter Maurice Co. Ltd., London/Shapiro, Bernstein & Co., Inc.

"Scatterbrain," 12/2, 12/16, 12/30, 1/6, 1/13—W and M: Johnny Burke, Frankie Masters, Kahn Keene & Carl Bean; Bregman, Vocco & Conn, Inc.

Top Three No. 1s

1. "Deep Purple" (tied with) "Over the Rainbow"
2. "Jeepers Creepers" (tied with) "South of the Border" (tied with) "Scatterbrain"
3. "And the Angels Sing" (tied with) "Wishing" (tied with) "Stairway to the Stars" (tied with) "Moon Love"

Academy Award Nominees and Winners
Music—Best Song

1934

"Carioca" from *Flying Down to Rio*, RKO Radio. Music by Vincent Youmans. Lyrics by Edward Eliscu and Gus Kahn.

* "The Continental" from *The Gay Divorcée*, RKO Radio. Music by Con Conrad. Lyrics by Herb Magidson.

"Love in Bloom" from *She Loves Me Not*, Paramount. Music by Ralph Rainger. Lyrics by Leo Robin.

1935

"Cheek to Cheek" from *Top Hat*, RKO Radio. Music and Lyrics by Irving Berlin.

"Lovely to Look At" from *Roberta*, RKO Radio. Music by Jerome Kern. Lyrics by Dorothy Fields and Jimmy McHugh.

* "Lullaby of Broadway" from *Gold Diggers of 1935*, Warner Bros. Music by Harry Warren. Lyrics by Al Dubin.

1936

"Did I Remember" from *Suzy*, Metro-Goldwyn-Mayer. Music by Walter Donaldson. Lyrics by Harold Adamson.

"I've Got You Under My Skin" from *Born to Dance*, Metro-Goldwyn-Mayer. Music and Lyrics by Cole Porter.

"A Melody from the Sky" from *Trail of the Lonesome Pine*, Paramount. Music by Louis Alter. Lyrics by Sidney Mitchell.

"Pennies from Heaven" from *Pennies from Heaven*, Columbia. Music by Arthur Johnston. Lyrics by Johnny Burke.

*Denotes winner.

*"The Way You Look Tonight" from *Swing Time*, RKO Radio. Music by Jerome Kern. Lyrics by Dorothy Fields.

"When Did You Leave Heaven" from *Sing Baby Sing*, 20th Century-Fox. Music by Richard A. Whiting. Lyrics by Walter Bullock.

1937

"Remember Me" from *Mr. Dodd Takes the Air*, Warner Bros. Music by Harry Warren. Lyrics by Al Dubin.

*"Sweet Leilani" from *Waikiki Wedding*, Paramount. Music and Lyrics by Harry Owens.

"That Old Feeling" from *Vogues of 1938*, Wanger, UA. Music by Sammy Fain. Lyrics by Lew Brown.

"They Can't Take That Away From Me" from *Shall We Dance*, RKO Radio. Music by George Gershwin. Lyrics by Ira Gershwin.

"Whispers in the Dark" from *Artists and Models*, Paramount. Music by Frederick Hollander. Lyrics by Ira Gershwin.

1938

"Always and Always" from *Mannequin*, Metro-Goldwyn-Mayer. Music by Edward Ward. Lyrics by Chet Forrest and Bob Wright.

"Change Partners" from *Carefree*, RKO Radio. Music and Lyrics by Irving Berlin.

"Cowboy and the Lady" from *The Cowboy and the Lady*, Goldwyn, UA. Music by Lionel Newman. Lyrics by Arthur Quenzer.

"Dust" from *Under Western Stars*, Republic. Music and Lyrics by Johnny Marvin.

"Jeepers Creepers" from *Going Places*, Warner Bros. Music by Harry Warren. Lyrics by Johnny Mercer.

"Merrily We Live" from *Merrily We Live*, Roach, Metro-Goldwyn-Mayer. Music by Phil Craig. Lyrics by Arthur Quenzer.

"A Mist Over the Moon" from *The Lady Objects*, Columbia. Music by Ben Oakland. Lyrics by Oscar Hammerstein II.

"My Own" from *That Certain Age*, Universal. Music by Jimmy McHugh. Lyrics by Harold Adamson.

"Now It Can Be Told" from *Alexander's Ragtime Band*, 20th Century-Fox. Music and Lyrics by Irving Berlin.

*"Thanks for the Memory" from *Big Broadcast of 1938*, Paramount. Music by Ralph Rainger. Lyrics by Leo Robin.

1939

"Faithful Forever" from *Gulliver's Travels*, Paramount. Music by Ralph Rainger. Lyrics by Leo Robin.

"I Poured My Heart Into a Song" from *Second Fiddle*, 20th Century-Fox. Music and Lyrics by Irving Berlin.

*"Over the Rainbow" from *The Wizard of Oz*, Metro-Goldwyn-Mayer. Music by Harold Arlen. Lyrics by E. Y. Harburg.

"Wishing" from *Love Affair*, RKO Radio. Music and Lyrics by Buddy De Sylva.

◀▼ Appendix C ▼▶

NARAS Hall of Fame Recordings

1931 "Mood Indigo"—Duke Ellington (Brunswick)
1937 "I Can't Get Started"—Bunny Berigan (Victor)
1937 "One O'Clock Jump"—Count Basie (Decca)
1937 "Sing, Sing, Sing" (Original recording)—Benny Goodman (Victor)
1938 "Begin the Beguine"—Artie Shaw (Bluebird)
1938 "September Song"—Walter Huston (Brunswick)
1939 "Body and Soul"—Coleman Hawkins (Bluebird)
1939 "God Bless America"—Kate Smith (Victor)
1939 "In the Mood"—Glenn Miller (Bluebird)
1939 "Over the Rainbow"—Judy Garland (Decca)
1939 "Strange Fruit"—Billie Holiday (Commodore)

Date noted is year of release.

✥ Appendix D ✥

Theme Songs

1930

"Au Revoir, Pleasant Dreams," signature theme of Ben Bernie and His Orchestra

"Bye Bye Blues," Bert Lown and His Hotel Biltmore Orchestra

"Falling in Love with You," *The Studebaker Champions* (radio show)

"Give Me a Moment Please," violinist Dave Rubinoff

"It's a Lonesome Old Town When You're Not Around," theme of Ben Bernie and His Orchestra

"Memories of You," Sonny Dunham and His Orchestra

"A Porter's Love Song to a Chambermaid," Freddie Bergin and His Orchestra

"Rockin' Chair," Mildred Bailey

"So Beats My Heart for You," Freddie Rich and His Orchestra

"Someday I'll Find You," *Mr. Keen, Tracer of Lost Persons* (radio show)

"Time on My Hands (And You in My Arms)," *The Chase and Sanborn Hour* (radio variety series)

"The Waltz You Saved for Me," Wayne King and His Orchestra; *Lady Esther Serenade* (radio musical series)

"Was I to Blame for Falling in Love with You," The Casa Loma Orchestra

"When the Bloom Is on the Sage," *Tom Mix Ralston Straight Shooters* (radio series)

"You Brought a New Kind of Love to Me," *A New Kind of Love* (film)

1931

"Adios," Enrique Madriguera and His Orchestra

"Got a Date with an Angel," Skinnay Ennis and His Orchestra

"Home (When Shadows Fall)," Smith Ballew and His Orchestra

"I Surrender, Dear," Red Norvo and His Orchestra

"I'll Love You in My Dreams," Horace Heidt and His Musical Knights

"Marta," theme song and radio signature of Arthur Tracy, "The Street Singer"
"Paradise," Russ Columbo
"Smile, Darn Ya, Smile," theme song of comedian Fred Allen's radio show
"Wabash Moon," Morton Downey
"When It's Sleepy Time Down South," Louis Armstrong and His Orchestra
"You Call It Madness (But I Call It Love)," Isham Jones and His Orchestra
"You're Just a Dream Come True," Isham Jones and His Orchestra

1932

"(I Would Do) Anything for You," Claude Hopkins and His Orchestra
"Chant of the Weed," Don Redman and His Orchestra
"Contented," the *Carnation Contented Hour* (radio show)
"I Gotta Right to Sing the Blues," Jack Teagarden
"I'm Getting Sentimental Over You," Tommy Dorsey and His Orchestra
"It's Over Because We're Through," Willie Bryant and His Orchestra
"(I'd Love to Spend) One Hour with You," Eddie Cantor's radio show
"The Party's Over Now," used as signature theme by Noël Coward in cabaret ap-
        pearances
"Smile for Me,"*The Fitch Bandwagon* (radio series)
"You're an Old Smoothie," Del Courtney and His Orchestra

1933

"Blue Prelude," Woody Herman and His Orchestra
"Deep Forest," Earl Hines and His Orchestra
"I Cover the Waterfront," title theme for film
"The Old Spinning Wheel," radio theme of child singer Mary Small
"On the Trail," Philip Morris radio commercial
"One Minute to One," Gray Gordon and His Orchestra
"Oodles of Noodles," Jimmy Dorsey and His Orchestra
"Smoke Rings," Glen Gray and the Casa Loma Orchestra

1934

"I'm Popeye the Sailor Man," *Popeye the Sailor* cartoon series
"Let's Get Together," Chick Webb and His Orchestra
"Lost in a Fog," The Dorsey Brothers Band
"Love in Bloom," used as theme by Jack Benny and for comic violin solos
"Out of Space," Jan Savitt and His Orchestra
"Sandman," The Dorsey Brothers Orchestra
"Wild Honey," George Hamilton and His Orchestra

1935

"A Blues Serenade," Henry King and His Orchestra
"Good-bye," closing signature theme of Benny Goodman and His Orchestra
"Hobo on Park Avenue," Will Hudson and His Orchestra
"I Can't Get Started," Bunny Berigan and His Orchestra
"It Must Have Been a Dream," Les Hite and His Orchestra
"Let's Dance," Benny Goodman and His Orchestra
"Moon Over Miami," Dean Hudson and His Orchestra
"The Most Beautiful Girl in the World," Ted Straeter and His Orchestra

"She Shall Have Music," Jack Hylton and His Orchestra
"Summertime," Bob Crosby Band
"Wail of the Wind," Red Nichols and His Orchestra
"When a Gypsy Makes His Violin Cry," Emery Deutsch and His Orchestra
"You Are My Lucky Star," Enoch Light and His Orchestra

1936

"Blue Rhythm Fantasy," Teddy Hill and His Orchestra
"Christopher Columbus," Fletcher Henderson and His Orchestra
"Manhattan Merry-Go-Round," *Manhattan Merry-Go-Round* (radio show)
"The Milkman's Matinee," *Milkman's Matinee*, all-night radio show on WNEW (NYC)
"Thinking of You," Kay Kyser and His Orchestra

1937

"It Seems Like Old Times," Arthur Godfrey's radio show (and later his TV show)
"Nightmare," Artie Shaw and His Orchestra
"Quaker City Jazz," Jan Savitt and His Top Hatters
"Stardust on the Moon," Emery Deutsch and His Orchestra
"Study in Brown," Larry Clinton and His Orchestra
"(Oh, How I'll Miss You) When Summer Is Gone," Hal Kemp and His Orchestra
"Where or When," theme for *Gaby* (film)

1938

"Apurksady," Gene Krupa and His Orchestra
"I'll Be Seeing You," featured by Liberace in 1950s as closing theme on his radio and TV shows
"Sunrise Serenade," Frankie Carle and His Orchestra
"While a Cigarette Was Burning," Fred Waring's *Chesterfield Time* (radio show)
"You Go to My Head," Mitchell Ayres and His Orchestra

1939

"Blue Rain," Alvino Ray and His Orchestra
"It's a Wonderful World," Jan Savitt and His Orchestra
"Low Down Rhythm in a Top Hat," Al Donahue and His Orchestra
"Scatterbrain," Frankie Masters and His Orchestra
"What's New?," Billy Butterfield and His Orchestra

❧ Appendix E ❧

Cotton Club Parades

1930

"Linda." W: Ted Koehler; M: Harold Arlen. *Brown Sugar.*

1931

"Kickin' the Gong Around." W: Ted Koehler; M: Harold Arlen; Introduced by: Cab Calloway in *Rhythmania.*

"Minnie the Moocher (The Hi-De-Ho Song)." W and M: Cab Calloway, Irving Mills, & Clarence Gaskill.

1932

"I've Got the World on a String." W: Ted Koehler; M: Harold Arlen; I: Aida Ward.

"Minnie the Moocher's Wedding Day." W: Ted Koehler; M: Harold Arlen; I: Cab Calloway.

"That's What I Hate About Love." W: Ted Koehler; M: Harold Arlen.

"The Wail of the Reefer Man." W: Ted Koehler; M: Harold Arlen; I: Cab Calloway.

1933

"Calico Days." W: Ted Koehler; M: Harold Arlen; I: George Dewey Washington. 22nd Ed.

"Happy As the Day Is Long." W: Ted Koehler; M: Harold Arlen; I: Henry "Rubber Legs" Williams. 22nd Ed.

"Raisin' the Rent." W: Ted Koehler; M: Harold Arlen; 22nd Ed.

"Stormy Weather." W: Ted Koehler; M: Harold Arlen; Written for Cab Calloway and sung by Ethel Waters. 22nd Ed.

209

1934

"As Long As I Live." W: Ted Koehler; M: Harold Arlen; I: Lena Horne and Avon
    Long. 24th Ed.
"Breakfast Ball." W: Ted Koehler; M: Harold Arlen; I: Jimmie Lunceford and His
    Orchestra.
"Here Goes a Fool." W: Ted Koehler; M: Harold Arlen; I: Jimmie Lunceford and His
    Orchestra.
"Ill Wind (You're Blowin' Me No Good)." W: Ted Koehler; M: Harold Arlen; I: Aida
    Ward. 24th Ed.
"I'm a Hundred Percent for You." W and M: Irving Mills, Ben Oakland, Mitchell
    Parish.
"Like a Bolt from the Blue." W and M: Irving Mills, Ben Oakland, Mitchell Parish.
"Sidewalks of Cuba." W and M: Mitchell Parish, Irving Mills, Ben Oakland. 25th Ed.
"There's a House in Harlem for Sale." W: James Van Heusen; M: Jerry Arlen. 23rd
    Ed.

1935

"Truckin'." W: Ted Koehler; M: Harold Arlen; I: Cora La Redd. 26th Ed.

1936

"Alabama Barbecue." W and M: Benny Davis and J. Fred Coots. 27th Ed.
"Doin' the Suzy-Q." W and M: Benny Davis and J. Fred Coots. 27th Ed.
"Frisco Flo." W and M: Benny Davis and J. Fred Coots; I: Cab Calloway. 27th Ed.

Index

NOTE: FOR SONG TITLES, SEE SEPARATE INDEX, PAGE 231

Index of Songs